THE **ULTIMATE** GUIDE TO THE INTERNET

for the Christian Family

Christopher D. Hudson

BARBOUR
PUBLISHING, INC.
Uhrichsville, Ohio

THE **ULTIMATE** GUIDE TO THE INTERNET

The Ultimate Guide to the Internet for the Christian Family

Check out Barbour's exciting web site at: http://www.barbourbooks.com.

Developed and produced by the Livingstone Corporation.

Interior Design by Design Corps, Batavia, IL.

Cover Design by Robyn Martins.

ISBN: 1-57748-731-1
Published by Barbour Publishing, Inc., P.O. Box 719, Uhrichsville, OH 44683.

Printed in the United States of America.

Welcome to *The Ultimate Guide to the Internet for the Christian Family*—the most thorough and extensive Internet guide available for Christians. This book was created for:

- Christians who want to surf safely
- Parents who want to monitor their children's Internet access
- Educators, students, and homeschoolers who want more information on specific areas of study

This book will help you and your family feel safe as you easily find the information that you need.

How to Use This Book

The first part (pages 1–14) presents overviews of a handful of the best Christian Internet communities. For some readers, this will be the most important section of this book. These sites are so complete, some Christians use only these sites and the pages they link to.

The second part (pages 15–401) is an A-to- Z guide of the most popular subjects to many Christians. Sometimes we wrote brief descriptions; sometimes we let the sites speak for themselves. We've tried to bring the best information to you, whether it's from a Christian site or not. As Crosswalk.com, says, we've provided "information *for* Christians, not just *from* Christians."

Finally, the **third part** concludes with a glossary and index to help you navigate and enjoy it even more.

Special Notes

Throughout the book, you'll notice individual sites highlighted with two icons:

This icon indicates that we find this site to be especially interesting because it has the best information or is particularly well designed for the user.

 This icon indicates a good Christian site on a particular topic.

Three Ways to Personalize This Guide

Keep this guide near your computer. To make this book most useful, we suggest the following:

1) Keep a pen or pencil nearby and make notes in this book about the sites you find most interesting. We've included space throughout the book for you to write down the address of your favorite sites.
2) Circle or star those sites you find most helpful. It's very common to visit a particularly helpful site, then try to get back to it a day or two later but struggle to remember the address.
3) E-mail us your favorites and suggestions. Drop us a line as you find new sites that we should include in this book. E-mail *hudson@techie.com* with your suggestions.

What This Book *Can* and *Can't* Do

This book *can* help you feel more comfortable with the Internet, help you find what you are looking for, and help you control your on-line experience.

This book *can't,* however, take the place of a careful parent. The Internet changes rapidly. Web sites come and go, and on-line communities are bought and sold. We've done our best to review these sites and ensure sites that are suitable for all ages. We've alerted you if a site or topic might need special warnings.

We can't guarantee that our "safe" standards match yours, however. It's possible that content or advertising approved by webmasters may cause us to remove a site from future editions of this book. We'll be keeping up with the sites listed, but your comments on them are welcome, too.

Remember, *no book or filter can replace an informed, conscientious parent.*

God bless your efforts to be a wired, effective Christian in the twenty-first century. Happy surfing!!

Experienced surfers and newcomers to the net have important questions. So, before you begin surfing, check out these answers to the most frequently asked questions:

Is the Internet safe?

If used wisely, yes. But you should take a number of steps to protect yourself on-line:

- Limit your on-line purchases to secure web sites
- Refuse to give personal information (full name, age, passwords, name of your school, and your physical location) to strangers
- Choose your on-line chats and discussions carefully
- Practice safe surfing habits by using a web-filtering program and follow the other points listed on page viii.

If you surf safely, your Internet experience can be positive.

Isn't the Internet filled with pornography, violence, and gambling?

While such sites exist, they actually make up a small percentage of the Internet.

We reviewed thousands of sites while preparing this book. By practicing the safe-surfing suggestions we've outlined (pg. viii), we never once opened or stumbled across any pornographic sites.

Sure, those sites exist, but you can steer clear of them.

Should I allow my children access to the Internet?

We think so. Children quickly adjust to the Internet and learn to "surf" more easily than adults. We believe that part of being an effective Christian in the twenty-first century will mean understanding and being able to navigate our world—including the Internet. More and more schools, colleges, and jobs will require a basic confidence in using the Internet.

Does the good outweigh the bad?

Yes. Internet use requires self-discipline and safe-surfing habits. With these in place, the Internet can help you save time, learn more, and even grow spiritually.

How can the Internet help a person grow spiritually?

The Internet is filled with Christian sites. You can do Bible research, read classic Christian literature, listen to the Bible being read, enjoy Christian radio, engage in Bible study, exchange prayer requests, and meet new Christian brothers and sisters.

How do I get started?

First, get a computer. Most new computers are already Internet equipped (or powerful enough to be easily connected).

Whether you buy a PC or MAC is up to you. Over 90 percent of computers used to surf the Internet are PCs. But MACs also have a devoted and loyal following. We recommend the following:

- A modem of 14.4 kbs (kilobytes per second) or faster. The faster your modem the less time it takes to load graphics and the quicker you will interact with the selected program. Buy the fastest modem you can afford.
- A 486 microprocessor or Pentium microprocessor for the PC or a Macintosh with a 030, 040, or PowerPC microprocessor.
- Access to a live telephone line.

Next, you will need an Internet Service Provider (ISP). Some providers are free, and others require a monthly fee. Some require proprietary software; others allow you to dial in using a web browser like *Internet Explorer* or *Netscape Navigator*. Here's a list of popular Internet service providers.

Free Options	**Telephone Number**
(In exchange for their free service, these sites will barrage you with advertising and junk mail.)	
FreeI.net	1-253-796-6505
Netzero.com	1-805-418-2020

Fee-Based Options	**Telephone Number**
America On-Line	1-800-827-6364
AT&T	1-800-288-3199
Compuserve	1-800-292-3900

Is the Internet private?

Yes and no.

Yes, you can surf alone and feel anonymous. You can view many sites without being tracked by them.

No, many places on the Internet will keep track of you. They have the ability to monitor your buying and surfing habits. Their tracking is no different than your local grocery store, which monitors the items and brands you buy. (Your bank and credit card companies can profile your spending habits, too. They know how and when you spend your money.) Some websites and Internet Service Providers will track you in the same way.

Tips for Safe Surfing

You should stay clear of some Internet sites. These sites can be avoided by taking a few simple steps. These tips will help you enjoy the Internet.

- Use filtering software. This is your first line of defense. We suggest http://www.browsesafe.com.
- Limit the number of hours each day that you are on-line. Remember, the Internet can be addictive. Even innocent surfing can become time consuming and a big time waster.
- Keep your computer centrally located, in a well-trafficked room in your house. Isolated or secluded locations lead to temptation and are not easy for a parent to monitor.
- Keep your last name private. While you can confidently give it to secure on-line stores, resist the temptation to post it on a message board or reveal it in chat rooms.
- Have at least two E-mail accounts. Keep one private and only share the address with family and friends. Use the other account when you subscribe to Internet mailing lists or register as a user at a web page. This will help you limit your junk mail to one inbox. (Much junk mail is inappropriate for children.)
- Remember that you are not *completely* anonymous. Your computer lists the websites visited, and Internet Service Providers can watch you surf and create a profile about you.
- Talk to your children about the kinds of sites that are "off-limits." Make sure the guidelines are clear. Some parents let their kids write up and sign a contract (explaining rules and consequences).
- Never download programs or E-mail from the Internet without a good anti-virus system installed. We recommend Norton Antivirus, which can be downloaded from http://www.symantec.com/.

ACKNOWLEDGEMENTS

No *Ultimate Guide* can be completed alone. Some special, dedicated people have helped by suggesting sites, researching topics, and checking links. Special thanks are due to Amber Rae, Ashley Jones, Joan Woodhead, Katie Gieser, Ann Marie Clark, and Joy Easton. Your tireless help and thoughtful advice made this a good book. Thank you.

Thank you also to Susan Schlabach, Paul Muckley, and Kelly Kohl at Barbour Publishing. Thanks for believing in this title and in our relationship.

CONTENTS

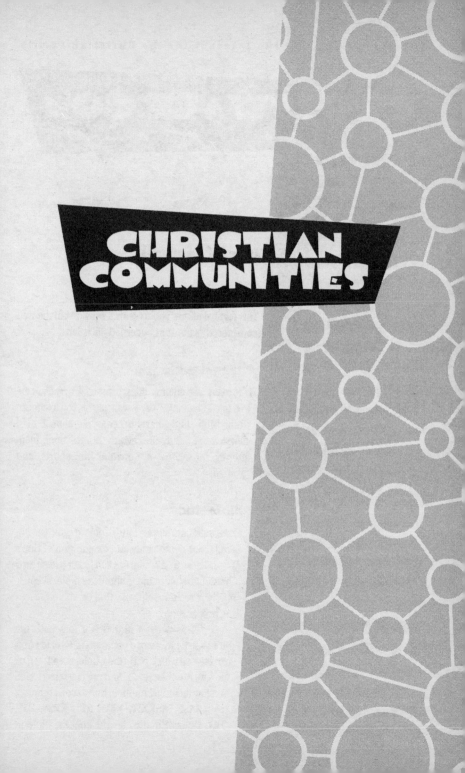

CHRISTIAN COMMUNITIES

CROSSWALK.COM

Crosswalk.com (http://www.crosswalk.com/) may be the largest and most popular Christian Internet community on the World Wide Web. It has 120,000 members in over 120 countries.

Crosswalk.com has created multiple interest channels dedicated to feed the mind, touch the heart, and move the spirit to action.

Because *Crosswalk* provides information for Christians, and not just Christian information, users can find the best of the entire web, from the latest headlines to sports, entertainment, culture, politics, business, and Christian life.

Special Features

SafeSearch

This feature allows you to search portions of the web considered "safe" for concerned Christians.

Channel guide

Like many web communities, Crosswalk organizes the web into "Channels." Crosswalk allows you to choose from: Bible study, careers, entertainment, E-mail newsletters, family life, health, homeschool, men, money, music, news, spiritual life, sports, and women.

Bible Study

Crosswalk.com's Bible Study Tools are designed to facilitate in-depth study and exploration of God's Word. These free resources can foster a desire for Christians to learn more about the Bible, deepening their relationship with God or in their teaching preparation

This section allows you to search the Bible—type in a word you want to look for. You can choose which part (the whole, the NT, OT, or the Law, Prophets, etc.). And you can select which version-including multiple translations (choices are: NASB, ASV,KJV, NKJV, NLT, NRSV, RSV, TEV, Douay-Rheims, World English, Bible in

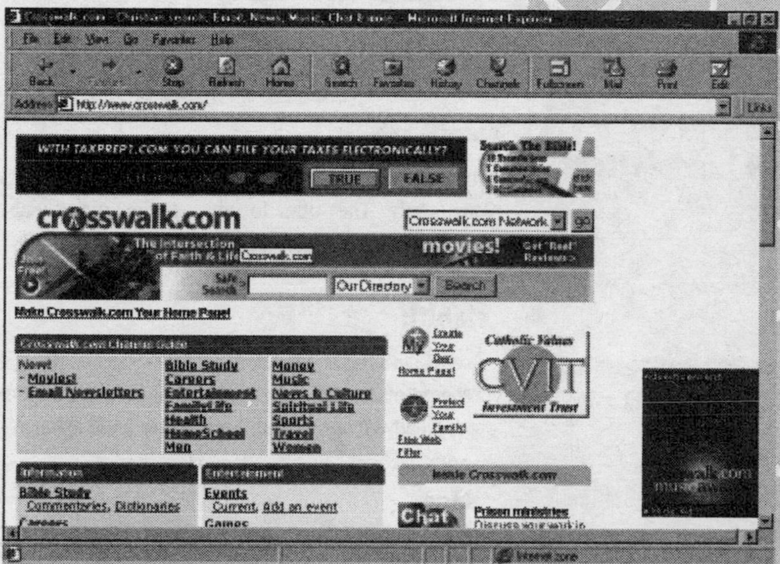

Basic English, Darby Translation, Hebrew Names Version, Webster Bible, Latin Vulgate, Young's Literal Translation, Wesley's New Testament, and KJV or NAS with Strong's Numbers.) You can also opt to use study tools including commentaries, dictionaries, lexions, an interlinear Bible, sermon helps, history books, and other resources.

Careers

Use Crosswalk to help you find a job or advance in your career. They give you access to the 2,000,000 jobs that are posted on-line.

Their Career Planning Service is provided by Birkman International, which includes comprehensive career assessment testing, using the Birkman Method that provides a personalized career planning report.

At Crosswalk, you can sign up for E-mail newsletters about:

Entertainment
Jokes, Riddles, Trivia, Movie Reviews and other fun stuff

Church & Devotional
Games, Bible Info, Church Resources

Family and Personal
Family Relationships, Parenting Helps, Life Stages

Internet & Computer
Best Web sites, Computer Use and Tips, Webmastering

Educational
Your Continuing Education, Teacher's Lounge, Homeschool

Society & Business
News, Culture

Entertainment

The Entertainment Channel provides music videos, movie reviews, humor, and the latest entertainment news.

Family Life

Crosswalk's FamilyLife section is committed to strengthen your family. They offer forums, studies, devotionals, tips, articles, and an on-line store.

Health

Crosswalk's Health Channel will give you a health tip, a receipe of the day, a daily devotion for dieters, and expert advice on nutrition, motivation, and aging.

Men

Here you'll find articles on fathering, maintaining your witness in the business community, and even tips on discipleship ministries.

Money

This section features: market data, news and commentary, articles from financial experts, and financial calculators.

Music—Crosswalk Radio

Six commercial-free stations for every taste in Christian music — listen while you surf!

Sports

You can look up information for each sport/organization by clicking on tabs along the top of page: NFL, NBA, MLB, NHL, NCAA football and basketball, golf, tennis, racing, MLS. Also find testimonies from Christian athletes and links to sports ministries as well as sports forums.

Women

Features geared toward women are women at home, marriage, women in the workplace, relationship advice ,and women's history.

Goshen Search Engine Directory

Goshen's web directory allows you to search the Internet and find links to "safe" sites.

CrossingGuard—Free Web Filter

Crosswalk offers CrossingGuard, a comprehensive filtering solution, for free! CrossingGuard will work to protect you from inappropriate material while you surf.

At Crosswalk, you can read the following devotionals on-line:

Daily Guideposts

Moments Together for Couples

Morning and Evening

Wisdom from the Psalms

Devotional For Dieters

Streams in the Wilderness

Great is Thy Faithfulness

Marketplace Meditations

CHRISTIANITY ONLINE.COM

Christianity On-Line's (http:// www.christianityonline.com) goal is to cultivate a community that provides Christians with the opportunity to fellowship with one another, to encourage spiritual growth through abundant Christian content, and to communicate the depth and transforming power of the Gospel to all who visit this site.

Behind It All

Christianity On-line is owned by Christianity Today. It is, therefore, heavy on magazine content. From this site, users can access articles from *Christianity Today, Books and Culture, Campus Life, Christian Parenting Today, Christian History, Christian Reader, CO Magazine, Leadership, Marriage Partnership, Men of Integrity, Today's Christian Woman, Virtue,* and *Your Church.*

Community

This site has built itself a loyal set of surfers by creating a good, safe community. Each of these communities lets you post, read relevant articles, enjoy devotionals, chat, and shop. On-line communities exist for women, men, singles, marriage/family, kids, teens, seniors, and church leaders.

Explore Your Interests

This site also lets you search for information on the following subjects: churches and ministries, shopping, Bible and reference, spiritual devotion, books and software, schools and jobs, music and media, newsstand, fun, and games.

Advice/Q&A

With a wealth of information behind them, this site is able to easily offer great advice on love

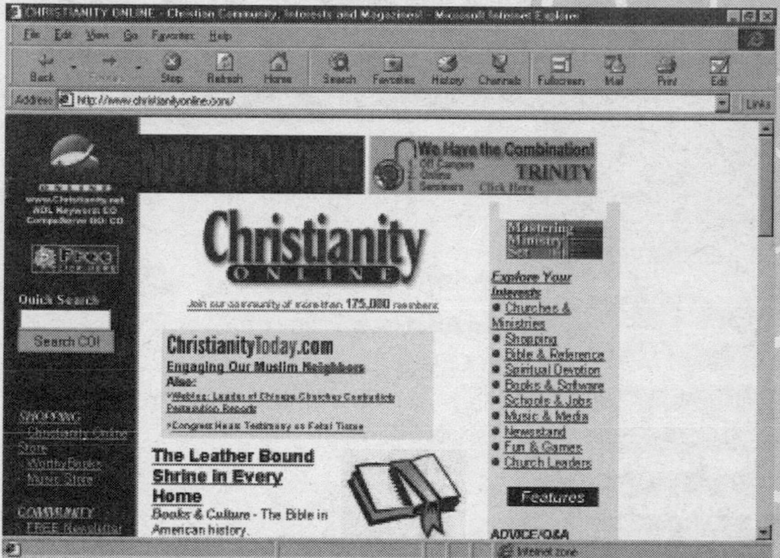

and marriage; dating; mother and child; and teen relationships.

Reviews

This site hosts reviews for church products, books, music, software, and web sites.

News and Trends

This site also includes a section to help you keep up on religion news, church news, church research. Other special features include columns from Chuck Colson and Philip Yancey.

GOSPELCOM.NET

Gospel Communications Network (http://www.gospelcom.net/) is the most frequently visited Christian site on the net. This site achieved this status by creating a devotional atmosphere and an alliance of over 170 Christian organizations dedicated to spreading the gospel over the World Wide Web.

An Alliance

This site serves as a hub, linking you to over 170 Christian organizations. Each day the site spotlights another member, allowing regular users to become aquainted with all of them.

Biblical Guidance—Life Answers

If you're struggling with life challenges or need help counseling someone who is, exploring the links in this section will bring up helpful messages on those subjects along with appropriate Scripture verses.

Shopping

At the Gospelcom Mall, you'll find over 100,000 items in this unique mall of more than twenty-five special Christian "stores."

Cool Features/Fun Stuff

Get a daily dose of humor with "Today's Cartoon," browse over three years' worth of humor at the archives, find out more about the author, or how to include cartoons in your publication.

Read On-line Magazines

This site links you to popular Christian magazines. Surf to this site to read from: *Charisma Magazine, Charisma Now, Christian*

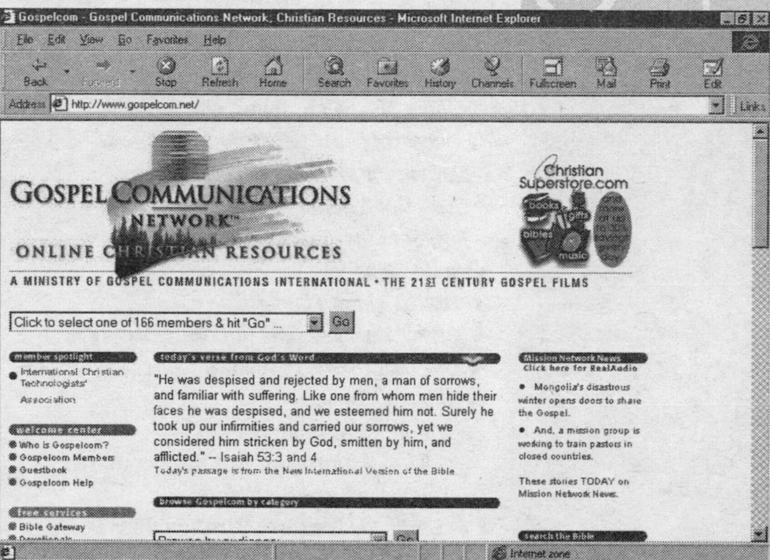

Computing Magazine, Christian Home & School, Crossroads Magazine, Discipleship Journal, Internet For Christians, Light Magazine, New Man Magazine, Pulpit Helps, Sharing the Victory, Sports Spectrum Magazine, Stewardship Solutions, Table Talk Magazine, Web Evangelism Bulletin

Devotions On-Line

In addition to reading and studying the Bible, this site allows you to read from many daily devotionals. Creating a devotional atmosphere has sent many users back to this site each day during their daily "quiet time."

Devotions are included from:

- *American Tract Evangelism Devotional*
- *A Little Daily Wisdom*
- *AMG Daily Devotion*
- *Daily Strength*

- *Back to the Bible Daily Devotionals*
- *Bible Minute*
- *Campus Journal Devotional*
- *Christian Quotation of the Day*
- *Daily Bible Booster* at Peggie's Place!
- *Today's Thought* by John Stott
- *Discovering Ancient Wisdom*
- *Early in the Morning Devotional*
- *God's Got A Better Idea*
- *Keys For Kids* - Devotional for Kids
- *In His Steps*
- *The NIV Quiet Time Bible*
- Oswald Chambers' *My Utmost for His Highest*
- *Our Daily Bread* Devotional
- *Tabletalk* Online
- *Words of Hope* Devotional
- *A Word With You* by Ron Hutchcraft
- Luis Palau's *Healthy Habits*
- *Smith Wigglesworth Devotional Series*
- *Devos & Gutsy Acts for Teens*

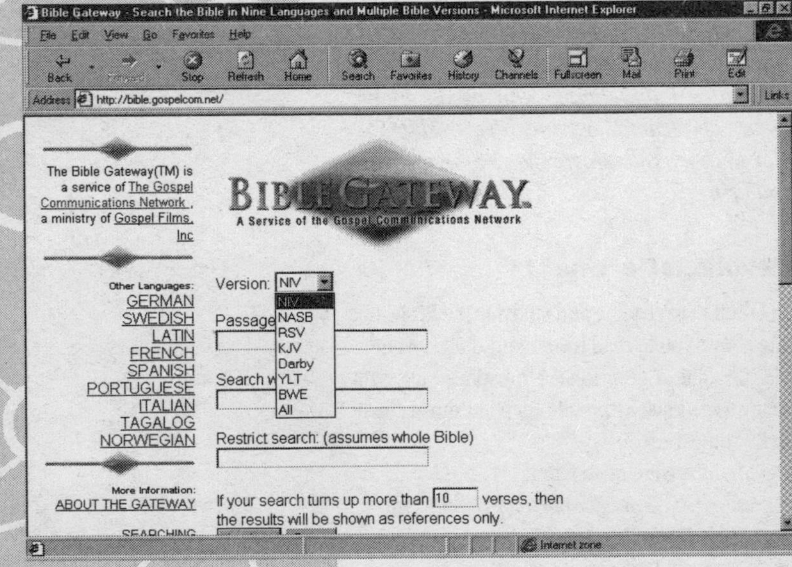

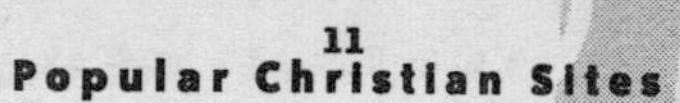

- *Daily Manna from the 'Net*
- *Words from the Well*

Bible Gateway

Currently, you can read and search the Bible from seven different Bible versions (NIV, NASB, RSV, KJV, YLT, BWE, and Darby) and ten different languages (English, German, Swedish, Latin, French, Spanish, Portuguese, Italian, Tagalog, and Norwegian). You can also search by topic—find out what the Bible says about over 22,000 topics.

IBELIEVE.COM

This is an Internet gathering place for Christians worldwide to come, experience, and grow in their faith. It is a lifestyle website for Christians and those concerned about family values and morality—encouraging users to incorporate biblical principles into their homes, places of work, and the world at large. On a regular basis, you'll find new articles as well as columns and stories from today's leading communicators, authors, artists, and ministries.

Membership

Registering as a member with iBelieve.com. is completely free and optional. There are several benefits for members, including exclusive newsletter updates and free e-mail service. For everyone who registers on their site, iBelieve.com will also make a donation to that month's featured ministry.

Chat events and Discussion Boards

Interact with Christian music artists, join a music discussion, find a kindred spirit at a mom's chat group, or share your work struggles. You'll find both moderated and unmoderated events.

My Faith

Here you'll find articles on spiritual growth, prayer, Bible study, and evangelism. You can check out an electronic library with classic essays and stories on living out your faith, ideas for your prayer life, ways to worship God, and more. Get involved in "e-prayer" by posting prayer requests and answers to prayer.

My Life

Find news, marriage and and family help, information on seminars and conferences, movie, video, music, and video game reviews from the Dove Foundation.

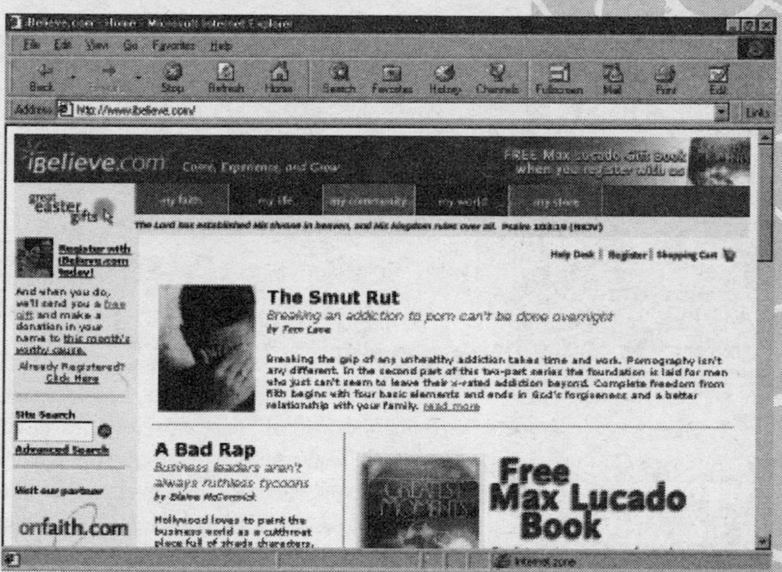

My Community

Check out articles on topics life golf, home decorating, self-image, fitness and health, and crafts. As well as submit a prayer request, and lets you send an e-card to someone in need of encouragement.

My Store

iBelieve.com has an exclusive partnership with Family Christian Stores. Thus, they are able to offer a wide selection of books, Bibles, music, gifts, stationery/cards, apparel, children's items, videos, and software. It is a secure shopping site with customer service always available via email or telephone. Check out new arrivals, top sellers, store highlights, or sale items.

A-Z GUIDE

ACADEMICS

Think you need to spend $50,000 in tuition to get access to libraries filled with information? Not true. Many great on-line resources will help you in your study or area of interest.

Many schools have a growing number of books, journals, and databases on-line.

Cal State

http://library.csun.edu/

California State University at Northridge offers some on-line tools to search humanities, business, and science databases. You'll also find the full text to electronic books you'd expect to find in the reference section of most libraries: encyclopedias, handbooks, dictionaries, and lots more.

Historical Resources

http://www.depts.drew.edu/lib/

Historical abstracts, Civil War newspapers, and many other historic resources are available for browsing on-line at Drew University Library.

Law and Education

http://www.niu.edu/libraries.html

Want to do education or legal research? The Northern Illinois University library includes these specialties as well as other typical university holdings.

Current Events

http://thorplus.lib.purdue.edu/

Grants access to NewsBank NewsFile Collection which catalogs 70,000 news stories a year.

Ivy League Power

Harvard

http://hul.harvard.edu/libinfo/

Think you need to travel to Massachusetts to have access to one of the greatest schools in the history of the USA? Here's instant access to one of the most exclusive academic libraries in the world.

Columbia University

http://www.cc.columbia.edu/cu/libraries/indiv/

The power of the Columbia University Library is at your disposal here. Browse the tremendous archives of one of New York's finest schools.

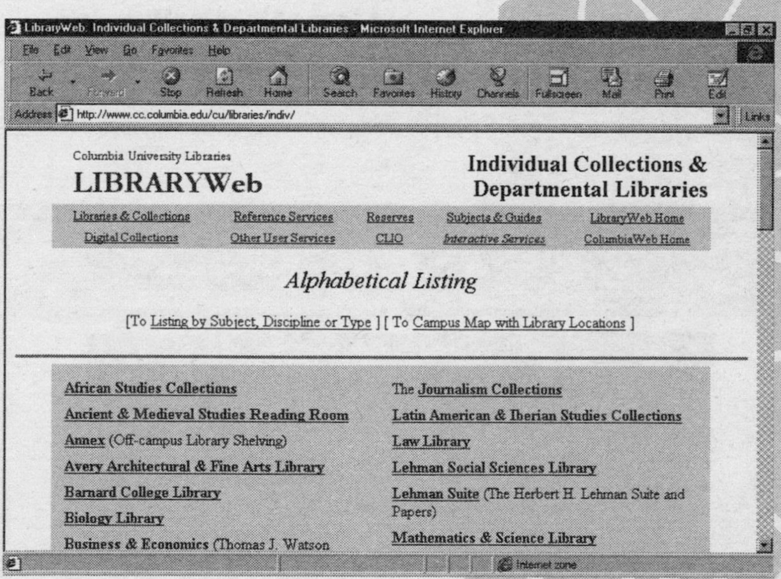

Yale University

http://www.library.yale.edu/htmldocs/collect.htm

Yale's collections speak for themselves, ranging from African studies to law. Find information on any topic of research—modern or ancient.

Christian Schools

Bob Jones University

http://www.bju.edu/resources/library/mackhome.htm

Bob Jones University brings its presence and some archives to the web.

Texas ChristianUniversity

http://library.tcu.edu/

The library holds nearly a million entries in its catalog. This mainstream Christian school has

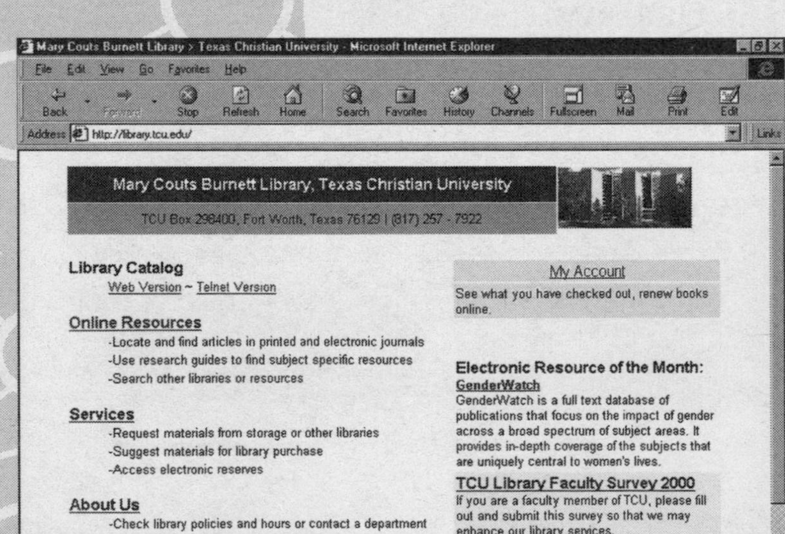

a growing number of on-line books available for use.

Wheaton College

http://www.wheaton.edu/learnres/

This site includes learning resources, special archives, and on-line catalogues to the college's libraries and special collections. Wheaton's special collections include archives on C. S. Lewis.

Academic Competitions

College Bowl

http://www.collegebowl.com/

College Bowl calls itself the "varsity sport of the mind." Other organizations exist at both the high school and university level, including the United States Academic Decathalon http://www.usad.org/ or try http://www.naqt.com/ to find the National Academic Quiz Tournament.

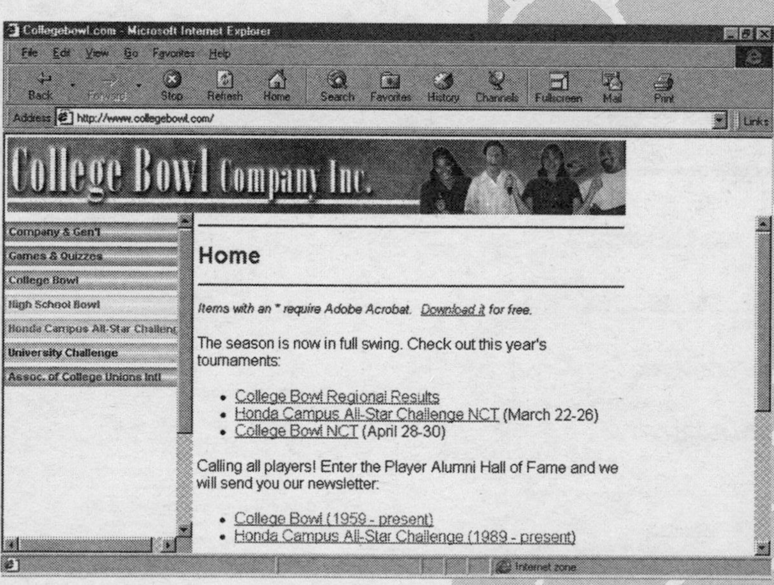

Ohio University

http://
www.library.ohiou.edu/

Stanford

http://www-sul.stanford.edu/

Christian Colleges

http://www.biola.edu/

http://www.taylor.edu/

http://www.olivet.edu/

http://www.gordon.edu/

http://www.calvin.edu/

http://www.moody.edu/

http://www.dts.edu/

http://www.ebc.edu/

Journals

Almost every major journal has a web presence. To best search for a specific journal or category, go to http://www.yahoo.com/ and search for JOURNALS. Browse until you find the topic or journal you are looking for.

ADVICE

When faced with a problem, some people can't relax. They fret, weigh options, and lose a lot of sleep. Now some of the advice you need is just a few mouse clicks away. Unlike your friend or your mom, this advice is available 24/7. Log on to these sites to find the *advice* you need. Then you'll be able to find the *sleep* you need.

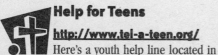

Dear Ann

http://creators.com/lifestyle/landers/lan.asp

The most widely syndicated columnist in the world, Ann Landers has an estimated readership of 90 million, and her column appears in more than 1,200 newspapers.

Christian Advice for Women

http://www.liveit.net/

Part of the crosswalk.com site, this site has lots of practical advice for women. It will help you keep your spiritual life alive, stay on top of a budget, and minister to your family.

No-Nonsense Advice

http://www.drlaura.com/

The queen of talk radio brings her moral advice to the web. Expect the same practical, moral advice you'd hear on her syndicated radio program.

Help for Teens

http://www.tel-a-teen.org/

Here's a youth help line located in New York City. It's a place designed for teenagers to call or chat with listening, helpful peers.

Talk about It

http://www.geocities.com/Athens/Academy/9894/

Christian Counsel on the IRC (Internet Relay Chat) is an on-line, nonprofit, nondenominational counseling and evangelism ministry. Here's a place you can talk about your problems as well as find other advice you might need.

More Advice

http://www.athomemothers.com/

http://www.christianityonline.com/tcw/features/marriage.html

http://www.hearthkeeper.com/

http://christianteens.about.com/

http://askandy.org/

Did You Know?

...that in 1999, there were five U.S. cities with greater than 50 percent Internet penetration among adults?

ANIMALS, INSECTS, & PETS

Help

http://petnet.detnews.com/
Pet news, advice, games, chat line, and even a virtual memorial park where previous users have posted memorials to their pets who have "passed on."

For Vet Quality Info

http://netvet.wustl.edu/
NetVet Veterinary Resources and the Electronic Zoo is a site maintained by a vet located in St. Louis. It contains a good collection of veterinary medical- and animal-related Internet resources as well as links to an on-line veterinarian library.

A Pet Portal

http://www.anancyweb.com/animals_pets.html
Anancyweb makes surfing for information about your cat or fish easy. Besides guides and loads of information, you'll find links to pet-related games and screen savers. If you want another option, try one with an Australian flair: http://www.ozsearch.com.au/Science_and_Technology/Biology/Zoology/Animals_Insects_and_Pets/

Learn More

http://dibbs.net/explore/pets.html
Want to learn more about your pet? Here's a

What do earwigs eat? What should you do if your dog gets sick? What's poisonous to cats?

Get access to veterinarian's answers and advice without trying to corral Fido or Fluffy into the car.

If owning a pet is not for you, how about enjoying a virtual pet? Browse one of the pet spy cams and enjoy a pet without ever cleaning the inside of a cage.

virtual classroom that will give you what you need. Once you load the page, click on the topic that interests you. You'll be taken to search results on the topic provided by the Mining Company.

Kid Pets

http://vax1.harf.lib.md.us/kid_pets.htm

Here's a home base for people who love pets. You'll also find veterinary information and information all about zoos, the U.S. Fish & Wildlife Service, and Endangered Species National Aquarium Spy Cam.

TOP SITE

Pet Spy Cams

http://www.campusware.com/turtles/

http://pbob.speeder.com/ferret/

http://www.atomicweb.com/antfarm.html

Want to enjoy an ant farm, a ferret, or a turtle without having to drop in food or scrub the sides of the tank? Watch live footage of pets that you can enjoy without needing to take care of them.

Keep Them Healthy

http://www.tznet.com/links/pets.html-ssi

Here's a site that links you to the other sites that you need to learn more about pets as well as keep them happy, loved, and healthy. Looking for information on newts or salamanders? It's here.

Kids and Insects

http://www.planetpets.simplenet.com/plntinsc.htm

It is estimated that there are a quintillion (1,000,000,000,000,000,000) individual insects populating the world. Here's a place to learn about them before you squash them.

Animal Immortality Book and Pet Resources

http://www.creatures.com/

Check out pet care tips, vet articles, animal stories and *Will I See Fido in Heaven*—a book about animals receiving eternal life.

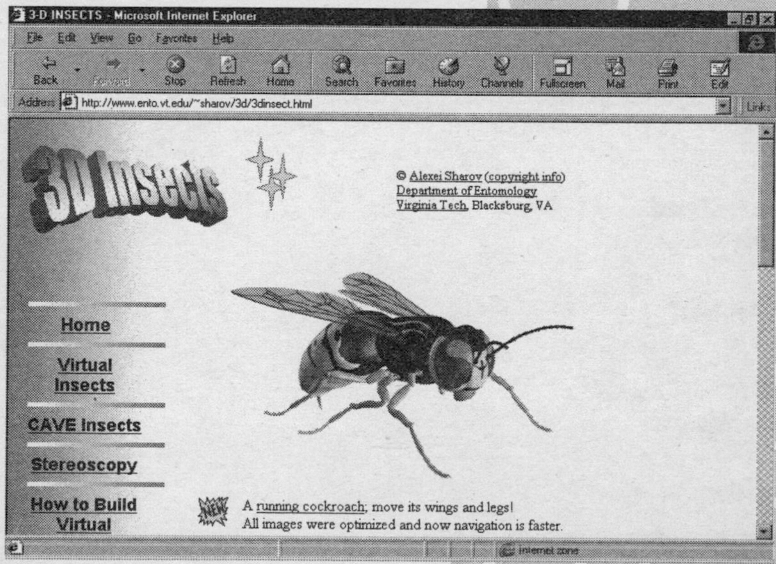

Pet Food Institute

http://www.800petfood.com

http://www.pfionline.org

http://www.gainespetfoods.com/

http://www.iams.com

http://www.sciencediet.com

http://www.purina.com

http://www.petco.com

Insects

http://www.insect-world.com

Fossil Amber

http://www.kadets.d20.co.edu/~lundberg/amber

Animal Sanctuary

http://www.bestfriends.com

3D Insects

http://www.ento.vt.edu/~sharov/3d/3dinsect.html

If you like real insects, you will love virtual insects because you can see them big without a microscope. Virtual insects are clean and have no smell; they will not bite or sting you. And sometimes they look even better than real insects.

The Butterfly Web Site

http://butterflywebsite.com/

This is a site where you can learn more about the fascinating world of butterflies. You can tour the photo gallery, learn how to plant a butterfly garden, take a field trip, find a pen pal, and chat with other butterfly lovers.

ANTHROPOLOGY & ARCHAEOLOGY

BibArch

http://www.bibarch.com/

Explore the lands of the Bible, encounter their ancient cultures, and learn more of biblical archaeology at this site.

Amazing Discoveries in Bible Archaeology

http://www.concentric.net/~extraord/archaeology.htm

Find out more about important archaeological discoveries that relate to the Bible.

Biblical Archaeology Society

http://www.bib-arch.org/

For over twenty-five years, the Biblical Archaeology Society has been presenting the excitement of archaeological discovery and groundbreaking Bible scholarship to a popular audience through magazines, books, videos, slide sets, and tours. This site features information on their organization, its publications, tours and seminars you can join, and a guide to archaeological digs this year.

What would it be like to walk on the roads on which Jesus walked? How did the earliest Christians live? What was life like for them and for societies before us? Archaeology brings us one step closer to answering these questions. While most archaeology is done in hot, dusty, and dry lands, the Internet brings interesting digs to your PC.

Archaeology

http://archaeology.about.com/education/archaeology/

http://archnet.uconn.edu/

http://emuseum.mankato.msus.edu/

http://www.fsu.edu/~library/subject/anthropology.html

Anthropology

http://home.worldnet.fr/~clist/Anthro/index.html

http://vlib.anthrotech.com/

Dig the Bible

http://www.digbible.org/

This web site is dedicated to Biblical Archaeology—where biblical studies and archaeology intersect. Its goal is to help individuals, particularly the layperson, gain a better understanding of the Bible through the use of archaeology. Take a guided on-line biblical archaeology tour of the Holy Lands, find out about joining an actual dig in the Holy Lands, learn more about biblical archaeology methods, check out links, and more!

Archaeology and the Bible Questions

http://www.christiananswers.net/archaeology/home.html

This site addresses archaeological discoveries from a Christian perspective.

ART

World Wide Arts Resources

http://www.world-arts-resources.com/

World Wide Arts Resources offers an interactive gateway to all exemplars of qualitative arts information and culture on the Internet. Artists, museums, galleries, art history, arts education, antiques, performing arts ranging from dance to opera, classified ads, resume postings, and more can be can be accessed from this site.

The Incredible Art Department

http://www.artswire.org/kenroar/

This visual arts site is for students, parents, and teachers. It includes art news, art lessons, art departments, art education, and thousands of links.

Artcyclopedia

http://www.artcyclopedia.com/

A guide to museum-quality fine art on the Internet, with a directory of both artists and museums. This site only provides references to sites on the World Wide Web where artists' works can be viewed on-line. Note that the site is primarily oriented to searching by artist name, although they intend to add more and more access by artistic movement, nation, time line, and medium.

You don't need a trip to an art museum to enjoy the full experience of a gallery. The web has many places that can become an art enthusiast's delight (and a place where the novice can learn a little, too).

While there are a lot of opinions about what is and what isn't art, we've limited our links to those sites that represent what you'd traditionally find in city museums. (Note: Even the classic masters drew nudes, so parents may want to excercise caution.)

Other Links

http://sunsite.unc.edu/louvre/

http://www.art.uiuc.edu/kam/

http://members.tripod.com/~artworkinparis/www11.htm

http://sunsite.unc.edu/wm/paint/auth/cezanne/

http://www.metmuseum.org/

http://www.rca.ac.uk/

Art Library On-Line

http://www.artlibrary.com/

This site aims to provide the most authoritative art reference information any professional, collector, or student will ever want at one address. Provides information on auctions, artists, galleries, museums, and the trade of art.

Museums

Museum Network

http://www.museumnetwork.com/

Features a topically organized directory of museums worldwide. Also provides information to museum professionals and aims to give educators easy access to museums' curriculum and other teaching materials.

Art Museum Network

http://www.amn.org/

Features exhibition calendar of the world's leading art museums, the Art Museum Image Consortium, and the Association of Art Museum Directors.

The Art Center

http://www.theartcenter.net/

This site lets you search the Internet for museums, galleries, artists, and exhibitions.

Art History

Art History Resources

http://witcombe.sbc.edu/ARTHLinks.html

A web directory organized by time period, region, and style. Also provides links to museums and galleries and research resources.

ArtHistoryTV.com

http://www.nichetv.com/arthistory/

Features an Internet-only TV channel with art history programs.

For Kids

Art for Kids

http://artforkids.miningco.com/kids/artforkids/mbody.htm

A good starting place for exploring art for kids, from your about.com guide.

Art Teacher on the Net

http://www.artmuseums.com/

Provides art resources and lesson plans for teachers that would also be of interest to parents and kids.

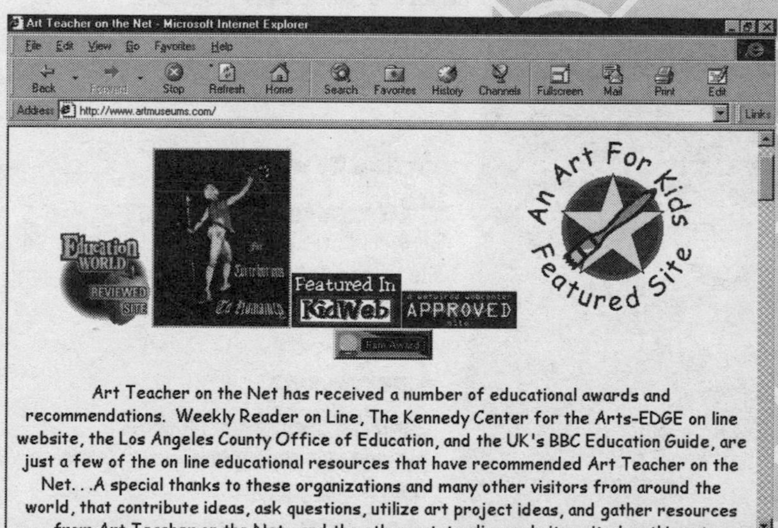
Art Teacher on the Net - Microsoft Internet Explorer
File Edit View Go Favorites Help
Back Forward Stop Refresh Home Search Favorites History Channels Fullscreen Mail Print Edit
Address http://www.artmuseums.com/
Links
Education WORLD REVIEWED SITE
Featured In KidWeb
APPROVED
An Art For Kids Featured Site
Art Teacher on the Net has received a number of educational awards and recommendations. Weekly Reader on Line, The Kennedy Center for the Arts-EDGE on line website, the Los Angeles County Office of Education, and the UK's BBC Education Guide, are just a few of the on line educational resources that have recommended Art Teacher on the Net. . .A special thanks to these organizations and many other visitors from around the world, that contribute ideas, ask questions, utilize art project ideas, and gather resources
Internet zone

AUCTIONS

Buying or selling items through auctions is one of the popular uses of the net. Some points to consider before you place your first bid:

1) Know what you're looking for before you begin browsing.

2) Be sure you know the retail price of what you're looking to buy.

3) Know your spending limit.

4) Participate in auctions that have published safeguards for both buyer and seller.

Auction Insights

http://www.auctioninsights.com/
This site provides insights for bidders and sellers from beginners to veterans; it includes tips, a message board and chat room, a newsletter, and more.

Auction Patrol

http://www.auctionpatrol.com/
Get on-line auction news, information, and tools. You can also participate in the discussion area.

Auction Row

http://www.auctionrow.com/
Site users can search multiple auction sites at once. Site also includes auction ad software, E-cards, and free auction tips e-zine.

Amazon.com

http://auctions.amazon.com/
Buy and sell on-line in a variety of categories from arts and antiques to toys and games.

eBay Home Page

http://www.ebay.com/

eBay offers a person-to-person Internet trading community. Buyers and sellers are brought together in an auction format to trade personal items. The eBay service permits sellers to list items for sale, buyers to bid on items of interest, and all eBay users to browse through listed items in a fully automated, topically arranged service that is available online around the clock.

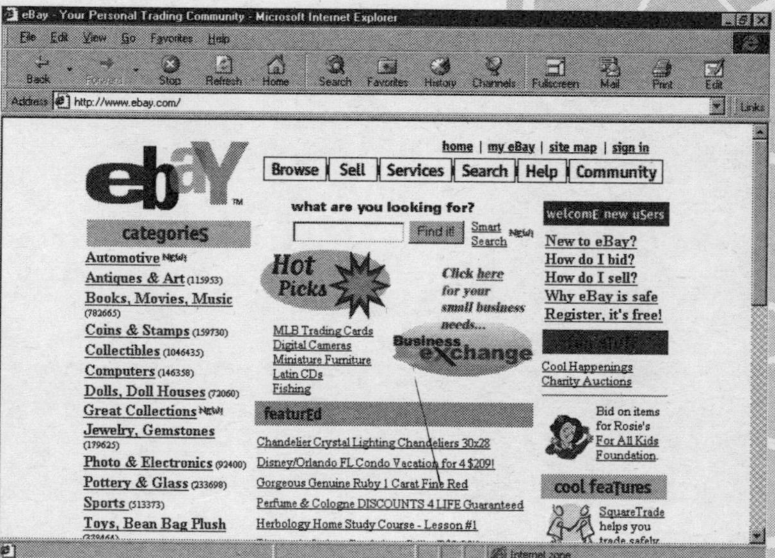

DealDeal.com

http://www.dealdeal.com/

DealDeal.com gives you deals on computer auctions, electronics auctions, software auctions, and more.

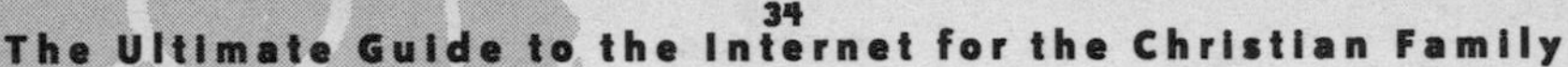

iWant.com

http://www.iwant.com/

A service for buyers to list what items, products, or services they want to purchase.

FAVORITE LINKS

Old-Fashioned Auctions

Internet Auction List

http://www.internetauctionlist.com/

An Internet resource listing for auctions. Here you'll find a directory of auction pages from all over the net: cars, art, antiques, and government auctions.

AUTOMOTIVE

Some people love grease under their fingernails. Others wouldn't recognize a spark plug if it lept up and shocked them. Either group can expand their knowledge of cars—repairing, purchasing, or financing.

You can learn to recognize common problems or get objective advice on what to buy.

TOP SITE

Yahoo! Autos

http://autos.yahoo.com/

Here you can research your car, buy or sell, learn how to best maintain your car, search for loans, or get an insurance estimate. Includes links to other automotive sites for shopping, news, net events, etc. You can even sign up for personalized services like oil change reminders and recall reports.

Popular Mechanics

http://popularmechanics.com/popmech/auto2/1HOMEAUTO.html

Popular Mechanics' Automotive section provides all the latest information on the automotive industry. Featuring reports on the newest cars, trucks, and motorcycles, automotive repair, and classic cars.

AutoNetwork

http://www.autonetwork.com/

Features include a buying service, car reviews, auto financing, automotive news, and consumer information. Twenty-four-hour automotive programming allows you to enjoy auto industry news via video while looking for the car of your choice and/or completing a credit application.

Auto Mequote

http://web-hou.iapc.net/~automeq/

Ever wondered whether your mechanic was trying to take advantage of you? This site offers a second opinion on the price and necessity of repairs.

American Automobile Association

http://www.aaa.com/

Find information about AAA membership benefits, on the road and at home; also get details on auto travel and automotive services, and member savings through their travel agencies partnerships.

Buying?

http://www.cars.com/

Cars.com simplifies new and used car shopping. Cars.com features quick access to automotive classifieds and dealers, price info, news and reports, performance data, recall notices, and auto reviews Try http://www.carmax.com for another option.

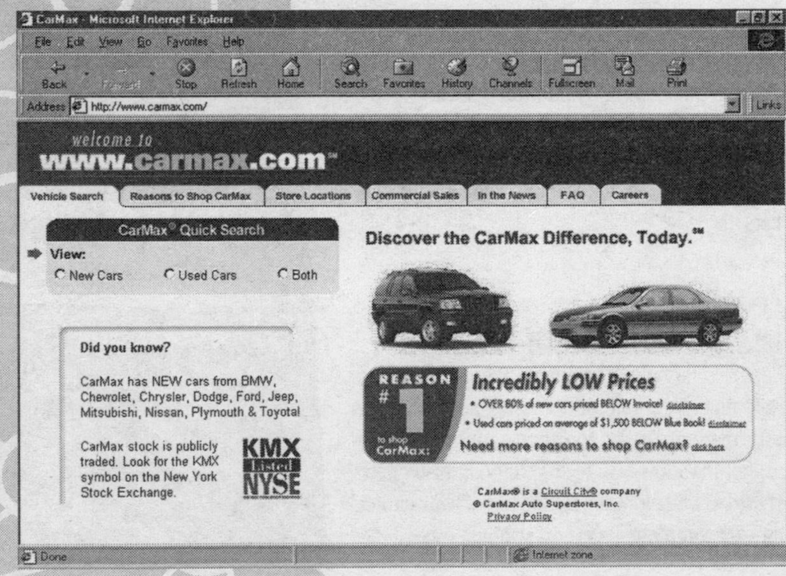

Motorcycles

On-Line Museum

http://www.tower.org/museum/

The Motorcycle Museum On-Line contains information on individual motorcycle models. Information on the individual cycles, images of those cycles, and links to related models can be found listed in chronological order of production with other cycles of the same marque. Vintage as well as modern models included.

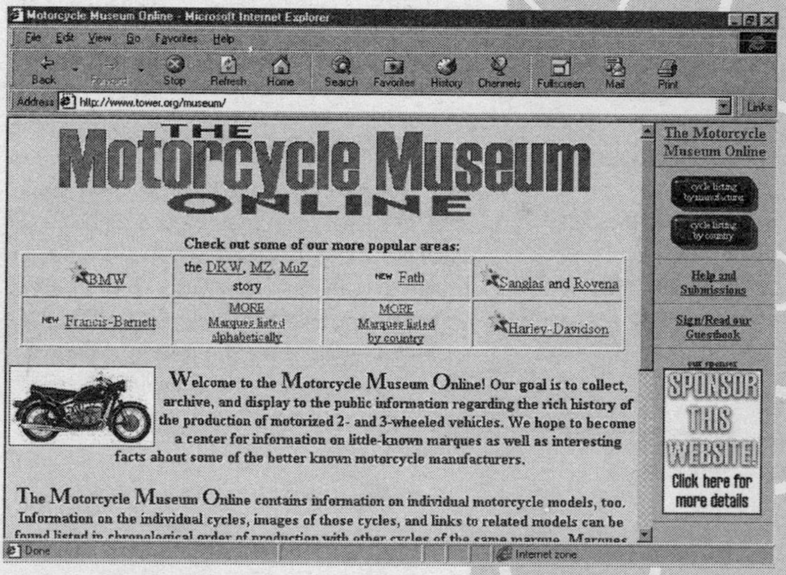

Open Road Radio

http://www.theautochannel.com/cybercast/openroad/

Open Road Radio, hosted by Gina Woods, Dan Schmitt, and Jim Viverito, is a two-hour weekly program focusing on various aspects of motorcycling. Visit this web site to check past programs and visit other links.

Car Maker

http://www.chrysler.com/

http://www.ford.com/

http://www.gm.com/

http://www.honda.com/

http://www.saturncars.com/

http://www.toyota.com/

Antiques

http://www.car-stuff.com/carlinks/classic.htm

http://www.autoclassics.com/

http://www.antiquecar.com/

http://www.hub-caps.com/

Christians and Cars

Christian Rods and Customs

http://www.geocities.com/MotorCity/Downs/9173/index.html

This site is the home of a group of interdenominational Christian car enthusiasts of all ages and backgrounds, with two major common areas of interest—Christianity and cars. They desire to be a positive witness and testimony for Jesus Christ, sharing God's love and His gospel with automotive enthusiasts.

Solid Rock Cruisers

http://www.solidrockcruisers.com/

Solid Rock Cruisers is an organization that combines a love for classic cars and a desire for fellowship in The Lord Jesus Christ. They are a family-based club, open to anyone—regardless of age or gender—with an interest in classic cars and trucks. Classic car ownership is not required. Members' vehicles range from dynamite show cars to fun projects.

AWARDS

The entertainment industry loves to give awards to its members. If you find yourself following the gossip columns or trying to watch award-winning programs or films, these sites are intended for you.

Dove Awards

http://www.doveawards.com/index2.html

The Dove Awards, gospel music's most prestigious awards, are broadcast each spring. The Dove Awards showcase performers who reflect the diversity in Christian music today.

Grammy Awards

http://www.grammy.org/awards/

Official site of the Recording Academy also known as NARAS, an organization of recording professionals that presents the Grammy Awards as well as numerous cultural, educational, professional development, and human service programs.

Tony Awards

http://www.tonys.org/

Keep up on the nominees, history, and awards of the prestigious Tony Award.

Golden Globe Awards

http://www.goldenglobes.org/

The Golden Globes are a much-sought-after award by TV actors. This site gives complete coverage.

BEAUTY

Makeup styles come and go, but a woman's need to purchase cosmetics remains the same. The web won't let you sample a few items at the counter, but if you know the product you're looking for, the web is a good place to pick it up. As well as purchasing, many of these sites give beauty treatment ideas or provide tips for looking better.

HealthnBeauty.com

http://www.healthnbeauty.com/

Discover the truth about good health, permanent weight loss, and natural beauty. Learn how to make your own beauty treatments at home. Sign up for the free monthly publication or chat with others about their experiences with health and beauty products.

Beauty Link

http://www.radio.dowco.com/dominelli/bl-live.html

A live net show featuring facts and myths from the hot growing industry of beauty services, skin and body care, and the latest trendy products.

Beauty Buzz

http://www.beautybuzz.com/

Site features a chat room, bulletin board, swap page, and reviews of various cosmetics, skin care, and body care products.

Beauty.com

http://www.beauty.com/

Offers a selection of cosmetics, skin, and hair care products, fragrances, and accessories. Also provides beauty tips and tricks. Chat live with a beauty advisor.

FAVORITE LINKS

Beauty Of A Site

http://www.beautyofasite.com/

Beauty Of A Site supports your desire for beauty. You'll find everything from the latest tips and trends in new products to a vast selection of the "classics." They stock over 5,000 professional products at 20–50 percent off retail salon prices.

American Discount Beauty Supply

http://www.adiscountbeauty.com/

Features low-priced, full-service beauty supply on the World Wide Web. This site stocks thousands of products—find everything you need for hair, skin, body, nails and beauty. They specialize in those hard-to-find items, and no challenge is too big. Also check out weekly blow-out specials.

Yahoo! Shopping: Bath and Beauty

http://shopping.yahoo.com/Bath_and_Beauty/

Find one-stop Internet shopping for bath and beauty products from featured stores like Macy's, Clinique, and Crabtree & Evelyn.

Dead Sea Company

http://www.deadseacompany.com/

Now, you too can enjoy the benefits of the Dead Sea and its internationally acclaimed spas in the comfort of your home—it's almost like being there. Find out about products and purchase them here.

MurielBell

http://www.murielbell.com/

A family-owned business featuring products for the mature or dry skin. Features four products that fully cover the needs for the basic care of any type of skin.

BIBLE

The B-I-B-L-E,
It's on the web for me,
I study and surf through
the Word of God,
The B-I-B-L-E.

Whether you want to listen to it, read it, or study it, the Bible is available on-line. In addition to different translations, you'll find study tools that help you get deeper into the meaning of a text. Even if you're especially attached to a particular Bible that you've had for years, give some of these sites a quick look. They won't take the place of your Bible, but they may enhance your reading of it.

Bible Study Tools

http://www.biblestudytools.net/

Crosswalk.com's Bible Study Tools are designed to facilitate in-depth study and exploration of God's Word. You can search the on-line study Bible for a particular word, phrase, or passage using any or all of more than fifteen Bible translations. Make use of the commentaries, concordances, dictionaries, lexicons, sermon helps, and church history books. Lots of resources in one place.

The Bible Gateway

http://bible.gospelcom.net/

Look for a passage or search for a word or words in a variety of Bible translations. Available in ten different languages. You can get cross-references in the NASB, and footnotes in the NASB and NIV. Also features a topical search.

Christianity On-line—Bible and Reference

http://www.christianityonline.com/bible/

Features links and articles from *Christianity Today*, PreachingToday.com, *Leadership Journal*, and more. Find Bible verses on-line in a variety of Bible translations—including the Blue Letter Bible. Available study tools include classsic commentaries like *Matthew Henry* and the *Treasury of Scripture Knowledge*, concordances like *Nave's Topical* or *Strong's Exhaustive*, dictionaries, lexicons, and other resources like Fox*'s Book of Martyrs* and the *Early Church Fathers*. Browse these tools or do a topical search of the tools of your choice. You can also find quotes and sermon illustrations here.

The Study

http://www.iexalt.com/spirituallife/thestudy.shtml

Search the Bible in a wide variety of translations. Enjoy insights from one of many devotionals including *My Utmost for His Highest* and *Our Daily Bread*. Check out the on-line Bible studies or advanced Bible studies. Utilize the Bible study helps like Read Through the Bible in One Year or How to Read the Bible. Or link to Bible study tools like the Bible study time line or the Antioch On-line Bible Study.

American Bible Society

http://www.americanbible.org/

This site includes a daily Bible reading, history of the Bible, historical time line, library, art, search function, Bible learning center to help you learn about the Bible, and an on-line catalog of Scripture products.

God's Word for Each Day

http://www.godsword.org/

Click on the God's Word for Each Day link to help get you started. This site will lead you through the entire Bible, providing Scripture passages for each day of the year. All you need to do is set aside a few quiet minutes each day for studying God's Word. Site also features other links on Bible study and Bible reading.

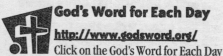

FAVORITE LINKS

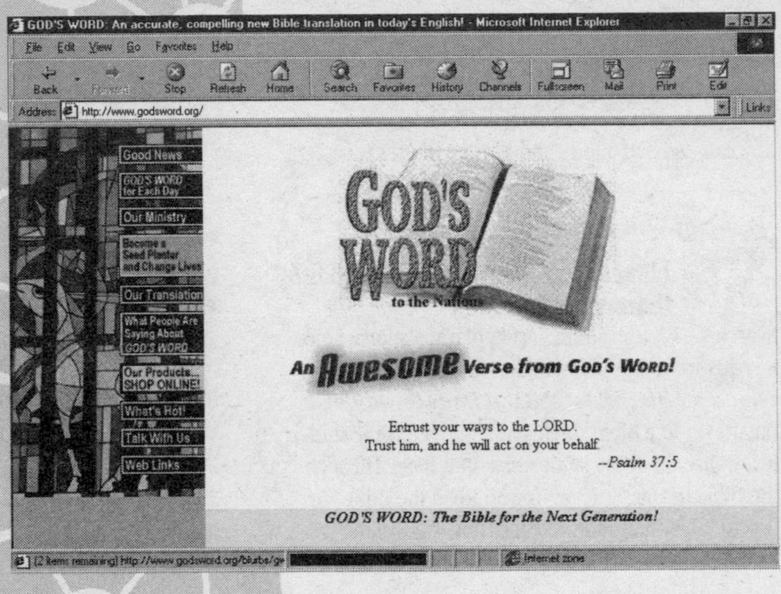

Audio Bible

http://www.audio-bible.com/index.html

Listen to the King James Version of the Bible on-line using Real Audio. Other translations are available at http://www.talkingbible.com

A Devotional Bible Study

http://mydevotion.com/

On-line Bible study. Post your devotional insights to share with other Christians. Read KJV and NIV side by side. Bookmark your favorite verses and read topical verses on faith, anger, stress,etc. Also features devotions from Spurgeon, *Easton's Bible Dictionary*, and *Matthew Henry's Concise Commentary*. For fun, you can download a free animated cartoon talking Bible screen-saver.

Did You Know?

...that the Barna research Groups says "Our research indicates that by 2010 we will probably have 10% to 20% of the population relying primarily or exclusively upon the Internet for its religious input"

Bible Answer Machine

http://bibleanswermachine.ww7.com/index.html

Provides answers to your Bible questions, with the option of selecting and saving answers to accumulate for later copying or printing.

Bible Quizzes

http://www.biblequizzes.com/

Quizzes on an assortment of topics, updated periodically. Also has crosswords and a free Bible Reading Planner.

Bible Quizzes from TwoPaths

http://www.twopaths.com/biblequizzes.html

Test your knowledge of the Bible with these automatically scored quizzes. Some quizzes include illustrations and background music.

BILINGUAL

Hola.
Shalom.
Bonjour.

Speak a second language? The Internet is international, so it doesn't take much to find sites in the language that interests you. Here are some sites that help you study bilingualism or find a job using your second language.

Studying Bilingualism

http://www.cal.org/cal/html/links/be.htm

Interested in improving communication through better understanding of language and culture? The Center for Applied Linguistics allows you to do just that by providing links to the hottest bilingual issues of today.

Pacific Rim Careers

http://www.asia-net.com/

Japanese, Chinese, and Korean bilingual-speaking jobs. Asia-Net serves the Asia/Pacific-Rim business community by providing career information to professionals.

Bilingual Jobs

http://www.bilingual-jobs.com/

Bilingual-jobs.com is a career resource for bilingual job seekers searching for international employment in Europe, Asia, and North America. This site gives bilingual job seekers the opportunity to submit resumés and receive job information via E-mail as well as allows bilingual employers to post job openings for free and search for candidates on-line.

Bilingual Electronic Postcards

http://www.abcard.net/

This site lets you send or receive an electronic postcard in either Spanish or English.

Bilingual Education

http://www.federalregister.com/hpage2/obemla.html

This commercial site provides rapid access to large amounts of federal and state data and services concerning bilingual education.

IJBEB

http://www.catchword.co.uk/titles/13670050.htm

Interested in learning more about bilingual education? This site posts full-text documents from the *International Journal of Bilingual Education and Bilingualism*.

National Association for Bilingual Education

http://www.nabe.org/

Promoting educational excellence and equity through bilingual education, the National Association for Bilingual Education (NABE) is the only national organization exclusively concerned with the education of language-minority students in American schools. Learn more about NABE by connecting to this site.

FAQ

http://www.ed.gov/offices/OBEMLA/q_a.html

The Office of Bilingual Education and Minority Languages Affairs answers your questions about bilingual education.

Dutch Search Engines

http://www.bluewindow.ch

Spanish Search Engines

http://www.radar.com.mx/

French, Dutch, Italian Search Engines

http://www.sitexplorer.com/

Bilingual Radio

http://www.bmradio.net/

Four Spiritual Laws

http://www.ccci.org/laws/index.html

BOOKS

The World Wide Web has not (and won't) rid the planet of books. Instead, the web does make it easier to review and purchase products. Some sites allow you to read books on-line or listen to audio versions.

When it comes to purchasing books, the best deal is not always at the biggest names. Take time to browse different sites—including the small stores for the best prices and experience.

Books and Literature

http://digital.library.upenn.edu/books/

The On-Line Books Page is a directory of books that can be freely read right on the Internet. It includes an index of thousands of on-line books and pointers to significant archives of on-line texts and special exhibits.

Classics

http://www.columbia.edu/acis/bartleby/

Looking for great books on-line? The Bartelby Library publishes the classics of literature, nonfiction, and reference—free of charge for the home, classroom, and desktop.

Classics and Reference

http://www.bibliomania.com/

Bibliomania, a vast on-line library, has what you're looking for. On this site you'll find over sixty classic novels, dictionaries, and important classic nonfiction works, all full-text searchable html. (Want another option? Try http://www.1stbooks.com/).

Hard to Find

http://www.alibris.com/cgi-bin/texis/searcher/

Searching for that one special book? This site brings you to books you thought you'd never find. Locate a loved one's favorite book, your treasured songbook, or find a repair manual for your '65 Mustang.

BookFinder.com

http://www.bookfinder.com/
This site is a search engine that immediately finds the best buys from over 15 million new, used, rare, and out-of-print books.

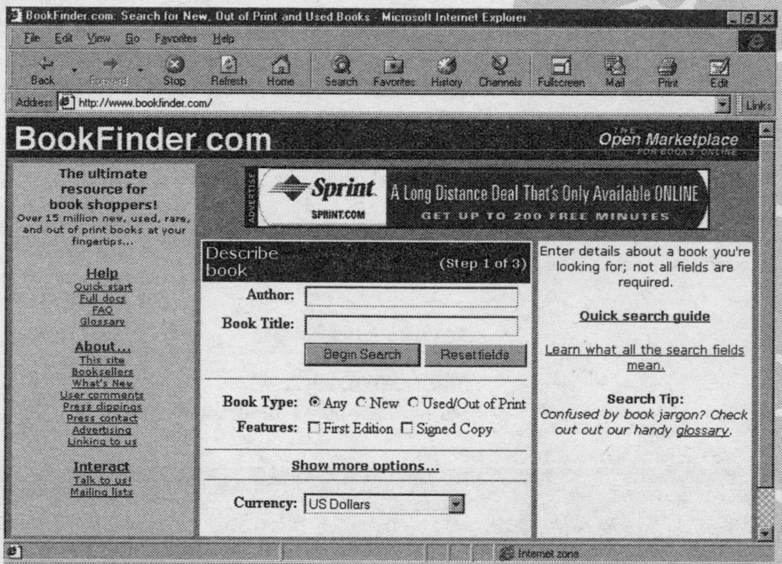

From Down Under/

http://www.timebooksellers.com.au
Time Booksellers, established in 1979, specializes in rare and collectible books, bringing you the best of Australian literature.

9000+ Free Books/

http://www.books-on-line.com
Books-On-Line—home page of 9,454 free

books. This site catalogues all known books available for downloading. There is also a free newsletter to tell you when new titles become available.

Bible Gateway

http://bible.gospelcom.net/bible/

This site allows you to search multiple versions of the Bible in seven different languages. Search by keyword, location, or concept.

Recipe Books

http://onlinebiz.com/recipes/recipes.html

If you love cooking, this site's for you. Download free electronic recipe books and get involved in a recipe exchange with other people on-line.

Booksellers

Barnes and Noble

http://www.bn.com/

Barnes and Noble's direct site to get you the books

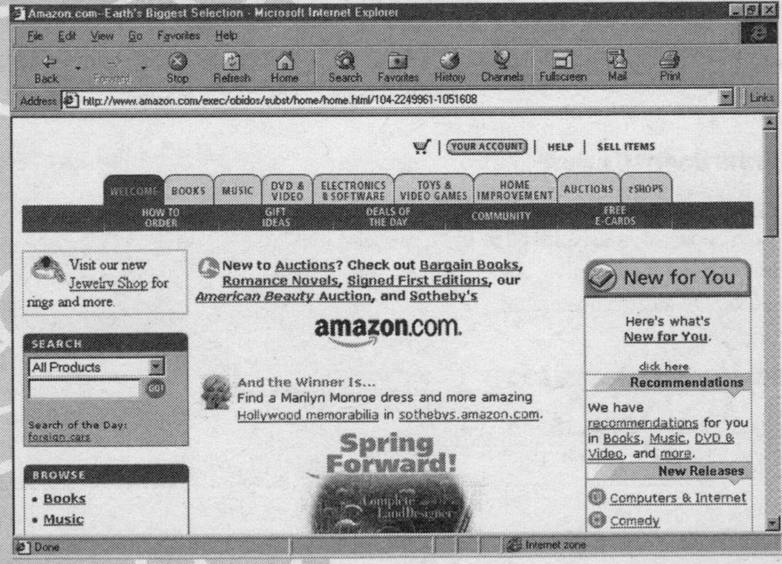

you need. Search for bargains, gifts, and even books that are out of print. This site gets you to a name you know and trust.

Amazon

http://www.amazon.com/

Browse books, music, videos, electronics, software, video games, and much more. Amazon provides a fast, easy way to purchase the products you need.

Borders

http://www.borders.com/

Ten million items: books, CDs, and music. Search for the newest best-sellers or hear stories of books that change lives.

Books for Auction

http://www.ebay.com/

Looking to make a deal? Place your bid for the book of your choice and have fun buying and selling on the web.

Finding Publishers

http://www.lights.com/publisher/

The number one spot for finding publishers on the web. This site provides you with links to all known publishers' home pages. Parental guidance is suggested, as some non-Christian publishers produce material you may not find appropriate.

Kid Books

http://www.kidsbooks.com/

Kidsbooks is your source for children's books. For nature, science, educational, and illustrated classics, visit this site.

Christian Publishing Companies

http://www.barbourbooks.com/

http://www.americanbible.org/

http://www.amginternational.org/

http://www.augsburgfortress.org/

http://www.bakerbooks.com/

http://www.bethanyhouse.com/

http://www.broadmanholman.com/

http://www.cph.org/

http://www.cookministries.com/

http://www.chariotvictor.com/

http://www.gospellight.com/

http://
www.grouppublishing.com/

http://www.guideposts.org/

http://
www.howardpublishing.com/

http://www.ivpress.com/

http://www.kirkbride.com/

http://www.kregel.com/

http://www.moody.edu/

http://www.navpress.org/

http://thomasnelson.com/

http://urbanministries.com/

http://
www.wordpublishing.com/

http://www.zondervan.com/

Technical Books

Fatbrain.com

http://www.fatbrain.com/

For a comprehensive selection of computer, programming, and technical books, interactive training and certification—such as MCSE—Fatbrain.com should be your first stop.

TechnicalBooks.com

http://www.technicalbooks.com/

Here you'll find a huge selection of technical books listed by category. Over 800 distinct categories specializing in computer, computer hardware, software, programming, and much more.

Best Buys

Compare Prices

http://www.bestbookbuys.com/

Best Book Buys is one of the first shopping comparison sites that searches several stores to help consumers find who's selling products they are seeking at the best prices. Best Buy Books can search over twenty bookstores simultaneously to find the lowest price.

Windows Booksellers

http://www.antiqbook.com/windows/

Find books on theology, biblical studies, church history, philosophy, and intellectual history.

Christian Booksellers

CBD On-Line

http://www.christianbook.com/

The Christian mail-order bookseller is also on-line. Log on to find the same good deals you expect through the mail. If you can't find what you're looking for, try changing the address slightly and pay a visit to http://www.christianbooks.com/.

Christian Chains

http://www.ibelieve.com/

The Christian chains are on-line, too. Try the address above to reach Family Bookstores. Try http://www.parable.com/ or http://www.providentbookstores.com/ for other options.

Heartsong Presents

http://www.getset.com/hsal/

Love stories are rated G! That's for godly, gratifying, and, of course, great! The home page of some of the Heartsong authors. Learn more about them and their books.

Independant Christian Bookstores

http://www.sonshinebookstore.com/

http://www.hackmans.com

Did You Know?

Did you know that there are 7.3 billion commercial E-mail messages sent each day in the U.S.?

CAREER

Put your job to work for you by applying the information you find here. Everything from finding a job, to surviving an interview, to asking for a raise.

If you work, or would like to, the Internet is becoming a standard tool for refining your job skills and landing the job that fits you best.

Newspapers

TOP SITE

USA Today Career Center

http://www.usatoday.com/careers/careers.htm

Your one-stop resource linking employers, job seekers, and career information. This site gives you the chance to find out who's hiring and the hottest companies on the market today.

Chicago Tribune Career Path

http://cgi.chicago.tribune.com/career/

This site provides job listings from the *Chicago Tribune,* plus employment news and advice. You can also post your resumé on-line or learn more about potential employers.

Job Tools

Job Interviews

http://www.job-interview.net/

Here's a guide to job interviews with strategy and job-specific tips; find sample interview questions and answers, and practice/mock interviews.

Able Career Planning

http://www.hawk.igs.net/~jobs/employmentplanning/

Do you require guidance in vocational

exploration? Obtain test information on this site about your interests, abilities, and readiness for employment. Such information is very useful in comparing psychological attributes of the individual with the demands and characteristics of a job activity.

Absolute Career Services

http://www.absolutecareer.com/

This site comes your way providing analysis and preparation of resumés, cover letters, and interviewing techniques. It also features career development consulting services for individuals and businesses, including job search, career change, transition assistance, career management, executive coaching, workshops, and support groups.

Celia D. Crossley & Associates

http://www.crosworks.com/

Assists individuals working on their own or through their company in developing a strategic plan for their career and achieving career satisfaction and success. In these career management services, you'll find career coaching and career transition guidance for individuals and groups. Also provided are career appraisal and assessment, career relocation assistance, and the Birkman Method Assessment Tool.

Yahoo! Jobs

http://dir.yahoo.com/Business_and_Economy/Employment_and_Work/Jobs/Career_Fields/

Search for careers in the field of your choice. Potential job opportunities are listed in alphabetical order for your convenience in researching.

Find a Job

http://www.monster.com/

Workplace Wisdom

http://www.wowi.net/

Career Choices

http://www.cybermall2000.com/stores/career/

Career Impact Ministries International

http://www.careerimpact.org/

Christian Career Center

http://www.gospelcom.net/ccc/

Career Action Center

http://www.careeraction.org/CACpub/index.html

The Career Action Center provides resources and encouragement, helping people understand and address their work-life needs, so they can take control of their careers and become more career self-reliant.

Career Enhancement Resources

http://www.cerseminars.com/

Whether you are an entry-level job seeker or an experienced professional, this site helps you take a *positive* step toward enhancing your job search and your career. Career Enhancement Resources comes your way offering interactive seminars that teach job-search methods.

Free Agent

http://freeagent.com

A powerful hub for freelancers, consultants, and contract professionals.

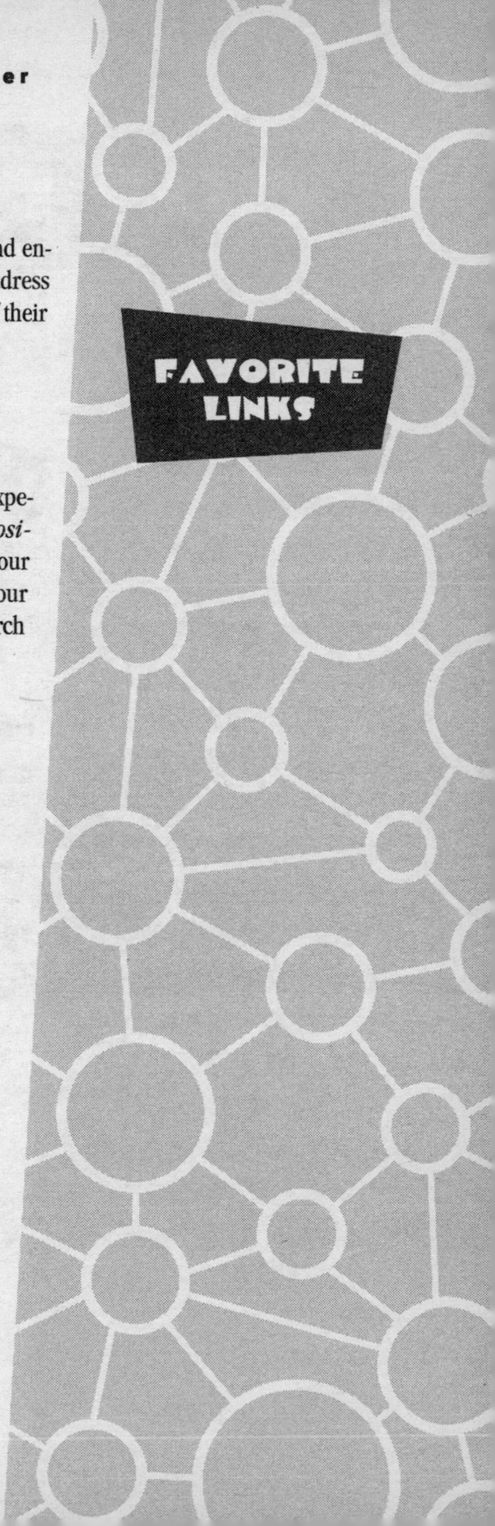

CHAT FOR KIDS

Chat rooms can be dangerous places for kids. The anonymity that people have in chat rooms can cause them to behave badly and speak inappropriately. You've probably also heard about pedophiles who stalk children in chat rooms.

Kids are, nonetheless, often drawn to chat rooms. Responsible parents need to know where their children are chatting and provide their own monitoring. The sites listed in this section are often monitored and considered "safe."

Christian Chat for Kids

http://www.christcenteredmall.com/kids/chat.htm

Christian Chat is a Christ-centered chat room that is fun, free, interactive, and family friendly. Enjoy the options of a Kids Zone Directory that allows you to choose between teachings, cartoons, profiles, and much more.

FreeZone

http://www.freezone.com/

FreeZone, a safe interactive community for kids and teens, brings free chat, E-pals, bulletin boards, home pages, cyber postcards, games, and more.

Kids Nation

http://www.kidsnation.com/index.html

Visit Kids Nation where children can chat, play games, enjoy storytime, and learn at the same time. Kids can express themselves with sounds, props, and games. This site allows you to meet and chat live with new friends from all over the world.

i-SAFE Kidz and Teenz Connection

http://www.legalpadjr.com/chat.htm

This site brings you chat rooms available 24 hours a day complete with live kids, teen hosts, and adult room monitors.

TOP SITE

KidChatters

http://www.kidchatters.com/

Clean, safe, and secure family-friendly chat rooms for kids ages six to twelve. KidChatters value keeping kids safe, happy, and productive on-line.

KidSurf On-Line

http://www.kidsurf.net/kidsport/chat/

Kids and teens love to chat around a table full of friends, ice-cold cokes, and of course—pizza. KidSurf On-Line welcomes you to an on-line pizza place. You're invited to join in the discussions and make new friends.

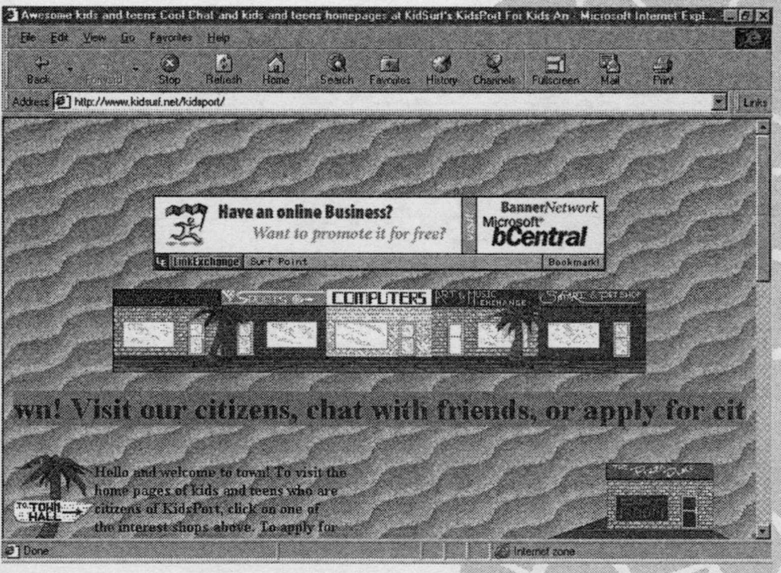

Headbone Zone

http://www.headbone.com/cgi-bin/hbzchatc.cgi?Start.x=1&ChatPath=friends/chat

This chat site for kids offers theme rooms, green rooms, and even private rooms. Pick the room of your choice and have fun.

Freezone's Chat Box

http://chat.freezone.com/

This site has celebrity chat times when kids can chat with their favorite TV star. Choose from five different rooms or opt to play some on-line games.

KidzChatz

http://www.kidzchatz.com/

Enter into a cool chatting experience for Kidz from all over the planet. This site is safe, clean, free, and friendly.

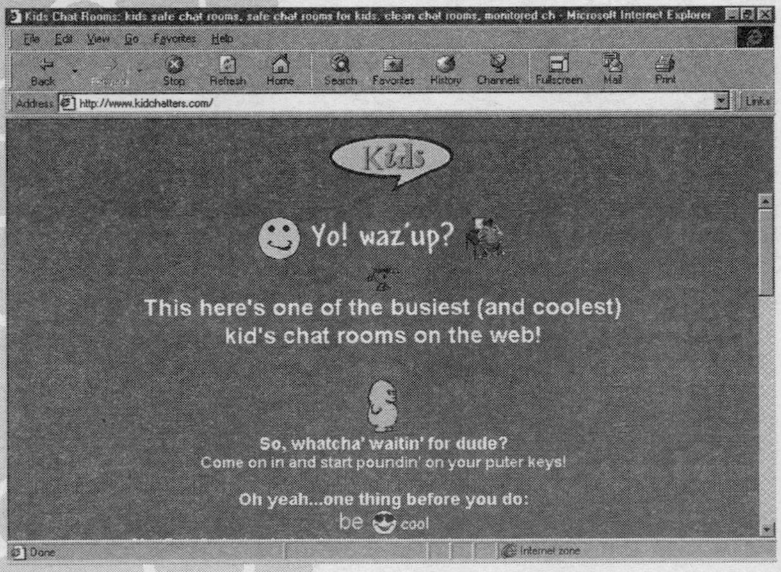

Crosswalk Chats

http://chat.crosswalk.com/

These Christian hub allows you to create your own chat room to discuss a topic that interests you. While there are not many formal kids chat rooms, you're free to create your own.

ibelieve.com

http://www.ibelieve.com/

This site has both scheduled chats and regular informal chats. Like many Christian sites, these sites are open to members only (this kind of policy helps keep chats clean).

Teens

http://www.tel-a-teen.org/

Six to Twelve Year Olds

http://www.angelfire.com/az/thepinkdollhouse/living.html

Christian Adult

http://www.crosswalk.com/

http://www.ibelieve.com/

http://www.gospelcom.net/chat/

Submit a Site

hudson@techie.com

CHEMISTRY

Neutrons. Protons. Electrons. Reactions. Lab experiments. The periodic table.

The net has thorough resources for those who've always enjoyed chemistry or need accessible information for class.

Use these sites to stay on top of chemistry news and research or simply get the study help you need.

Chemistry & Industry Magazine

http://ci.mond.org/

Chemistry & Industry provides a twice-monthly roundup of international and interdisciplinary news, features, comments, and views. It covers chemistry, biotechnology, health, the environment, energy, agriculture, food, materials, and education; and the chemical, pharmaceutical, biotechnology, and food industries.

The *Journal of Biological Chemistry*

http://www-jbc.stanford.edu/jbc

This site provides a wide range of information. Choose from a listing of articles and essays written on important issues in today's science world. View or search the archives, read a current issue, or find out future article titles.

Chemistry and Environmental Dictionary

http://environmentalchemistry.com/yogi/chemistry/dictionary/

This dictionary contains definitions for many chemistry, environmental, and other technical terms.

Chemistry Central

http://users.senet.com.au/~rowanb/chem/

Chemistry Central brings you basic atomic information on the periodic table of elements, chemical bonding, and organic chemistry. Check out the many chemistry links that this web site provides as an added feature.

ChemScope

http://chemscope.com/

Find and conduct business with life-science suppliers or biopharmaceutical companies by visiting this site. ChemScope provides a comprehensive chemistry site that includes complete daily biotechnology, medical devices, pharmaceutical magazine news, FDA updates, jobs, suppliers, and products.

Knowledge By Design

http://www.knowledgebydesign.com/tlmc/tlmc.html

Interactive technology applied to chemical education on the net, including a periodic table game and titration applets and interesting on-line interactive exercises to increase your chemical common sense with instant feedback. Also to be found on this site is visualization of molecular models and atomic orbitals and computer animation such as QuickTime, MPEG movies, GIFs, VRML, and Macromedia Shockwave files. This site also provides hundreds of links to other chemistry sites.

The Nobel Prize Internet Archive

http://www.almaz.com/nobel/chemistry/

Check out all the chemistry Nobel Prize winners from 1901 to the present. This site is fully interactive and gives you an annotated, hyperlinked list of all Nobel laureates. If you have an interesting and useful Internet link about a particular Nobel laureate, you can add your link instantly to that laureate's home page.

World of Chemistry

http://www.chemsite.com

Other Links

http://soulcatcher.chem.umass.edu/cgi-bin/pickPage.cgi?downloads.html

http://web.jjay.cuny.edu/~acarpi/NSC/index.htm

http://library.thinkquest.org/3310

http://www.chemcenter.org

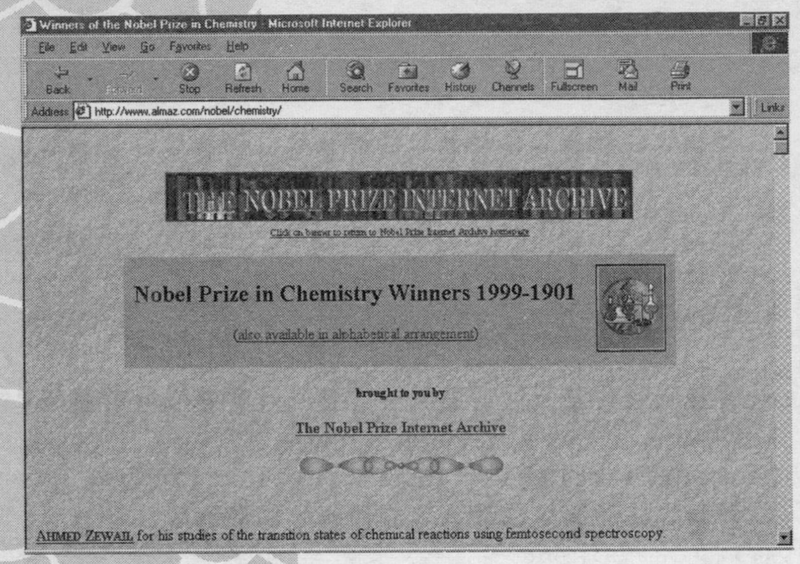

Biochemist On-Line

http://www.biochemist.com/main.htm

This site's mission statement is: 1) To serve as a site where visitors can learn and ask questions about biochemistry. 2) To provide biochemists with links to reference material found on the Internet. 3) To provide an on-line message board where individuals can post questions or comments about ongoing research.

TOP SITE

ChemConnect

http://www.chemconnect.com/news/journals.html

ChemConnect has a list of almost 600 links to various chemistry magazines and journals and has been maintained since April 1996. If you know of any publication that has been missed, you can send the URL and it will be added with the next update.

Did You Know?

...that 1.9 billion dollars was spent on advertising on the Internet in 1998? (And that 106 billion was spent on outdoor advertising?)

CHILDREN'S HEALTH

Virtual Children's Hospital Home Page

http://vch.vh.org/

The Virtual Children's Hospital digital library was created in 1994 to help meet the information needs of health care providers and patients and families. The goal of the Virtual Children's Hospital digital library is to make the Internet a useful medical reference and health promotion tool for health care providers and patients and families.

Mommie's Love

http://members.aol.com/Solhouse5/

The purpose of this web site is to inform parents about other resources on the Internet relating to parenting education and skills as well as physical and spiritual health.

Chronic Illness, Children, & Health Education

http://funrsc.fairfield.edu/~jfleitas/contents.html

This is a site about growing up with medical problems. Its goal is to help people understand what it's like, from the perspective of children and teens.

Parents tend to be concerned with their children's health. While no web site can replace a trip to the doctor's office, some sites do give good general health recommendations. Some will help you look for certain symptoms to help you determine if a trip to the doctor's office is necessary.

Basic Health Sites

http://www.personalbest.com/

http://www.cfhinfo.org/

http://vm.cfsan.fda.gov/list.html

http://www.americasdoctor.com/

http://www.drkoop.com/

Cardiovascular Health Promotion for Children

http://www.jhbmc.jhu.edu/cardiology/partnership/kids/kids.html

Health habits developed in childhood including a diet high in fat, cholesterol, and calories, physical inactivity, and smoking increase the risk for adult heart disease. The Partnership for Community Health teaches children to make healthier food choices, to increase physical activity, and to avoid smoking.

Infectious Diseases in Children

http://www.slackinc.com/child/idc/idchome.htm

This site bring you key articles from current and past issues of *Infectious Diseases in Children*. Take part in a real-time discussion with a panel of experts and peers from around the world. You can also seek news and advice—and give news and advice—in an ongoing newsgroup discussion.

KidsDoctor

http://www.kidsdoctor.com/

Check out the award-winning articles this site has to offer arranged by both category and anatomy. The question-and-answer section is helpful for answering your health-related questions. You can also use the search tool for quick, convenient access to our database of children's health topics. Go to the Reading Room where you'll find books on many topics, some of which are directly related to the KidsDoctor articles.

KidsHealth—Children's Health & Parenting Information

http://kidshealth.org/

Looking for expert health information for the

entire family? KidsHealth.org has the latest on everything from chicken pox to dyslexia in easy-to-read articles. Created by the medical experts at the Nemours Foundation, KidsHealth.org has trainloads of information on infections, behavior and emotions, food and fitness, and growing up healthy, as well as cool games and animations.

ParentsPlace

http://www.parentsplace.com/health/

The Health section of ParentsPlace features different topics each day and provides tools to help answer your questions.

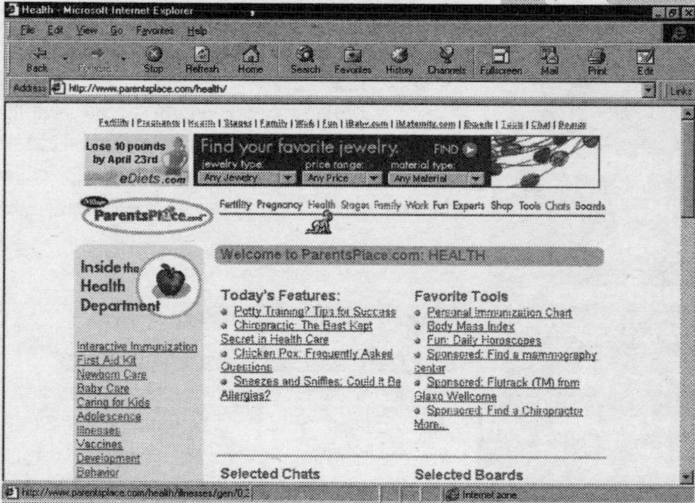

Wellness

http://www-hsl.mcmaster.ca/tomflem/child.html

This site brings you health care information resources. Find links to sites on children's health.

Did You Know?

Did you know that 37 percent of parents say their children watch less television since they were introduced to the Internet?

CLASSIFIEDS

The classifieds in your local paper are limited. They're limited by region and word count—only including the words and phrases that fit the seller's budget.

Internet classifieds are easier to use. They're searchable, longer, free, and reach a nationwide readership. If you're someone who combs the classifieds each week, consider picking out a site or two on the net that you can surf instead. The AdHound at the Classified Warehouse may be a great way for you to keep an eye out for what you're hunting for.

World Wide Classified

http://www.wwclass.com/

This site specializes in automotive, real estate, books, music, employment, jobs, and many other searches.

TOP SITE

The *News & Observer*

http://www.news-observer.com/classified

Looking for something special? Sign up today for The *News & Observer's* customized classified ad notification. Check out the marketplace or find what you're looking for in the classified ad index.

Classified Warehouse

http://www.classifiedwarehouse.com/

Classified Warehouse helps you find jobs, cars, housing, and more. This site's AdHound automatically searches and E-mails you the results from each day's new postings.

AmericaNet

http://www.americanet.com/Classified/busopp.html

You can choose the type of ad you would like to look at in the category of your choice. Searching is made easy by using the image map to navigate the Business Opportunity ads. This site features special buttons that display the ads in order of when they are received.

E-Swapper

http://www.eswapper.com/
E-Swapper is your neighborhood and worldwide shopping mart to buy and sell goods and services through classified ads. Sell or buy everything from airplanes to zip drives. Use the advanced search engine to notify you when someone places a classified ad in E-Swapper selling the product you want.

Classify-It

http://www.classify-it.com/
Free classified ads. This site offers over twenty-five categories for you to place ads or find the ads that you need.

The Multilevel Classified Zone

http://worldentre.com/thezone.htm
This site links you to the MLM classified advertising on the World Wide Web. Post your ad, make a web page submission, visit the zone mailer or the message boards, and check out the most recent ads placed.

Web-Cat's Free Classifieds

http://www.web-cat.com/classifieds/
Free Classified ads for home, auto, business, sports, and life. Choose from the category of your choice and view or post ads. Over thirty categories to search from.

Crosswalk Classifieds

http://www.christianclassifieds.net/
Crosswalk.com's Christian Class-ifieds is a place for you to post a classified ad and read existing ads. You'll find everything from Job Seekers to Personal Announcements. This site also includes help-wanted ads, job openings,

Writing Your Ad

http://www.freebiereports.com/

http://www.mlmcentral.com/marketingstation/dodont.html

http://www.reslight.addr.com/info/r0008.html

http://www.goldnbear.com/docs/ad.html

http://desktoppub.miningco.com/compute/desktoppub/library/weekly/aa980717.htm

positions wanted, announcements, education, events, business opportunities, real-estate ads, retirement services, conventions, financial consultation, and fundraisers.

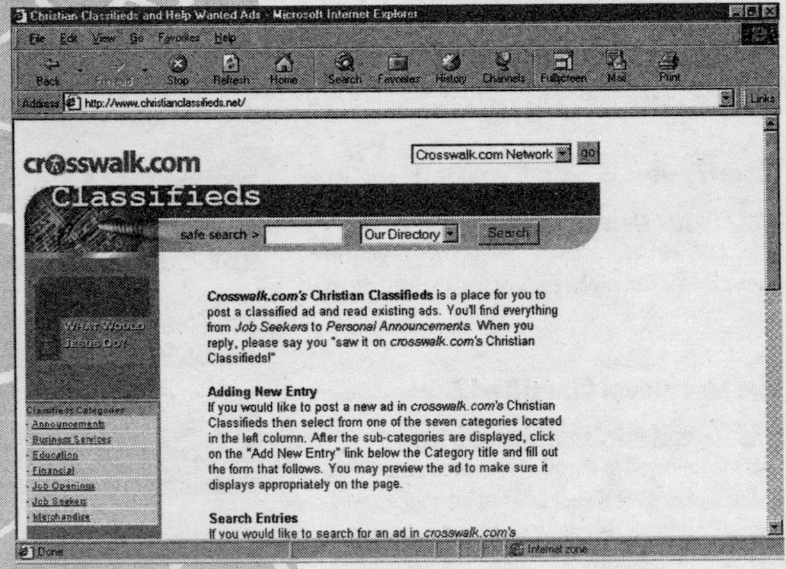

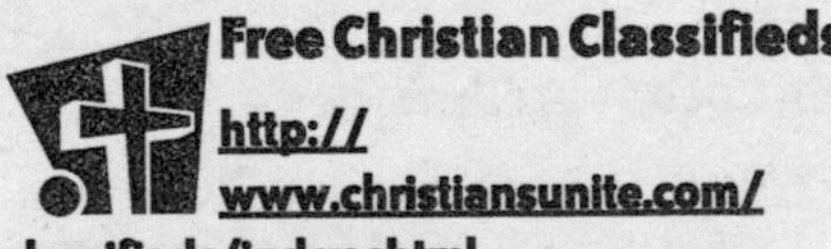

Free Christian Classifieds

http://www.christiansunite.com/classifieds/index.shtml

http://www.christiancompanies.com/

http://www.christianweb.net/

Try these sites to reach a Christian readership.

DID YOU KNOW?

...that 10 percent of people remember a banner ad from a web site, while 12 percent remember a TV ad?

COLLEGE

College Is Possible

http://www.collegeispossible.org/

Thinking about college? You probably have a lot of questions: How does the application process work? What sort of college is right for me? How much will college cost? America's colleges and universities have prepared this site to guide you to the books, web sites, and other resources that admissions and financial aid professionals consider most helpful.

The College Board

http://www.collegeboard.org/

The College Board prepares, inspires, and connects students to colleges and opportunities by preparing students academically for college entrance, helping students earn college credit and placement, and securing financial aid information.

College Quest

http://www.collegequest.com/

This site is a personal organization tool. Includes school descriptions, on-line applications, and financial aid advice.

U.S. News On-Line

http://www.usnews.com/usnews/edu/

U.S. News helps you find a college or grad school, see the national rankings, apply on-line, find a scholarship, and discover what the best jobs are.

What should today's student major in? Which colleges are the best? How can you afford college with today's tuition?

While college has never been more expensive, it's also never been easier to collect information on the schools that interest you. Today's college web sites have links to their libraries, pages devoted to student life, and some even have on-line courses.

Some colleges have web cams set up on campus, which take live pictures of the campus—allowing parents to "visit" with their son or daughter more often.

Christian College Guide

http://www.whatsthebest-college.com/

Which Christian college best meets your needs? This site offers a guide for Christian colleges. It simply provides you with the information you need to select the right school. WhatsTheBest-College exists solely to help you in your quest to find the right school for you. Your selection of a college is extremely important — you do spend at least four years there.

BestSchoolsUSA

http://www.bestschoolsusa.com/

BestSchoolsUSA provides comprehensive information on: applying to colleges, applications and admission requirements and procedures, college admissions criteria, and the weight allotted to grades by various colleges, AP courses, SAT, ACT, sports, volunteer work, essays, references, etc. They also have tips on choosing colleges, preparing college applications, writing essays, getting recommendation letters, preparing for interviews, etc. The comprehensive surveys provide answers which colleges themselves gave on application and admission requirements and procedures.

Campus Tours

http://www.campustours.com/

CampusTours is the definitive on-line source for virtual college tours, interactive maps, college web cams, QuickTime virtual reality tours, campus movies, and pictures. Every day thousands of prospective students visit CampusTours to take virtual excursions of colleges across the United States.

The College Bound Network

http://www.collegebound.net/

Looking for advice and resources on money, technology, sports recruiting, or application? The College Bound Network can answer your questions.

American University in London

http://www.aul.edu/

Student Debt

http://www.studentcredit.com/

http://www.educaid.com/

UK colleges

http://www.liv.ac.uk/~evansjon/university.html

Washington, D.C. Internships

http://www.twc.edu/

Employment

http://www.summerjobs.com/

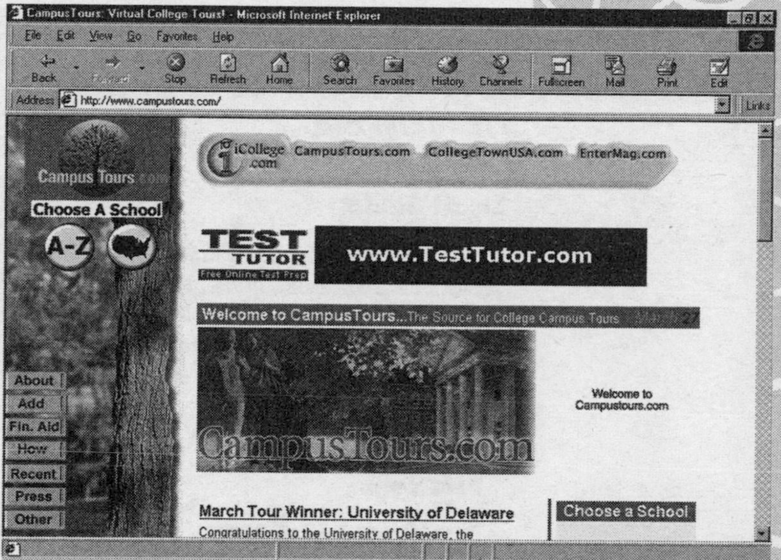

College Reviews

http://www.review.com/college/templates/temp1.cfm?body=index.cfm

Looking for the right college for you? Review.com has expert opinions and custom searches. Let the search begin. Wondering where you can find the best education? The poshest dorms? The coolest classmates? The most interesting professors? This site has done the research for you. Check out the best 331 colleges on the list this site prepared for you. And don't sweat the college application process. Get organized and take control; just visit the apply section. You'll love the search, selection, and application tools. . .customized to your personal likes, needs, preferences, and priorities.

Criterion Productions

http://www.criterioninfo.net/vcd/

This site is an easy way to view college information on the web. From this page, you can call up college videos through an interactive map, or if you'd prefer a simpler way, through the alphabetical college listing.

Financial Aid

Smart Guide

http://www.cs.cmu.edu/afs/cs.cmu.edu/user/mkant/Public/FinAid/finaid.html

FinAid, The Smart Student Guide to Financial Aid, is a comprehensive free resource for objective and unbiased information about student financial aid on the World Wide Web.

Petersons

http://www.petersons.com/

This is a comprehensive web resource on education and careers. Research and connect to the school, camp, college, study-abroad program, graduate program, or job of your dreams.

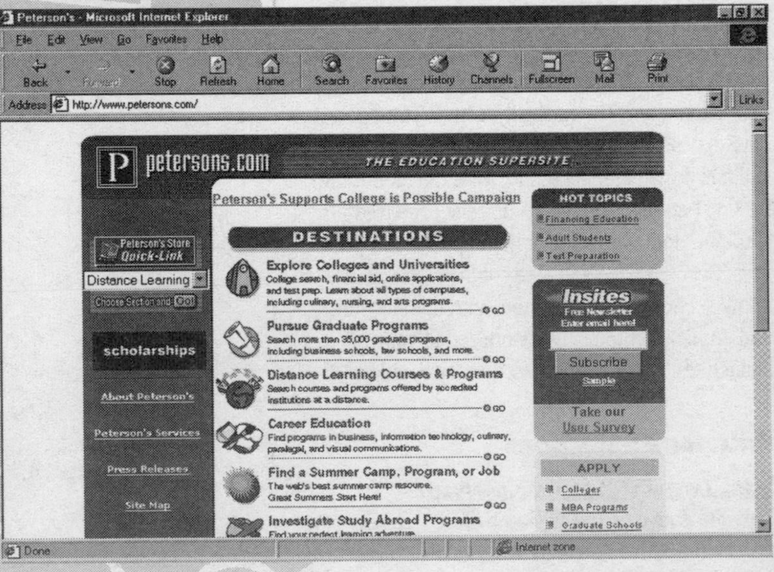

Student Financial Assistance

http://www.ed.gov/offices/OSFAP/Students/
The Student Financial Assistance Programs are the largest source of student aid in America, providing over $40 billion a year in grants, loans, and work-study assistance. Here you'll find help for every stage of the financial aid process, whether you're in school or out of school.

Fast Web

http://www.fastweb.com/
Find scholarships and colleges. . .free. Need money for college? Use the free FastWeb on-line Scholarship Search.

Kaploan

http://www.kaploan.com/
From Kaplan Educational Centers, this site lets you request information and an educational loan application on-line. Find out more about scholarships and finance packages. Learn to make wise decisions, and have enough money for tuition and late-night pizza.

CollegeNET

http://www.collegenet.com/
CollegeNET is the complete on-line guide to colleges, universities, graduate programs, and financial aid. With CollegeNET you can find the perfect college for you with the college search engine, apply to that college on-line, then get the funds to pay for it.

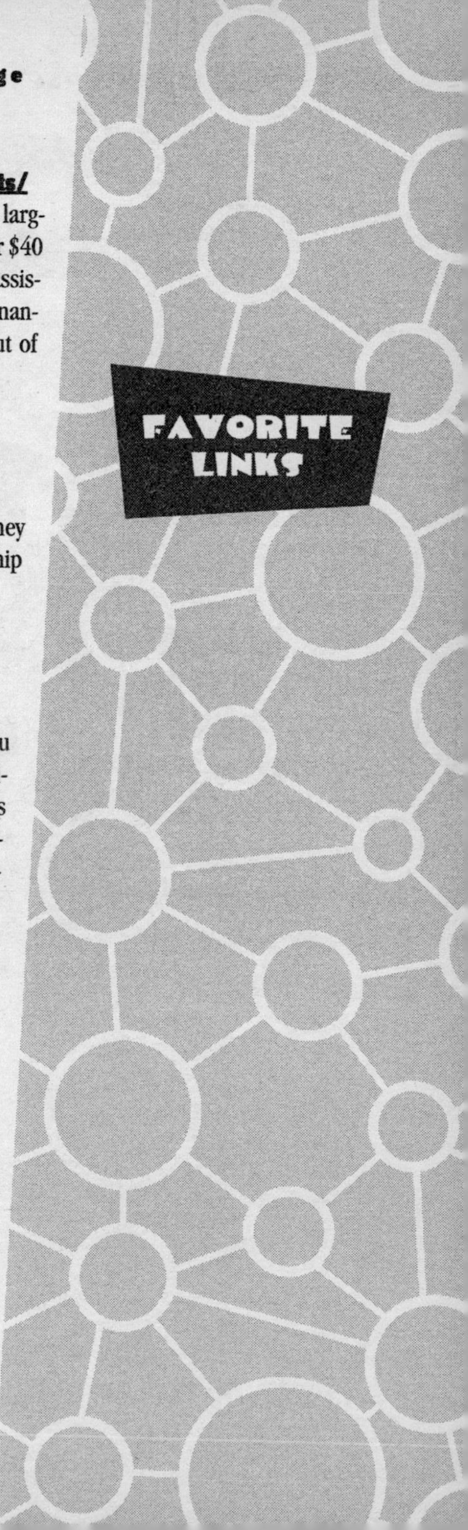

COMICS

Everyone needs a good laugh—that's why one of the most read parts of many newspapers is the comics page. If your job or life is stressful, consider beginning today's surfing session with a cartoon. The lighthearted humor might help you regain your perspective as you get ready to tackle the day ahead of you.

Christian Cartoons

http://www2.itexas.net/~jwt

The Christian Cartoon web site invites you to learn something through the cartoon characters they have created. Laugh at the animation while you learn a valuable lesson about how to live for Christ in today's world.

The Christian Cartoons Showcase

http://www.ChristianCartoons.com/

Christian cartoons and comics showcase is a resource center for Christian cartoonists. If you're interested in becoming a cartoonist for Christ, your work can be featured on this site.

Christian Comics

http://members.aol.com/ChriCom/

This page contains news, reviews, and previews of Christian Comics products and projects around the world. See how comics can be and are being used for evangelism.

Kidzweb

http://www.kidzweb.org/

Kidzweb endeavors to provide great Internet content that teaches biblical values to a global community of children. It's a fun and safe place on the Internet that provides comic stories that are written by a pastor.

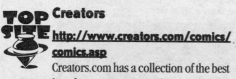

The Two Edged Sword

http://hooray2u.com/

The Two Edged Sword is a comic book for kids ages seven through fourteen (and their parents). Visit this site and see hot graphics and cool Bible lessons while learning Scripture and laughing. For cartoon and Bible fun, check out the Two Edged Sword.

TOP SITE

Creators

http://www.creators.com/comics/comics.asp

Creators.com has a collection of the best comics on-line for you to enjoy. This site has all your favorites from Heathcliffe to the Rugrats. Check out the archive to read the comics that were written in the past.

United Media

http://www.unitedmedia.com/comics/ab.html

Comic Search is a one-of-a-kind service that enables you to reprint comic strips on the topics you want without the hassle of searching through years of strips. Just describe the type of strip you're looking for and this site does the rest.

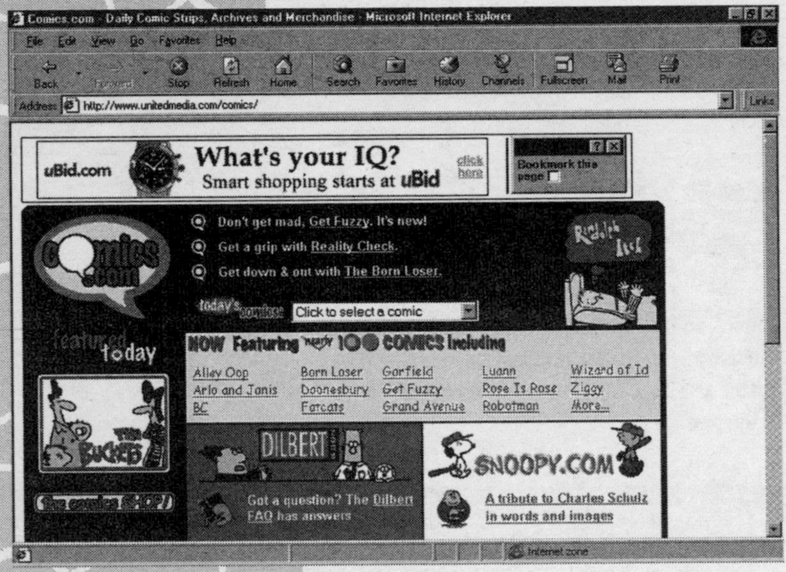

Animations

Animation Library

http://animation.simplenet.com/

This site offers over 4,000 excellent free animations for you to use on your web site, plus articles, reviews, tutorials, and everything else related to animated graphics. You can also use the Postcard Center to develop your own personal postcards.

Did You Know?

Did you know that 58 percent of new Internet users in the U.S. in 1999 were women?

Disney

http://panda.tierranet.com/vu/animation.htm

Check out all the Disney animations. This site links you to lots of cartoon clips from major movie productions. If you like Disney movies, you'll love this web site.

Toonshoppe Character Animation

http://www.toonshoppe.com/

Toonshoppe Media, Inc. provides the very best in digital media, including cartoon-style character animation and original entertainment.

Aspiring Artists

http://stats.bls.gov/k12/text/mus_005t.htm

http://www.kaleidoscapes.com/current.html

National Society

http://www.reuben.org/

Fun Stuff

http://www.saunalahti.fi/~animato

http://www.pixar.com /

http://www.mcdonalds.com/mcdonaldland/whatsnew/happy_meal

COMPUTERS

Just because you enjoy the web doesn't mean you know a lot about computers. If you don't, you're in good company and these sites are awaiting you. You'll find the information and education that you need to keep ahead of the changes in the world of computing.

Computer News

http://www.zdnet.com/

Zdnet is one of the premier computer sites on the web. Use it to read reviews of new software, download programs, and keep up on the computer industry.

Help!

http://www.computer.com/

Valuable information, shopping and support functions in one easy-to-use, comprehensive web site aimed at the novice technology user. Here you'll find easy-to-follow technical support and recommendations from experts.

Microsoft

http://www.microsoft.com/

The granddaddy of them all. Find support for Microsoft products, updates, and downloads.

Apple

http://www.apple.com/

The official Apple web page for all Macintosh devotees.

MacWorld

http://macworld.zdnet.com/

Read up and purchase the latest in Macintosh computing and accessories.

Shopping

http://www.ComputerShopper.com/
http://www.insight.com/
There are many good computer-catalog companies. Try these sites to browse for the latest in technology.

Finding the Best Price

http://www.pricewatch.com/
This site will do the price comparison for you. Select the item you wish to purchase and let it connect you with the cheapest retailer.

Software

Egghead.com

http://www.egghead.com/
This store used to be made of brick-and-mortar. Now it exists exclusively on the web. It's a good choice for a comprehensive list of the software titles you need.

Antivirus

http://www.symantec.com/
No computer should be connected to the Internet without running up-to-date antivirus protection. Norton Anti-Virus is an industry leader and offers free, monthly updates to their software.

Gateway

http://www.gateway.com/

Dell

www.dell.com/

Catalog Comanies

http://www.insight.com/
http://
www.tigerdirect.com/

Ink Cartridge Refills

http://www.out-of-
ink.com/printer.htm

CONSUMER REVIEWS

You know you need a certain kitchen appliance, but which brand is better? Which car is the better choice for you? Many of these sites are free and offer the ratings and reviews that you're looking for. Deja.com is one of the best, offering opinions and reviews from people who have already purchased what you're looking for.

Consumer Reports

http://www.consumerreports.org/

This site features a fee-based service that includes product recalls, shopping guidance, ratings, recommendations and advice, and message boards. The categories of the product and service reports are: cars and trucks, appliances, electronics, house and home, home office, money, health and food, personal and leisure. There is a free area that provides information and advice about products and services and how to shop for them, about safety issues and late-breaking consumer news; this section is updated weekly.

Epinions.com

http://www.epinions.com/

Features both professional and volunteer-supplied reviews of consumer goods. Includes such topics as autos, colleges and universities, computers, electronics, finance, food and drink, home and garden, kids and family, media, restaurants, services, sports and outdoors, and travel. Includes a search feature so you can find exactly what you're looking for.

ConsumerReview.com

http://www.consumerreview.com/

Features product reviews by consumers for family items, autos, electronics, sports gear, computers, and more.

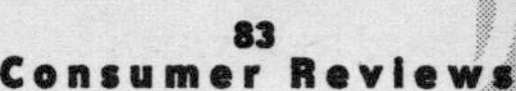

Product ReviewNet

http://www.productreviewnet.com/splash.html

This site offers links to product reviews from a variety of sources. Check out review information on everything from appliances to zip drives. Also provides a key word search feature.

Deja.com

http://www.deja.com/

Deja., unites all of the essential product research and buying tools consumers seek in one integrated, intelligent, and intuitive service. Their unbiased Precision Buying Service features consumer-generated product ratings and reviews, professional reviews, in-depth product specifications, highly intuitive product comparison tools, discussion forums for personalized product inquiries, and a comparison shopping service that far surpasses competitive services currently available to consumers. This site will help you find the product that you want and will direct you, armed with competitive pricing information, to merchants who have that product in stock.

Reviewboard Magazine

http://www.reviewboard.com/

This site offers product reviews written for the consumer without clutter or complexity. Focuses on computer hardware and software, but you can also find a number of reviews for cellular phones, home fitness, home and car audio, home and garden, automotive, and home electronics items.

Consumer Direct Warehouse

http://www.consumer-direct.com/index.htm

This site offers on-line ordering of home video/audio equipment with product pictures and reviews.

CyberStuff

http://www.cyberstuff.net/what_is_cyberstuff.htm

This is a consumer publication written from a non-technical pespective that provides reviews of unique, useful, and/or bizarre web sites, new software and hardware products, as well as technology trends.

Access Magazine

http://www.accessmagazine.com/scripts/home.cfm

Distributed by newspapers across the US, this site publishes weekly reviews of consumer web sites.

Financial Reviews

http://ctcr.investors.net/

This site reviews futures products and provides information for trading.

Recreation and Leisure

Innstar B&B Guidebook Reviews

http://www.innstar.com/

This site rates all the B&B Guidebooks on the web from the consumer's viewpoint. It's designed to help travellers find the on-line guide that will best help them find an Inn.

DID YOU KNOW?

...that men bookmark an average of 55 pages, whereas women bookmark an average of 12 pages?

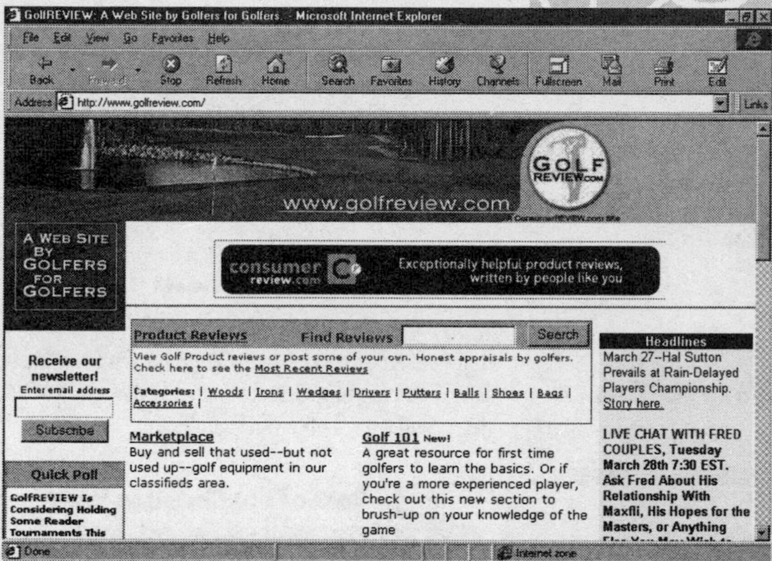

Golf Review

http://www.golfreview.com/

This is a web site by golfers for golfers—focusing on consumer reviews of products and equipment.

OutdoorReview.com

http://www.outdoorreview.com/

Features include consumer-generated gear reviews, trail reviews, a photo gallery, marketplace, outdoor manufacturer links, message boards, and more.

Video Fitness Consumer Guide

http://216.33.170.198/videofitness/

This site contains reviews of exercise videos submitted by consumer reviewers.

BookPage

http://www.bookpage.com/

A monthly general interest book review,

BookPage covers the best in new releases. In the past ten years, BookPage has interviewed everyone from John Grisham to Norman Mailer, and typically reviews up to 100 of each month's new fiction, nonfiction, business, children's, spoken word audio, and how-to books. The tone is upbeat and literate, focusing on best-sellers as well as new discoveries.

Motorcycle Consumer News

http://www.mcnews.com/

Find consumer reporting for the motorcycle enthusiasts, including model and product reviews, safety articles, and a used bike value guide.

Best of the Christian Web

http://www.botcw.com/index.shtml

Reviews and rates Christian web sites and software.

Christianity On-Line

http://www.christianityonline.com/

CCM Full Review

http://www.geocities.com/ccmfullreview/page2.html

Completely Free Software

http://www.completelyfreesoftware.com/cd_rom_tw.html

eXtreme Christianity Reviews

http://php.iupui.edu/~blgroce/

COOKING

Four pints make up a gallon. . .or is that three pints?
If you like to cook, but don't have all the answers, check out these sites. Whether you're a novice and just learning the difference between certain spices, or if you're a regular Martha Stewart, these sites can help you add more than a garnish to your next meal.

About.com: Food

http://home.about.com/food/index.htm

Everything you ever wanted to know about all different kinds of cooking from your About.com guide—a network of sites providing Internet best-link directories, original content and perspective, community features and E-shopping opportunities. Includes cooking topics like barbecues and grilling, busy cooks, Chinese cuisine, home cooking, Italian cuisine, low-fat cooking, Southern U.S. cuisine, and vegetarian cuisine.

The Inquisitive Cook

http://www.inquisitivecook.com/

While many agree that the preparation of food can be an art form, few consider that it's also one of the oldest forms of science; this site is dedicated to helping you understand the science of cooking. It features cooking, baking, and culinary answers. You'll find recipes, free software, hints, tips, discussion. Tune into the Inquisitive Cook's own version of talk radio. This hands-free presentation offers a lively sampling of a selection of questions and answers from the "You Asked Us" section. There's also a monthly contest with a great prize.

TOP SITE

Cooking.com

http://www.cooking.com/

Cooking advice, recipes, and shopping all in one location. Purchase the best in kitchen and tableware items, select specialty food items, or visit the gift center for that perfect gift. Then check out the cooking resources—including menus and menu-planning helps, recipes, a cooks' glossary, and product tips.

Culinary Café

http://www.culinarycafe.com/

An informative cooking site where only the best recipes are available in a handpicked searchable recipe archive with in-depth information about ingredients and techniques to make cooking more enjoyable. Also features a spice and herb encyclopedia, suggestions on kitchen necessities, hints and tips, food chat, and bulletin boards.

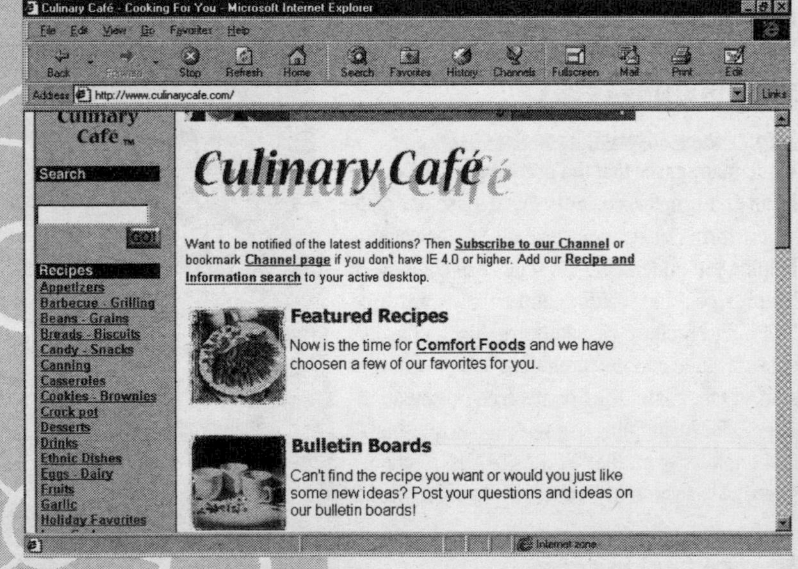

Creative Cooking

http://www.creativecomputing1.com/cooking/kitchen.htm

Site features a database of recipes—including some unique, old-fashioned recipes. Also has a special sections for kids' cooking and cooking/household tips and tricks.

Gourmet

http://www.epicurious.com/a_home/a00_home/home.html

This site is on-line host to *Gourmet* and *Bon Appetit* magazines. A key ingredient of the web site is the Recipe File, an easily searchable database of 10,000 recipes from *Gourmet* and *Bon Appétit* magazines and other sources, such as current and classic cookbooks. Content on Epicurious covers the gamut of cooking and dining, such as basic and advanced cooking techniques, menus, comprehensive wine and restaurant resources, and regular columns on food in France, Italy, and throughout the United States. More Epicurious highlights include a library of over seventy cooking videos, weekly cookbook reviews, a large section on Jewish cooking, a vintage cookbook search, food and wine dictionary, recipe swap, and chef finder.

Cooking Light On-Line

http://www.cookinglight.com/

Texas Beef Council

http://www.txbeef.org/

Cooking Together Chinese Style

http://www.cookingtogether.com/

Cooking Recipes

http://cooking.langenberg.com/

http://www.cookiereceipe.com

CRAFTS

Every season of the year has opportunities for new crafts. If you enjoy unpacking the glue gun, take a few minutes and get stuck on these sites. They're filled with ideas as well as links to purchase whatever supplies you might need.

Crafts Search

http://www.bella-decor.com/search.htm

This site features a search engine just for crafts and crafters. Satisfy all your gift giving needs with handmade crafts by people from around the world. Check out links to crafts newsgroups, downloads, and other crafting sites. And check out the latest in craft headlines.

Arts and Crafts Internet Mall

http://www.artcraftmall.com/index.html

Arts and crafts originals-what the Arts and Crafts Internet Mall is all about: angels, primitive angels, dolls, Barbie clothes, embroidery, woodcrafts, carvings, wreaths, ceramics, dried flowers, clocks, craft kits, jewelry, clothing, quilts, candles, clothing, Noah's Ark, a Victorian store, porcelain, gifts, greeting cards, mosses, and more. Site also has links to crafting associations, organizations, publications, and museums; printed catalog information; crafters on-line help room; magazines; classifieds; and consignment opportunities.

Art and Craft Shows.net

http://www.artandcraftshows.net/

This is a directory of craft fairs which lists more than 2,000 shows, events, and festivals. Searchable by date, city, state, or region.

CraftSearch.com

http://www.craftsearch.com/Craft/

This site features two Internet search engines. The first will help you find a local store that specializes in your craft needs, and the second will connect you with the manufacturers of crafts-related products.

Craft Links Galore

http://www.massachusetts.net/nozzle/crafts/

Find just about everything you need here. The links here are categorized by type and also by location to make them easy to find. Descriptions of each site are on their individual pages.

Pofessionals and Hobbyists

http://www.crafter.com/

Are you a crafter who loves to learn, share, and have fun? If so, then this site was meant for you. Includes shows, malls, suppliers, projects, tips, industry articles, bulletin board, and chat room.

Ruglady Studio

http://www.ruglady.net/

Find rag rug kits, along with hints and tips for this craft. This site also allows women to use their talent of crocheting to make money from home. Check out this site for more information.

Chrismon Snowflakes

http://www.geocities.com/Eureka/Enterprises/4322

Find Christian crafts and Bible games that point to Jesus. Also featuring Chrismon Snowflake ornaments; Chrismons are symbols of faith ornaments to decorate your Christmas tree. Site offers a free pattern.

Aunt Annie's Craft Page

http://www.auntannie.com/

Michael's

http://www.michaels.com/

Crafts, Inc.

http://www.craftsinc.com/

Making Friends: Crafts for Kids

http://www.makingfriends.com/

Kid's Spot

http://www.kids-spot.com/crafts.htm

Kids and Stuff—Crafts for Kids

http://www.angelfire.com/ca/kidsandstuff/crafts.html

Christian Crafting

http://www.geocities.com/Heartland/6580/

Crafty Lady

http://www.getcrafty.com/

Dedicated to making art out of everyday life, this site includes tips for throwing parties, sprucing up your apartment or house, and fashioning your own lovely crafts.

Better Homes and Gardens Magazine—Crafts

http://www.bhglive.com/crafts/

Check out articles, find free projects, join a talk group, or enter a contest. You can also link to other craft magazine web sites.

Did You Know?

...that in 1967 IBM built the first floppy disk?

DESKTOP CUSTOMIZATION

Christian Themes

http://www.geocities.com/christian_today/christiandesktopthemes.html

This site has themes in the following categories: scriptural, inspirational, Easter, Thanksgiving, and Christmas. Also has calendar wallpapers.

Desktop Themes

http://www.infonet.ee/arthemes/

Find themes filled with love and light. Find spiritual themes and themes with art from the old masters.

BiblePower

http://www.biblepower.com/

Bible Power contains 100 percent original Christian clip art, screen savers, wallpaper, and sounds.

BibleVerseArt.com

http://bibleverseart.com/

This site features images that share the Word of God. Find Christian art gallery,

Who says that Microsoft needs to determine what the screen of your computer looks like? You can customize your desktop, screen saver, cursor, and web browser to reflect your interests or personality. Consider installing a kid-theme to help make your computer more accessible to children. Other adaptations can make your computer feel friendlier.

Ministry E-Cards, desktop wallpapers, screen savers and a weekly devotional.

Christian Wallpapers

http://www.christianwallpapers.freeservers.com/

Check out Christian wallpapers and startup screens.

TOP SITE

Free Desktop Themes

http://freedesktopthemes.webjump.com/

Choose from a wide variety of desktop themes—James Bond, Dr. Seuss, and I Love Lucy are just the beginning. This site also features links to other free desktop themes and Theme Making 101—a lesson in how to create your own desktop themes.

Digital Meltdown

http://www.ibbo.fsnet.co.uk/

This site offers desktop-textures backgrounds and themes, tileable wallpaper, and icons.

Kristy's Desktop Creations for Kids

http://www.kwebdesign.com/kdesk/

Designed to encourage young computer lovers to personalize their computers with original icons, cursors, and desktops. Includes downloadable examples and graphics resources.

Georgina's Winnie the Pooh Page

http://members.tripod.com/~eeyore98/

This site includes several desktop themes.

HOT LINKS

Christian

http://www.geocities.com/christian_today/christiandesktopthemes.html

Cars

http://www.users.globalnet.co.uk/~anchsa/home2.htm

Kids

http://kidsstuffpage.tsx.org

Submit a Site

hudson@techie.com

DIET

Surfing the Internet usually won't help you drop a few pounds. Here's a part of the book that may be an exception to that rule. These sites will give you the encouragement and accountability you need to lose weight. They'll also give you good, healthy weight loss ideas. Need to loose a few pounds? Join the club and log on.

CyberDiet

http://www.cyberdiet.com/

This site addresses issues related to adopting a healthy lifestyle. It includes self-assessment tools like an ideal body weight calculator, nutritional profile, and body mass index. The diet and nutrition section includes topics like the daily food planner, recipe index, and food facts. Also features a free newsletter, live chat, and a help desk.

Diet Analysis

http://dawp.anet.com/

This site provides a diet analysis. A diet analysis lets you enter the foods you've eaten for one day and then reports a complete nutritional review of your diet based on the Recommended Dietary Allowances for your demographic.

Delicious Decisions

http://www.deliciousdecisions.org/

Hosted by the American Heart Association, this site offers healthy eating tips and suggestions. Packed with recipes and other helpful resources.

What We Eat

http://www.csmonitor.com/durable/2000/02/16/eatflash.htm

Features an interactive look at changes in U.S. dietary patterns, food advertising, dining out, and world meat consumption from the *Christian Science Monitor*.

Shape Up, America

http://www.shapeup.org/

This site provides the latest information about safe weight management, healthy eating, increased activity, and physical fitness—by Dr. C. Everett Koop. Check out their new Shape Up and Drop 10 program. This site will help you achieve your personal weight loss and shape up goals in the privacy of your own home.

Weigh Down Workshop

http://www.wdworkshop.com/home.htm

The Weigh Down Workshop is a Bible-based weight loss program and more. At their site, you can find out more information about the program (including a new self-paced program for individuals), check out testimonials, or join the E-mail list.

Weight Focus

http://www.weightfocus.com/

ThriveOnline - Weight

http://thriveonline.com/weight/

Christian Women's Weight Loss Support

http://www.cyberenet.net/~cclemens/Hebrews12.html

Calorie Counter

http://www.caloriescount.com/calculator.html

Calorie Control

http://www.caloriecontrol.org/

DISTANCE LEARNING

Aletheia Tutorial Service

http://www.vidnet.net/~aletheia/

Aletheia Tutorial Service is a live, on-line teaching service for homeschoolers and anyone who wants to learn from home by computer. Available courses include New Testament Greek, New Testament Survey, and God's Law and the Civil Government.

Biblical Hebrew Made Easy

http://www.biblicalhebrew.com/

This is primarily the home page for a correspon- dence Biblical Hebrew course developed by a Hebrew and Theology teacher for all ages and abilities. Additionally, at this site you can get an introduction in Hebrew, learn the Hebrew alphabet, check out word studies, learn about the application of Hebrew to New Testament studies, gain insights from Judaism, check out other links, and more. Whether or not you order the correspondence course, this site has useful information for anyone interested in Biblical Hebrew.

Baker's Guide to Christian Distance Education

http://www.ccde.org/

Baker's Guide to Christian Distance Education is an on-line reference center for prospective distance learners and others interested in Christian

Distance learning used to be a version of correspondence schools. You'd sign up, wait for the tapes or assignment to arrive in the mail, do course work, and return your homework by certified mail.

Today, many courses are available on-line. Even more traditional distance learning programs utilized the web to pass class work between teacher and student. Today's instant access to professors, teachers, and tutors can help take the apparent "distance" out of distance learning.

distance education. Find out about accredited Christian distance learning programs, gain assistance in finding the appropriate program for you, and check out the suggested reading list. You can also subscribe to the newsletter to keep up with the latest happenings in Christian distance learning.

TOP SITE

Education Search

http://www.educating.net/

Family oriented education search engine with homeschooling, distance learning, college and university degrees, K-12 resources, references, news sources, and resources for people of all ages and stations. This is a great doorway to all forms of education with something for everyone.

Links Galore

http://www.links2go.com/topic/distance_learning/

Go to this site for links and topics related to distance learning. Find out where you can go to chat in real time about distance learning and other related topics.

Eduport.com

http://www.eduport.com/

Eduport.com is a specialized search engine directory for professional development, education, and distance learning, offering access to information and resources in the areas of education, business, technology, and medicine.

Degree.net Central

http://www.degree.net/

Here you'll find news, books, guides to specific topics like accreditation or MBAs, links, and a database of distance learning programs. Learn how to earn a bachelor, master, or doctorate

Classical Education

http://www.gbt.org/

Home Study International

http://www.hsi.edu/

Village Learning Center

http://www.snowcrest.net/villcen/vlchp.html

Tutorials

http://www.schola-tutorials.com/

degree entirely by distance learning or by credit from prior learning, using mail, phone, or the Internet. Bear's Guide is a classic in distance learning and in evaluating the quality of programs.

Distance Learning Resource Network

http://www.wested.org/tie/dlrn/
Check out the on-line interactive community, find other distance learning programs, locate sites with web-based instruction, read literature reviews and reports, and more.

Peterson's

http://www.petersons.com/
A great educational resource, this site helps you take inventory of your educational needs, search for courses and programs with detailed descriptions of each, and apply for scholarships for on-line courses. You can also use the search feature to look for a key word, and you can get information on technical degrees and certificates.

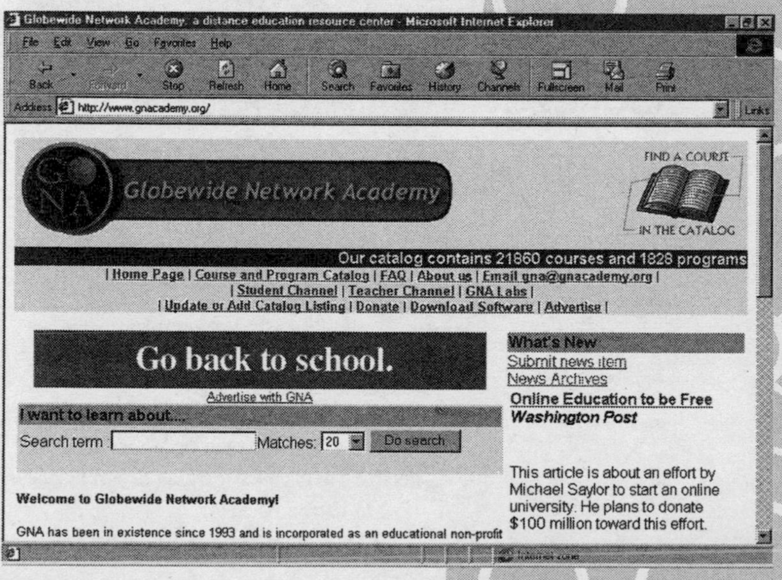

Globewide Network Academy

http://www.gnacademy.org/

Distance education resource center web site with a free on-line course catalog containing thousands of courses and programs, an on-line bookstore, and academic support services.

Furbello.com

http://furbello.com/

Furbello.com provides an interactive learning directory for individuals seeking guidance and information about on-line learning resources. You can find courses and resources under such topics as education, business, recreation, computers, science, and home improvement. Additionally, this site offers resources for organizations aspiring to deliver courses or training on-line; and it provides consulting, content development, hosting, and brand promotion services.

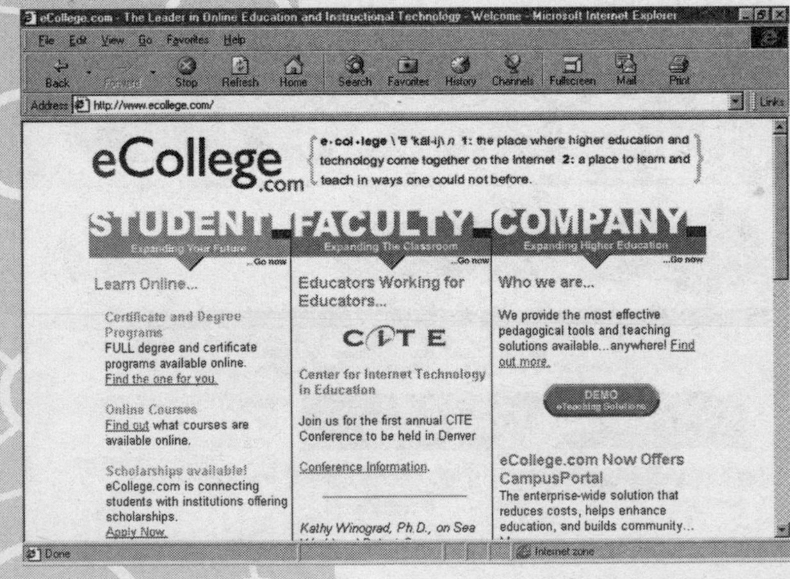

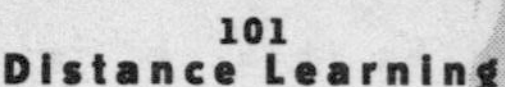

FAVORITE LINKS

World Wide Learn

http://www.worldwidelearn.com/

World Wide Learn is a directory of courses, tutorials, classes, and workshops offered exclusively on-line. Maybe you want to learn something new, continue your education to get a better job, take up a new hobby, improve on your existing skills, or just learn something for the fun of it. If so, check out this site.

eCollege.com

http://www.ecollege.com/

Interested in learning from the comfort of your own home? Find out about full degree and certificate programs available on-line. See what courses are available on-line. Short on cash? Apply for a scholarship. This site also features services and resources for educators and businesses.

Does It Have Merit?

http://www.academyonline.com/

Includes insightful essays and editorials that delve into new forms of education. Interact with the leaders and innovators in distance education.

EDUCATION

Whether it's preschool, elementary school, secondary school, or home-school, education is often on our minds. We want the best education for our kids and hope to see them excel in it.

These sites will help students of all ages study better and help educators stay atop of their field.

TOP SITE

Kid Info

http://www.kidinfo.com/

This starting point allows students, teachers, and parents to spend quality time on the web. Find on-line children's stories and games, homework help and reference resources, teacher tutorials and lesson plans, parenting tips and college information—and those are just some of the topics covered here.

Education Index

http://www.educationindex.com/

Here you'll find an annotated guide to education-related sites on the web. Resources are indexed by subject and life stage. Includes games and life-stage-specific chat groups.

Education Planet

http://www.educationplanet.com/

This site helps teachers, students, and parents find on-line educational resources. Also includes forums, teacher training, and sites of the week.

Education World Search Engine

http://www.education-world.com/

Dedicated to educators and students, this site features education news, chat forums, education site reviews, and links to commercial sites.

ScholarStuff

http://www.scholarstuff.com/
Check out links to all things related to education from scholarships and financial aid to education software and job-search tools.

SchoolNet

http://hudmark.com/schoolnet/
An annotated directory of educational resource links.

Study Web

http://www.studyweb.com/
This is a comprehensive, searchable, categorized index with reviews of over 17,000 educational and reference web sites. Great for students and educators alike.

Early Childhood Care Givers

http://www.educarer.com/
Here you'll find information, articles, and resources for infant caregivers.

Child Fun

http://www.childfun.com/
A wonderful resource for child-care providers, educators, and preschool teachers, this site provides a support network with discussion lists, chat rooms, and message boards. Loaded with crafts for kids, preschool activities, curriculum plans, and parenting advice. Features include an Ask the Teacher column and a free greeting card system, too.

Child Development Web Site

http://idealist.com/children/
This site includes a tutorial, a message forum, links to off-site resources, and more.

Other Sites

http://www.edunet.ie/links/aus.html

http://www.schoolnet.ca/

English

http://www.access2020.com/new.html

http://www.speech.cs.cmu.edu/cgi-bin/cmudict

http://www.geocities.com/~spanoudi/quote.html

http://www.starlingtech.com/quotes/search.html

http://www.bdd.com/teachers/

http://www.edunet.com/english/clinic-h.html

http://www.vicnet.net.au/~typo

Early Childhood Education

http://www.ume.maine.edu/~cofed/eceol/welcome.shtml

This site offers support and opportunities for information exchange through its on-line community. Go to the ECEOL web site for a web directory of topics related to early childhood education.

Baby School

http://www.babyschool.com/

This site includes articles about teaching infants to read and a downloadable software program.

Did You Know?

...that in April 1975 Bill Gates and Paul Allen founded Micro-Soft? (The hyphen is later dropped.)

Early Childhood

http://www.earlychildhood.com/

Geared toward educators but also useful for parents, this site features an arts and crafts section, a sharing board, articles, links, and an on-line store.

Early Childhood Educators Web Guide

http://www.ecewebguide.com/

The Early Childhood Education Web Guide seeks to provide child-care professionals with the most up-to-date Internet resources. Sites are checked on a weekly basis to ensure their reliability and integrity. Find sites on child development, cultural diversity, discipline and guidance, and other areas.

Web Directory: Resources for Early Childhood Educators

http://eceresources.iwarp.com/

Check out links under such topics as Dramatic Play, Art Area, Circle Time, Quiet Area, and much more.

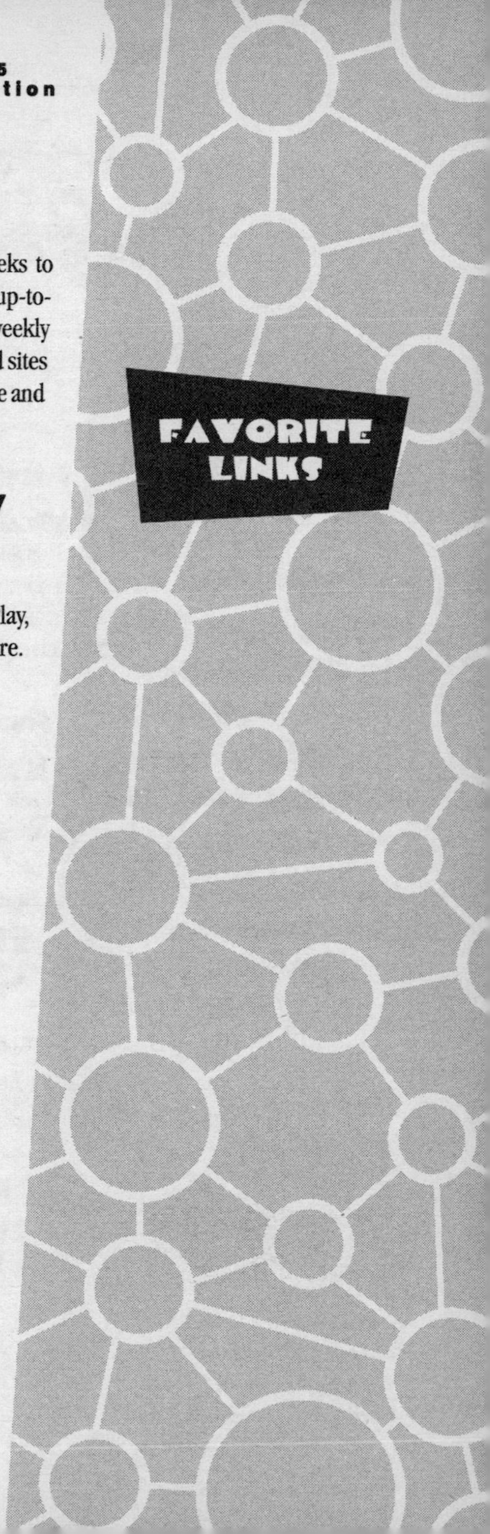

E-MAIL

Many sites are now offering "free E-mail for life." Sign up for E-mail at one of these sites to help keep a simple E-mail address no matter what ISP you use or how many times you change your ISP. A site like http://www.mail.com/ offers many different E-mail domains, allow you to select one that best fits your personality or vocation.

E-Mail Today

http://www.emailtoday.com/

This site publishes current news on E-mail technology (server and client software, E-mail plug-ins), E-mail use, bulk and target E-mail, bulk E-mail issues, and a directory of services—including E-mail providers.

Free E-Mail Address

http://www.free-email-address.com/

This site provides reviews of web-based E-mail services and links to get you there if you're interested.

TOP SITE

AltaVista E-Mail

http://altavista.iname.com/member/login.page/

Free E-mail service. AltaVista partners with another site to give many E-mail choices, i.e., yourname@doctor.com or yourname@unforgettable.com.

Katchup

http://www.katchup.co.nz/

Here travelers can get a permanent E-mail address and home page to catch up with friends and family no matter where their travels may take them.

Every Mail

http://www.everymail.com/

Free web-based E-mail that allows you to compose and receive mail in over thirty different languages.

NetAddress

http://www.netaddress.usa.net/

Get free lifetime E-mail addresses. This service allows you to change providers as many times as you wish but keep the same E-mail address.

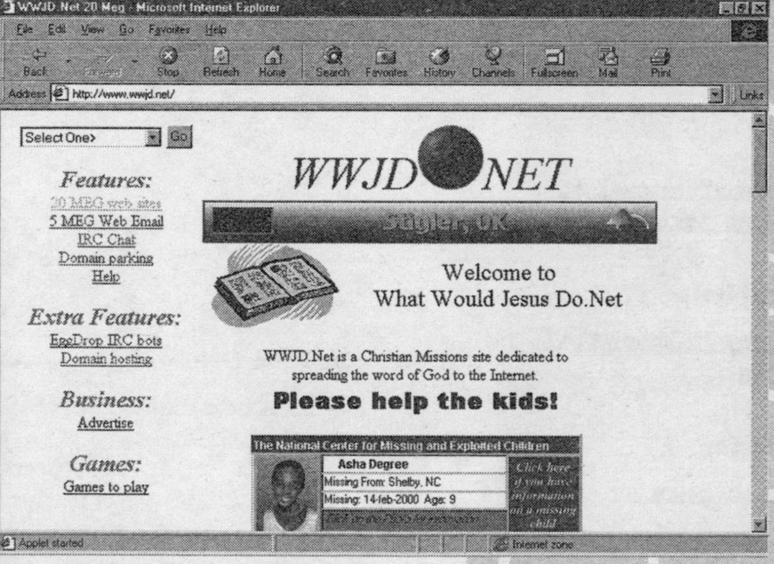

ChristianWeb.net

http://www.christianweb.net/

ChristianWeb.net is devoted to providing free Internet resources—including lifetime E-mail accounts, a web site directory, Christian yellow pages, and free classifieds advertising site.

Submit a Site

hudson@techie.com

Christianmail.net

http://www.christianmail.net/

This is a free Christian web-based E-mail service. It's easy to set up your own E-mail account here.

WWJD.net

http://www.wwjd.net/

WWJD.net is a Christian missions site dedicated to spreading the word of God through the Internet. They offer free home pages, free web-based E-mail, free Christian banner exchange, and even clean, safe web-based Christian chat.

Beginners Guide

http://www.webfoot.com/advice/email.top.html?Yahoo

Tips

http://everythingemail.net/email_help_tips.html

General Help

http://www.iwillfollow.com/email.htm

Anti-Spam

http://www.cauce.org

Christian E-mail

http://www.christianmail.net/

http://www.christianweb.net/

http://www.truthmail.com/

EMBASSIES & CONSULATES

TOP SITE

Embassy Web

http://www.embassyweb.com/

This site features a searchable diplomacy database with over 50,000 addresses, phone numbers, and E-mail addresses of diplomatic posts worldwide. The Embassy Web also turns its spotlight onto web sites maintained by foreign representations all over the world. You can find reviews of diplomatic web sites as well as many other resources.

U.S. Embassies & Diplomatic Missions

http://usembassy.state.gov/

Find links to U.S. embassies around the world. Also here are links to international organizations like NATO.

Embassy World

http://www.embassyworld.com/

Here you will find an embassy and consulate search engine along with a directory of embassies and consulates.

The Electronic Embassy

http://www.embassy.org/

This site is a resource of and for the Washington, D.C. foreign embassy community. Find information on all of the foreign embassies of

The World Wide Web can help your world-wide travel.

Do your research on-line as you make your plans. Keep track of news in the countries you will be visiting or the countries your loved ones are in.

Washington, D.C., along with an events calendar, help and resource center, international business center, and virtual library and gallery.

Worldwide Embassies and Consulates Search Engine

http://consulate.travel.com.hk/

This is a searchable database for addresses, telephone numbers, E-mail addresses, and web sites of world embassies and consulates.

Representations in Foreign Countries

http://www.gksoft.com/govt/en/representations.html

A directory of links to web sites of embassies, consulates, permanent missions, tourist offices, cultural institutes, trade commissions, etc.

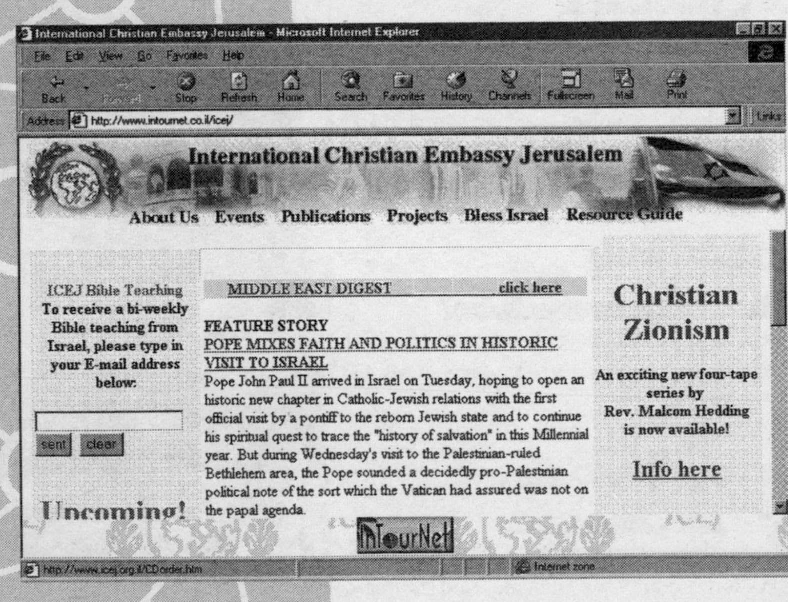

International Christian Embassy Jerusalem

http://www.intournet.co.il/icej/

This is the web page for the International Christian Embassy Jerusalem, which opened after the international community condemned Israel for declaring Jerusalem the "eternal and indivisible capital" of the reborn Jewish state in 1980. As thirteen nations moved their embassies from Jerusalem to Tel Aviv due to a threatened Arab oil embargo, 1,400 Christians from forty countries decided to open their own embassy in Jerusalem as an act of solidarity with the Jewish people's 3,000-year-old connection to their holy city. Today, Christians everywhere have an embassy representing them in Jerusalem, an effective channel for their concern and love for Israel. At this site you will be able to find news and information.

The Diplomatic List

http://www.state.gov/www/about_state/contacts/diplist

State Department

http://www.state.gov/www/dept.html

Protocol

http://www.meetings-conventions.com/issues/0298/features/feature5.html

Did You Know?

...that Finland ranks first in the number of Internet hosts per capita?

EMPLOYMENT

Looking for a job in the newspaper classifieds takes a lot of time and is limited in its information.

The Internet is quick, easy to search, global, and has no space limitations. These sites let you search for a job that fits your skills—no matter the field. Want more? Search by locality or by the salary you'd like to command.

Power Searching for Your Next Job

http://www.firstwebnet.com/

A guide to using on-line resources for job seekers, this site features a free course and other information.

Christian Jobs On-Line

http://www.christianjobs.com/

Are you looking for a Christian employer? Looking for a Christian employee? This site provides a location for Christian employers and Christian job seekers to find each other.

Ministry Search

http://www.ministrysearch.com/

A Christian ad job listing offering available church openings, ministry positions, and ministers seeking jobs. Fee required to register as a candidate.

College Grad Job Hunter

http://www.collegegrad.com/

One-stop entry-level job-search shopping for college students and recent grads. Includes info on resumés, jobs, interviewing, offer negotiation, and more.

FAVORITE LINKS

Senior Staff

http://www.srstaff.com/

SeniorTechs collects and markets current job information for the American workforce over fifty.

Cool Jobs

http://www.cooljobs.com/

Look through the database and get the scoop on some of the coolest jobs on the planet. Submit an opening for a cool job or information on how to get one. Enter the contest for the coolest job idea. Think you've already got a cool job? Take their two-minute survey and find out.

JobMonkey

http://www.jobmonkey.com/

Get information on summer, seasonal, or year-round work in unique industries such as cruise ships, national parks, Alaskan fishing and tourism, and beach and ski resorts.

JobReviews.com

http://www.jobreviews.com/cgi-bin/index.pl

While offering a variety of employment resources, this site specializes in user-generated reviews of different aspects of the job-hunting process, including interviews, salaries, and the job position itself. This site will help you get the inside scoop about the jobs and careers you are seeking.

Yahoo! Careers

http://careers.yahoo.com/

This site features weekly articles, helpful links, and job and relocation resources like the job search and resumé pages.

Monster.com

http://monster.com/

Here you can search jobs, personalize your career tools, or find the employees you need.

Career.com

http://www.career.com/

Career.com lets you search jobs by company, discipline, location, hot jobs, new grad, or by your own key words.

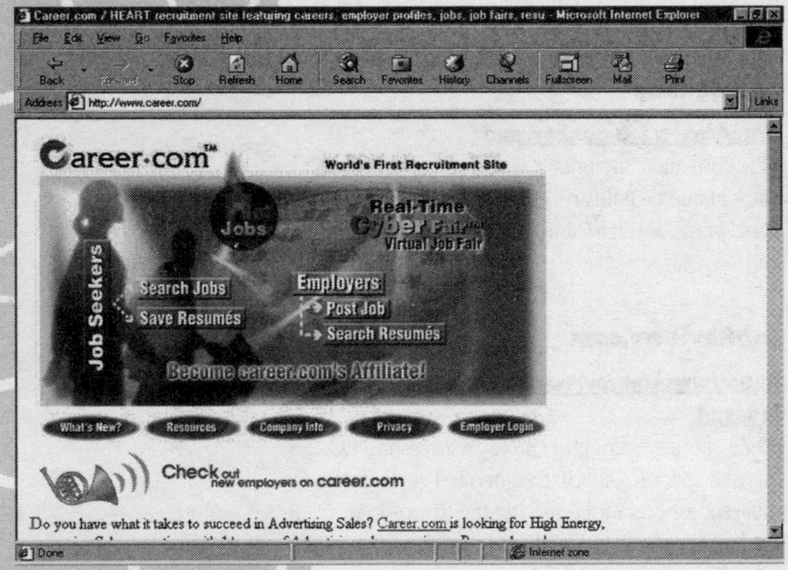

CareerWeb

http://www.cweb.com/

This is a global recruitment center and one-stop shop for learning about the top technical employers, browsing job opportunities, applying for jobs on-line, and testing and polishing your "career fitness."

Did You Know?

...that more people access the net from home then anywhere else? Here's the breakdown: home (72 million), work (46 million), school (28 million), and other (32 million).

CareerCity

http://careercity.com/

Here you can search the job database and submit your resume on-line. Also offers a career center, resumé samples, and interview strategies.

Help Wanted Pages

http://www.helpwantedpage.com/

Features employment ads from across the U.S., career resources, convention and job fair updates, job opportunities, and loads more.

Jumbo Classifieds

http://www.jumboclassifieds.com/

This site features searchable employment ads.

Job Interview

http://www.scrtec.org/track/tracks/t00489.html

http://www.quintcareers.com/intvres.html

For Teens

http://www.bygpub.com/books/tg2rw/resumes.htm

Job Search

http://www.peachnet.edu/galileo/internet/jobs/jadvice.html

Tips

http://www.stcc.cc.tx.us/main/careers.html

ENGINEERING

What keeps bridges from collapsing? Why do rail cars remain attached to each other? How deep should the foundation of a new building be? *Engineering* contains the answers. This art and science is behind many of the things we take for granted.

Ask an Engineer

http://www.expage.com/page/askanengineer/

A service of the Society of Women Engineers, this is the place to ask questions about engineering principles and what engineers do on a day-to-day basis.

National Science Foundation

http://www.nsf.gov/

Opportunities for research and education funding in all areas of engineering from the National Science Foundation.

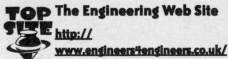

TOP SITE

The Engineering Web Site

http://www.engineers4engineers.co.uk/

Engineering web site for professional engineers. Electronic, electrical, consulting, design, mechanical, software, etc. Find links to vast sources of engineering information.

Engineering Resources On-Line

http://www.er-online.co.uk/

A practical guide to engineering products, companies, and resources on the Internet.

Virtual Library

http://www.spec-net.com.au/
http://www.buildingindex.com/

An information source for building, construction, and engineering. Spec-Net provides an easy link to thousands of construction and engineering products and suppliers.

Engineering and Technology

http://galaxy.einet.net/galaxy/Engineering-and-Technology.html

Annotated links are organized under many branches of engineering—from agricultural to mechanical engineering with lots in between.

American Society for Engineering Education

http://www.asee.org/

The American Society for Engineering Education is a nonprofit member association, founded in 1893, dedicated to promoting and improving engineering and technology education. A great resource for anyone seeking information about engineering.

Christian Engineers

http://www.emiusa.org/

If you are involved in architecture, engineering, or surveying, and have a desire to serve God, you may be interested in this site. Engineering Ministries International is a nonprofit organization committed to involving architects, engineers, and surveyors in short-term Christian ministry projects. These projects include the design of hospitals, schools, water systems, and orphanages.

Achievements

http://www.greatachievements.org/

Yahoo! Engineering

http://dir.yahoo.com/Science/Engineering/

Students

http://www.expage.com/page/askanengineer/

Mesa

http://mesa.ucop.edu/about/

Theme Park Engineering

http://www.themedattraction.com/

Competitions

http://www.sciserv.org/isef/index.asp

ENTERTAINMENT

The entertainment world is one of the largest segments of our economy. Many books, media—even much of the web—falls under the category of entertainment. These sites will help you stay informed in the areas that interest you most.

TVLink

http://www.timelapse.com/tvlink.html

A film and television web site archive with tons of links to movie and TV sites.

Internet Movie Database

http://www.imdb.com/

This is the place for everything you ever wanted to know about every movie ever made.

Nitpickers Site

http://www.nitpickers.com/

This is the place to post and review those little mistakes and details in movies that you always seem to notice.

Christian Movies Theater On-Line

http://www.angelfire.com/mt/BibleTruths/MovieCenter.html

Grab the popcorn and the kids and go to the movies—at home. Using Real Audio and Video Player—free to download. This is a fun family entertainment site.

Entertainment Network News

http://www.enn2.com/

Find entertainment news, an industry info megasite, and lots of information on radio, TV, movies, music, rock, and video.

Star Seeker

http://www.starseeker.com/

Star Seeker is designed to allow quick and easy access to your favorite celebrity, movie, TV show, etc. One or more of the highest-quality sites are listed, with links to general search engines for additional information.

Mr. Showbiz

http://mrshowbiz.go.com/

Loaded with entertainment information. Lots of links on movies, TV, games, music, and celebrities. Check out the movie guide, news, and artist bios.

Acts Christian Search

http://www.actschristian.com/a/Entertainment/

The entertainment section of this Christian search engine and directory, Acts Christian Search has links to Christian sites for books, chat, movies, music, drama, games, and more.

The Amen! Page

http://www.amenpage.com/

The Amen! Page is a nationally syndicated news feature covering all forms of Christian entertainment and serving mainstream and religious newspapers and publications. They review the latest releases, check out the hot web sites, offer CD giveaways, and let readers know what's hot and what's not.

Rodeo

http://www.comp-unltd.com/~rodeo/clowns.html

Clowns

http://www.webdom.com/chof/

Ice Skating

http://www.world-skating-info.com/ice/rinks.html

Water Parks

http://dir.yahoo.com/Entertainment/Amusement_and_Theme_Parks/Water_Parks/

Theme Parks

http://travelwithkids.miningco.com/travel/travelwithkids/msubthemeparks.htm

Christian Music

http://www.phatt-music.com/phatt/index.html

FAVORITE LINKS

Travel & Entertainment Network

http://www.ten-io.com/index.html

Provides travel and entertainment information and arrangements.

Travel-Watch

http://www.travel-watch.com/

An on-line magazine including news, features, and profiles for travel, food, entertainment, skiing, and recreation. Published daily.

Total Travel and Tickets

http://www.total-tickets.com/

This company is engaged in buying and selling first-rate and sold-out tickets for local and national concerts, theaters, and sporting events. All tickets are a part of a complete package, which may include transportation, dinner, hotel, parties, or other amenities.

ENVIRONMENT & NATURE

The *World* Wide Web will only be useful as long as the *world* is still around. These sites will help you learn about the Great Blue Planet, how it works, and how to care for it.

Link up with organizations trying to protect our planet and keep the *World* Wide Web around a little longer.

Nature

http://www.pbs.org/wnet/nature/

Each week *Nature* on the web presents a web piece based on the program scheduled to be broadcast nationally by PBS.

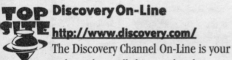

TOP SITE Discovery On-Line

http://www.discovery.com/

The Discovery Channel On-Line is your web guide to all things related to science, nature, animals, technology, history, adventure, and exploration. Features include up-to-the-minute science news, real-time international expeditions, fun and games, teaching resources, and a whole area just for kids.

Sierra Club Home Page

http://www.sierraclub.org/

The Sierra Club is an organization dedicated to protecting the environment. At their home page you can get environmental news, find an update on major issues, learn ways you can take action, get information on getting outdoors, and learn about the history of the Sierra Club.

Sequoia Ministry

http://www.angelfire.com/biz2/sequoiaministry/

Check out Christian nature and science programs from an ex-park ranger naturalist. Eight different programs are all Christ-centered and Bible-based, and they are tailored for schools, church groups, home educators, and camps. They emphasize hands-on learning while teaching Christian stewardship over the resources with which God has entrusted us.

World Wildlife Fund

http://www.worldwildlife.org/

Known worldwide by its panda logo, WWF is the world's largest and most experienced independent conservation organization with 4.7 million supporters and a global network active in some 100 countries. WWF's mission is to protect nature and the biological diversity we all need to survive. At this site you can learn more about endangered species and the places where they live, and the global threats that put all living things in harm's way.

USDA Forest Service

http://www.fs.fed.us/

The USDA Forest Service national headquarters web site. This acts as a gateway to all Forest Service web sites and is filled with links and information.

NRDC On-Line's Home Page

http://www.nrdc.org/

Natural Resources Defense Council is an environmental organization that uses law and science to protect the planet and to ensure a safe and healthy environment for all living things. Get the latest in news and information at this site.

Innovative Action for the Environment

http://www.earthisland.org/

This is an environmental organization that develops and supports projects that counteract environmental threats. This site provides in-depth information and resources from their project network, award-winning journalism from the *Earth Island Journal,* and tools to address the environmental challenges we face.

Best Environmental Resources Directories

http://www.ulb.ac.be/ceese/meta/cds.html

Selection of Internet environmental directories (list of lists) for about 500 environmental subjects.

Natural Products

http://www.greenmarketplace.com/greenmarket/

GreenMarketplace.com provides direct access

Other Links

http://hammock.ifas.ufl.edu/txt/fairs/19994/

http://rbcm1.rbcm.gov.bc.ca/

http://www.cabi.org/

http://www.igc.apc.org/ran/

http://www.sierraclub.ca/bc/

http://www.localcurrency.org/

Religious Sites

http://www.nrpe.org/

http://www.ozemail.com.au/~sjhop/prayer.htm

http://members.tripod.com/~treelife/

to quality natural products that are good for people and the environment.

Environmental Health

Environmental Health Information Service

http://ehis.niehs.nih.gov/

The Environmental Health Information Service is an on-line service of the National Institute of Environmental Health Sciences. The EHIS provides accurate and timely information on environmental health, toxicology, and cancer. Check out articles and publications, search the databases, or link to other interesting sites.

National Safety Council Environmental Health Center

http://www.nsc.org/ehc.htm

The Environmental Health Center is a division of the National Safety Council. This web site provides information on many environmental health topics.

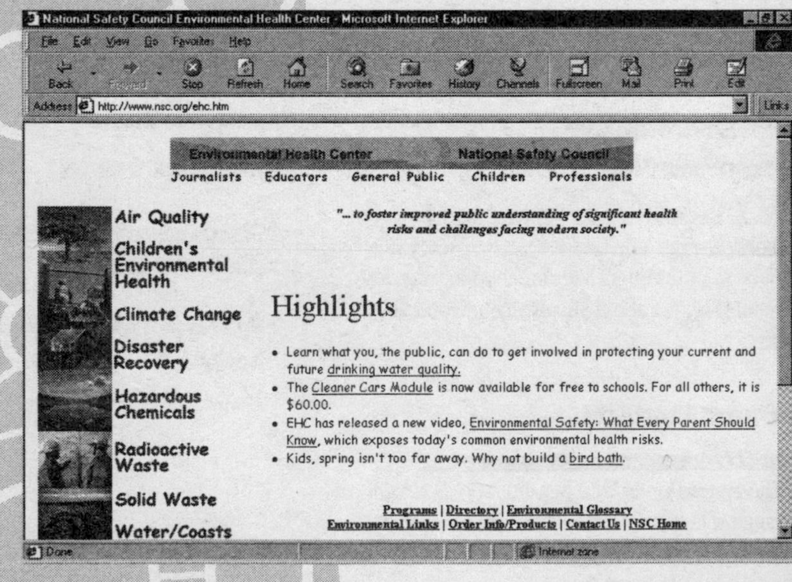

Toxicology and Environmental Health

http://sis.nlm.nih.gov/tehip.htm

This site is part of the National Library of Medicine's Division of Specialized Information Services. Find direct links to environmental health databases, check out the tutorials to learn more about environmental health, and get the latest news on this important issue.

Environmental Health Clearinghouse Home Page

http://www.infoventures.com/e-hlth/

The Environmental Health Clearinghouse provides substantive information and key documents on a variety of environmental health issues.

EcoMall

http://www.ecomall.com/

Find thousands of green, environmentally responsible eco-products that are good for people and the environment. Also get news, ask an expert, join eco chat, check out links (including a special section of links for kids), read articles, find out about vegetarian restaurants, experience the audio/video clips—and more.

Natural Health Super Site—Links to Natural Health and Environmental Sites

http://www.anaturalway.com/supersite/

Natural Health Super Site is a directory of links to Natural Health and environmental products and services.

Environmental Magazine

http://www.emagazine.com/

The *Environmental* magazine covers a wide range of issues—from recycling to rain forests, and from the personal to the political—always with a "what you can do" emphasis. This site features subscription information (you can get a free trial edition), along with on-line classifieds, links, and a marketplace of eco-goods and services.

EnviroLink Home Page

http://www.envirolink.org/

The EnviroLink Network, a nonprofit organization, provides the latest environmental news, information, products, and resources for the environmental community. EnviroLink also provides over 400 nonprofit organizations with free Internet services.

Destination: Earth

http://www.earth.nasa.gov/

Destination Earth is the official web site for NASA's Earth Science enterprise—taking the spirit of exploration and focusing it back on our own planet. You can see late-breaking Earth news, view Earth science

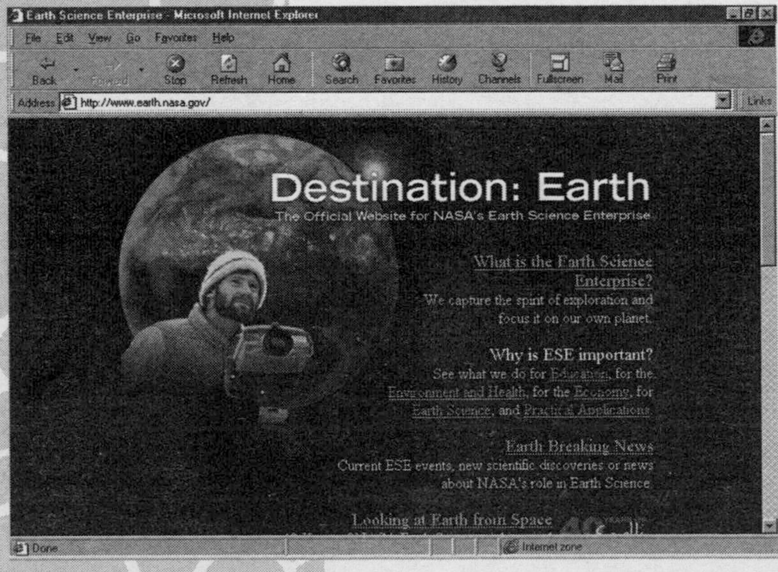

images taken from space, find educational materials for teaching Earth science, get information on research opportunities, or browse the multimedia library. There's also a great section for kids.

Discovery Channel School

http://www.discoveryschool.com/schoolfeatures/featurestories/earthalert/

Looking for disaster? You've come to the right place. Discovery Channel School presents nine classroom modules—each featuring background information and lesson plans—to help you teach some of Earth science's most important curriculum topics.

Earth and Environmental Science

http://info.er.usgs.gov/network/science/earth/

The U.S. Geological Survey maintains this registry of Earth and environmental science Internet resources as a service to the research community.

Virtual Library: Earth Sciences

http://www.geo.ucalgary.ca/VL-EarthSciences.html

Find links to Earth science organizations, current events, and resources.

Ecology

Ecology Protectors Society

http://www.eco-pros.com/

High-quality educational web site for children, pertaining to the ecology of the environment. Kids can come here to have fun and learn at the same time.

Did You Know?

...that the overall top shopping categories (shopping defined as researching and comparing prices, not purchasing) are:

1. **Cars/car parts—18.2 million,**
2. **Books—12.6 million,**
3. **Computers—12.4 million,**
4. **Clothing—11.6 million,**
5. **CDs and videos—11.4 million?**

Greenpeace International

http://www.greenpeace.org/

Greenpeace is an independent, campaigning organization which uses nonviolent, creative confrontation to expose global environmental problems, and to force the solutions which are essential to a green and peaceful future. Check out their international photo and video library, read the latest in environmental headlines and Greenpeace campaigns, and link to other environmentally friendly sites.

Christian Ecology Link

http://www.christian-ecology.org.uk/

CEL is a U.K. organization for Christians concerned about care of the environment. Features web links and information on their magazine called *Green Christians*.

The Ecology Center, Inc.

http://www.wildrockies.org/TECI/

The Ecology Center is a nonprofit conservation organization dedicated to protecting and restoring biodiversity and intact ecosystems. You can search the ecosystem defense library, learn more about programs, read the latest headlines, and more at this site.

Virtual Library: Biodiversity and Ecology

http://conbio.rice.edu/vl/database/

A directory of links related to biodiversity and ecology.

Did You Know?

...that Saturday is the busiest day of the week for surfing the net?
...And that Wednesday is the least busy day of the week for surfing the net?
...And that Friday is the second busiest, Thursday the third, Sunday the fourth, Monday the fifth, and Thursday the sixth busiest day of the week for surfing the net?

ETHICS

Is lying always wrong or does it depend on the situation? Is it wrong to steal bread if your family is starving?

These sites will make for interesting discussion as you develop God-honoring ethics in a world that emphasizes relativity.

Christian Ethics

http://gonow.to/ethics/

Young people are taught that morality, right and wrong, depends upon the situation. Leaders claim to be ethical. What does it all mean? This site describes Christian ethics and the ethics of today's world.

Religion-online.org

http://www.religion-online.org/

Religion On-Line provides full texts by recognized religious scholars. Topics include Bible, theology, ethics, history, sociology, church and society, culture, communication, pastoral care, counseling, liturgy, worship, and missiology.

Religion & Ethics NewsWeekly

http://www.pbs.org/religionandethics/

This is the web companion to the television show *Religion & Ethics NewsWeekly* on PBS. Read articles, check out related and featured web sites, view transcripts, and more.

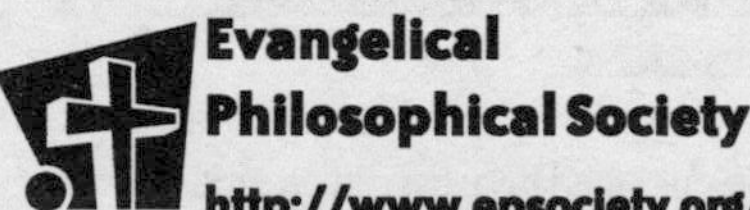

Evangelical Philosophical Society

http://www.epsociety.org/

The Evangelical Philosophical Society is

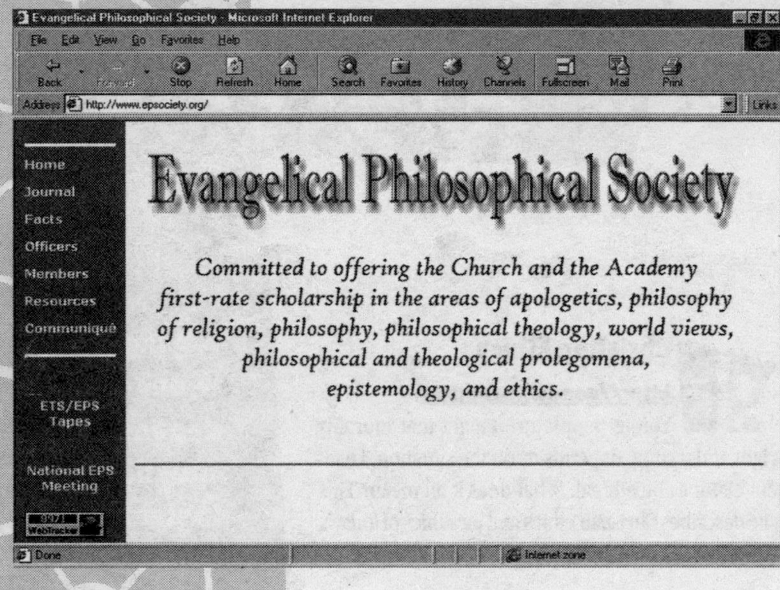

committed to offering the church and the academy first-rate scholarship in the areas of apologetics, philosophy of religion, philosophy, philosophical theology, worldviews, epistemology, and ethics. Their site features information on their journal as well as a listing of related links.

Ethics Updates

http://ethics.acusd.edu/

Ethics Updates is designed primarily to be used by ethics instructors and their students. It is intended to provide updates on current literature, both popular and professional, that relate to ethics.

Ethics Matters

http://www.ethicalculture.org/ethicsmatters

An on-line journal of ethics in today's world. Articles included here have been written by members of ethical societies, fellowships, and at-large members of the American Ethical Union.

The On-Line Journal of Ethics

http://condor.depaul.edu/ethics/ethg1.html
An on-line journal of cutting-edge research in the field of business and personal ethics.

Ethics for Scientists

http://onlineethics.org/
The On-Line Ethics Center for Engineering and Science is designed to provide engineers, scientists, and science and engineering students with resources useful for understanding and addressing ethically significant problems that arise in their work, and to serve those who are promoting learning and advancing understanding of responsible practice in engineering and science. This site features cases, research, letters, codes, and a help line.

Applied Ethics

http://www.ethics.ubc.ca/resources/
Find lists of WWW sites which may be of interest to people doing research in the various branches of applied ethics—from health care to media to environmental ethics. Note that these lists are not limited to sites about applied ethics.

Ethics on the Web

http://commfaculty.fullerton.edu/lester/ethics/ethics_list.html
This is a resource of ethical links on the World Wide Web within almost twenty categories.

Ethics Links

http://www.gac.edu/Academics/philosophy/lethics.html
http://galaxy.einet.net/galaxy/Humanities/Philosophy/Ethics.html
List of links to ethics sites on the web.

Ethics & Compliance Strategies

http://www.ethicscompliance.com/

Ethics & Compliance Strategies provides consulting and support services to develop ethics and compliance programs which support good business practices, encourage ethical decision making, assist in adherence to regulatory requirements, and meet the suggested elements for compliance programs as outlined in the Federal Sentencing Guidelines for Organizations. Each program is designed to provide real-world, workable solutions tailored for the specific needs of your organization.

International Business Ethics Institute (IBEI)

http://www.business-ethics.org/

The International Business Ethics Institute is a private, nonprofit, nonpartisan, educational organization founded in response to the growing need for transnationalism in the field of business ethics. At this site you can find out more about their

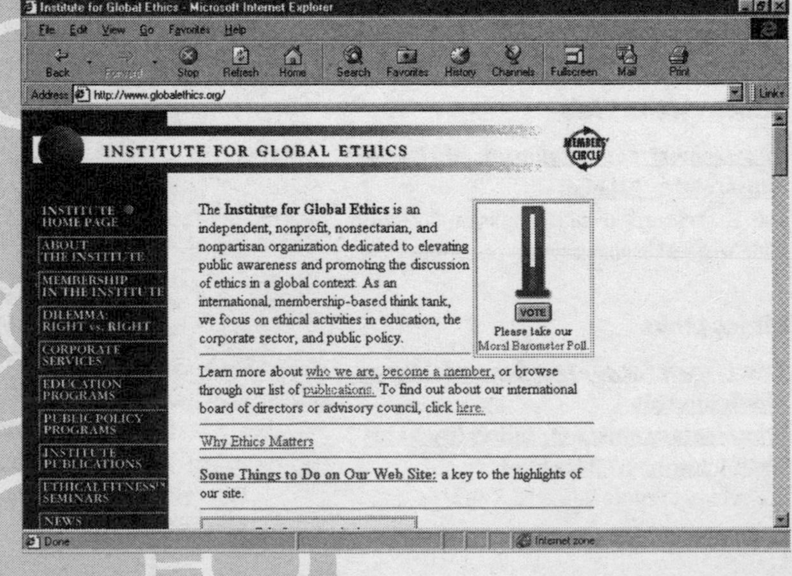

organization, check out publications, or utilize the resources and education sections.

Institute for Global Ethics

http://www.globalethics.org/

The Institute for Global Ethics is an independent, nonsectarian, and nonpolitical organization dedicated to elevating public awareness and promoting the discussion of ethics in a global context. This nonprofit think tank is an international, membership-based organization focusing on ethical activities for corporations, educators, professionals, and communities. Their site includes book reviews, interviews and speeches, ethics statistics, teacher tools, news releases, and more.

CataLaw: Legal Ethics

http://catalaw.com/topics/Ethics.shtml

The catalogue of catalogs about law. Links to sites relevant to the topic of legal ethics.

Other Links

http://www.mapnp.org/library/ethics/ethics.htm

http://www.josh.org/

http://www.cellgroup.com/

http://www.cmds.org/online_resources/Christian.html

Did You Know?

...that from 1994–1999, Internet access in schools increased from 35 to 95 percent?

ETHNIC STUDIES

This book is not about the World *White* Web. The web is global and helps define the new trendy phrase, "global Community."

The web allows differing cultures to become neighbors. If your own neighborhood is not culturally diverse, these sites will help you learn more about the different races and cultures that help make up our world.

Balch Institute for Ethnic Studies

http://www.libertynet.org/balch/

Located in Pennsylvania, the institute features a multicultural library, archive, museum, and education center and is dedicated to collecting and interpreting materials that reflect our nation's multicultural heritage. Online you'll find such features as a guide to their manuscript and microfilm collections, a catalog of holdings for the Balch Institute and the Union catalog of the Phildadelphia Area Consortium of Special Collections Libraries, a link of the week archive, and a directory of interesting on-line resources.

TOP SITE **UCLA Ethnic Studies Publications Catalog**

http://www.sscnet.ucla.edu/esp/

An interactive, searchable catalog of publications about African-American, Chicano/a, and Asian-American studies, including nearly three decades of journals.

National Association for Ethnic Studies

http://www.ksu.edu/ameth/naes/naes.htm

This organization provides an interdisciplinary forum for scholars and activists concerned with the national and international dimensions of ethnicity. At their site, find out information about the organization as well as links to ethnic studies programs, ethnic web sites, and other resources.

Other Links

http://www.fau.edu/library/ethnic.htm

http://www.newschool.edu/library/area.htm

http://www.peachnet.edu/galileo/internet/area/areamenu.html

Did You Know?

. . .that there are about four million Internet users in China alone?

ETIQUETTE

When is it appropriate to send a thank-you card? What kind of gifts are appropriate for different occasions? What cultural boundaries should you watch for when traveling internationally? Proper etiquette helps answer these questions. In earlier days, parents sent their children to finishing school. Today, the answers you need are a little easier to come by. Surf through these sites to learn how to show kindness and respect to others.

Etiquette for Today

http://www.homearts.com/gh/advice/1196ppf1.htm

Peggy Post will answer your questions about parties, family gatherings, invitations, and guests.

Ultimate Etiquette and Manners Resource Page

http://www.mindspring.com/~thinds/jmh/etiquetteurls.htm

Features links to etiquette sites for dining, wedding, business, children, church, history, cultural, and humor.

National League of Junior Cotillions

http://www.nljc.com/

This organization licenses directors to establish local cotillion programs. Their site features guidance on etiquette, ethics, and manners.

Etiquette Advice Reference

http://www.westernsilver.com/etiquette.html

This site features helpful hints for every dining occasion. The emphasis is on table manners for formal occasions with a focus on American traditions. Unsure about how to eat foods that require more than just a fork or spoon? Use the reference section to discover the proper way to eat certain foods. Not sure how to set your table for a formal dinner or buffet? Check out this site for the answers to these questions and more.

Epicurious: In Polite Company

http://www.epicurious.com/c_play/c02_polite/polite.html

This site provides a guide to coping with problem foods in public.

Computer Communication Etiquette

http://reality.sgi.com/relph/etiquette.html

This is a list of links to pages that may contain useful and practical information concerning the etiquette of on-line communications, especially concerning E-mail use.

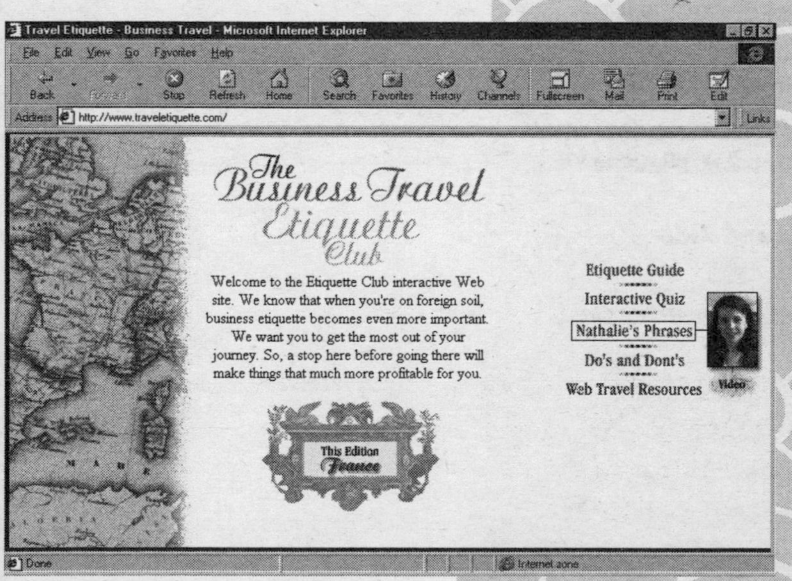

E-Mail Etiquette

http://www.tricityherald.com/biz/stories/story74.html

Golf Etiquette

http://www.mrgolf.com/primer.html

Travel Etiquette

http://www.traveletiquette.com/

Wedding Etiquette

http://www.ourmarriage.com/html/wedding_etiquette.html

Teens and Kids

http://www.etiquettesurvival.com/

The Business Travel Etiquette Club

http://www.traveletiquette.com/

When you're on foreign soil, business etiquette becomes even more important. Think of this web site as your travel advisor and silent companion. It's designed to acclimatize you to cultural differences and coach you on the business niceties of your destination. Each edition features a different place and provides an interactive quiz, dos and don'ts, helpful phrases, web travel resources, and an etiquette guide covering topics like dress, tipping, greetings, meetings, and courtesy.

Guide to Japan

http://www.japan-guide.com/e/e622.html

This is a guide to etiquette in Japan. This is a helpful guide for any foreigner in such areas as table manners, greeting, gifts, superstitions, bathing, using the toilet, and more.

FAMILY

Every generation of children has felt that their parents don't understand them. Every generation of parents has tried hard to relate to their children. As our world today is changing faster than ever, parents need to work hard at strengthening their family. These sites offer creative ideas for strengthening the bond.

TOP SITE Children's Television Workshop

http://www.ctw.org/

The CTW Family Workshop is specially designed for today's networked family, offering fun experiences for everyone from preschoolers to grandparents. Here parents can discover how to get the most out of the Internet while spending quality time with their kids since the activities are designed to be done together. You'll find stories to create, games to play, and interactive adventures to explore—all accompanied by additional learning suggestions developed by a trusted team of educational specialists. You'll also find kid-friendly crafts, activities, and games. Lastly, you'll discover Family Tech Tips to help parents become as web savvy as their kids.

Family

http://family.go.com/

A wealth of resources in one spot. This site offers localized activity calendars from various parenting publications. The activities section features a fun finder, craft ideas, birthday ideas, and TV-free activities. The food section features a recipe finder, favorite recipes, cookbook browser, and cook's dictionary. Other sections include holidays, pets, travel, baby and pregnancy, health, parenting, and learning. There's also a family shop where you can purchase products on-line, and a parent chat and message board feature.

Family Management

http://www.familymanagement.com/

This site hosts over 900 pages of resources for family members of all ages, as well as thousands of links to other sites. Some of the things you'll find at this site are help for parents, ways to stay in shape physically, great cooking recipes, ways to cope with job changes, resources to start your own business, books to read on-line or download, and forums for sharing your experiences. Use the Quick Family Resource index to find resources in categories like children and teens, parents and parenting, elderly and aging, and information for the child-care provider.

Focus on the Family

http://family.org/

Web site of Focus on the Family, is full of information focusing on families from a Christian perspective.

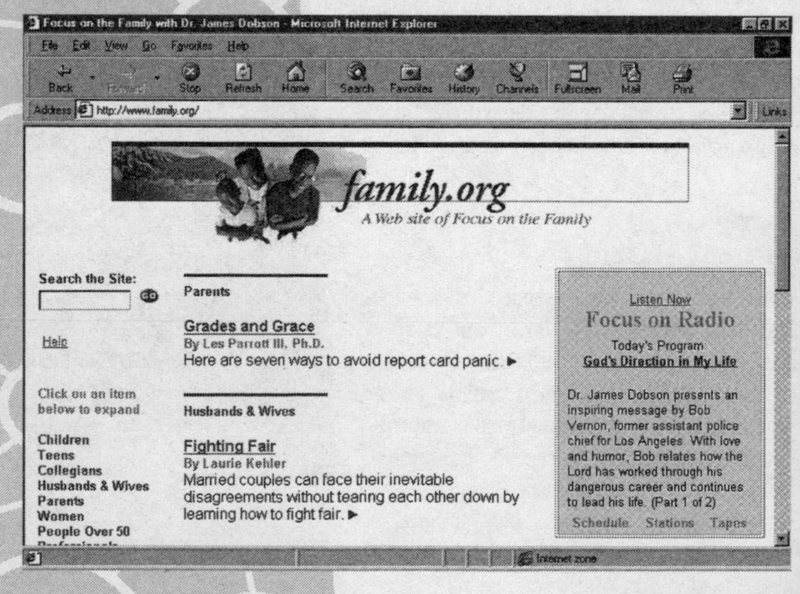

Family Play

http://www.familyplay.com/activities/

Hundreds of ideas of things to do with your kids. You can customize the choices by age, skill, location, or occasion.

Gospel Communications International

http://www.gospelcom.net/gci/column/

Site with a series of articles for building better family relationships.

Magazine

http://www.famunity-worldwide.com/

Building Family Strength

http://www.montana.edu/wwwpb/pubs/mt9506.html

http://www.cfm.org/

http://www.douglascamp.com/

Christian Family Network

http://www.cfnweb.com/

Adoption

http://www.adopting.org/

FAMILY SAFETY

One of parents' primary jobs is to protect their children. In today's world there are physical and health dangers, Internet threats, and many others.

These sites can help give you the tools you need to protect your children as they walk downtown or cruise the information superhighway.

Internet Safety

TOP SITE

Browsesafe

http://www.browsesafe.com/

PlanetGood is the best way for families to enjoy all of the best the Internet has to offer. The staff of Browsesafe constantly reviews web pages and grades them in thirty catagories (sex, violence, gambling, etc.). You customize the kinds of sites you want to access, and they will filter out the sites you don't want to see.

SmartParent.com

http://www.smartparent.com/

SmartParent.com is a resource dedicated to educating parents on the best ways to safeguard their children from the dangers presented by cyberspace. This site's goal is to help keep the on-line experience safe, educational, and entertaining for children. On SmartParent.com, you will find information on blocking and filtering software, valuable protection tips, and links to parent and child-friendly sites, as well as links to agencies and organizations that focus on Internet-related issues.

CrossSearch

http://www.crosssearch.com/Computers

A web resource page on computers from Cross Search (a Christian search engine). Many sites of interest on computing and information for a family deciding how and when to use the computer safely.

KidShield

http://www.kidshield.com/

Use KidShield tools and information to create a SafetyNet for your children on-line. Includes a section on laws being introduced to protect kids on the net, and the "NetScrubber," a reporting form for offensive sites.

NetParenting.com

http://www.netparenting.com/

Welcome to NetParenting.com. This site contains all the information a parent needs to know in terms of Internet safety, safe children's sites, software filtering, and more. This is a good source for parents with children on the Internet: safety, filtering, education, and entertainment. This site is written in an easy-to-understand format and is set up so that you, the parent, can enhance your child's on-line experience.

Physical Safety

SafeKids

http://www.safekids.org/

The National Safe Kids Campaign's mission is to prevent the number one killer of children—unintentional injury. By working at a national level through grassroots coalitions, Safe Kids educates adults and children, provides safety

Wildlife

http://www.boreasbackcountry.com/polaris/bear.htm

Desert

http://www.desertusa.com/Thingstodo/du_ttd_hike2.html

Hiking

http://www.wnyliving.com/outdoors/hiking_safety.htm

Animals

http://www.bcadventure.com/adventure/hiking/safety.htm

General Safety

http://www.healthcentral.com/mhc/top/001931.cfm

devices to families in need, and works to pass and strengthen laws that empower families and communities to protect children ages fourteen and under.

Fire PALS

http://www.firepals.org/tips.htm

Fire PALS is a nonprofit organization offering free life-safety education to schools, grades K–12. Life Safety Education Program highlights: fire safety, earthquake, tobacco prevention, bike safety, drug awareness, latchkey safety, and much more.

Kid Safe Search Engines

http://www.ajkids.com/

http://www.yahooligans.com/

http://www.alfy.com/

http://www.searchopolis.com/

http://www.studyweb.com/

BoatSafeKids

http://www.boatsafe.com/kids/

Site offering information for kids on boating safety. Home site offers info on boating courses, boating tips, boating safety, and boating contests.

Did You Know?

...that there are dogs with a URL on their name tags?

FASHION

Christ Illustrated

http://www.christillustrated.com

This site provides the Christian community with quality, attractive clothing that encourages others to ask them about their faith and the Lord Jesus Christ. Fashions are very conservative.

"That outfit is *soooo* 80s..."
"Retro is in."

Who can keep track of the latest fashions? The web will help you do your best to stay informed about the latest on the runway or the latest trends in Christian fashions.

Flash'N Fashion

http://www.media-motion.com/fshowf.htm

Flash'N Fashion is a commercial product designed to bring the world of sewing to young children. The program includes 22 patterns which fit 12" or 18" dolls, such as Barbie and American Girl. A child designs a fashion outfit, choosing desired garments and matching fabrics. Once designed, the child goes to the Sewing Room and follows the animated instructions to sew the outfit together. There is a free demo; however, the programs are sold separately from the demo.

Firstview

http://www.firstview.com/

Photo galleries of fashion and recent collections by designers worldwide. Fee required to view current season's collections; archives are free.

Leah Feldon

http://www.leahfeldon.com/

A style expert offers valuable fashion advice, tips

on finding good buys, and style alerts that provide the lowdown on the latest trends.

Business Casual

http://www.tiptop.ca/english/index2.html

Fashion Career

http://www.fashioncareercenter.com/fashion_colleges.html

Historic

http://www.public.iastate.edu/~shonrock/tc4.html http://www.shoesonthenet.com/resourc.html

Designers

http://www.anancyweb.com/fashion_designers.html

Links Galore

http://web.idirect.com/~klg/fashion.html

Other

http://www.birkenstockcentral.com/

Picky Ideas

http://www.picky.com/

This site is dedicated to discovering and celebrating the individual styles of real women with ideas, resources, and answers for fashion, beauty, and home.

Costume Image Database

http://www.lib.colum.edu/costwais.html

A searchable index of selected images used in the study of fashion and costume.

FINANCE & INVESTMENT

The American Association of Individual Investors

http://www.aaii.org/

The American Association of Individual Investors specializes in providing education in the area of stock investing, mutual funds, portfolio management, and retirement planning. This is a not-for-profit organization that arms investors with the knowledge and tools needed to manage their finances effectively and profitably.

Learn Investing

http://www.learninvesting.com/

This educational investment site has free simulations for teaching you, more advanced courses for a fee, and a beginner's corner for those just starting.

Douglas Gerlach's Invest-o-Rama

http://www.investorama.com/

Annotated directory of hundreds of Internet resources for investors, including feature articles on growth-stock investing.

InvestorGuide

http://www.investorguide.com/

Primarily an investing directory, InvestorGuide.com personally visits and handpicks each of the thousands of investing links on

One of the most well-known Bible verses is "The love of money is the root of all evil" (1 Timothy 6:10 KJV). Money *itself* is not evil. In fact, Christians are commissioned by God to be good stewards and are to manage their resources well. These sites will help you manage your financial resources and be a good steward of what God has entrusted to you.

their site and organizes them in a way for you to maximize your benefit from your on-line investing experience. By making it easy for you to find just what you need, and by focusing on the high-quality, free, objective information, InvestorGuide.com transforms the web from an interesting way to kill time into a powerful tool that helps you take control of your money and your financial future. Additionally, they have expanded this site to include an on-line investing community. Together with the Investorville message boards and InvestorWords site, the largest and most comprehensive on-line investing glossary, they offer on-line investors a one-stop shop for all investing needs.

Financial Supermarket

http://www.financialsupermarket.com/

At this directory, visitors can find information on every aspect of finances, including stocks, bonds, futures,

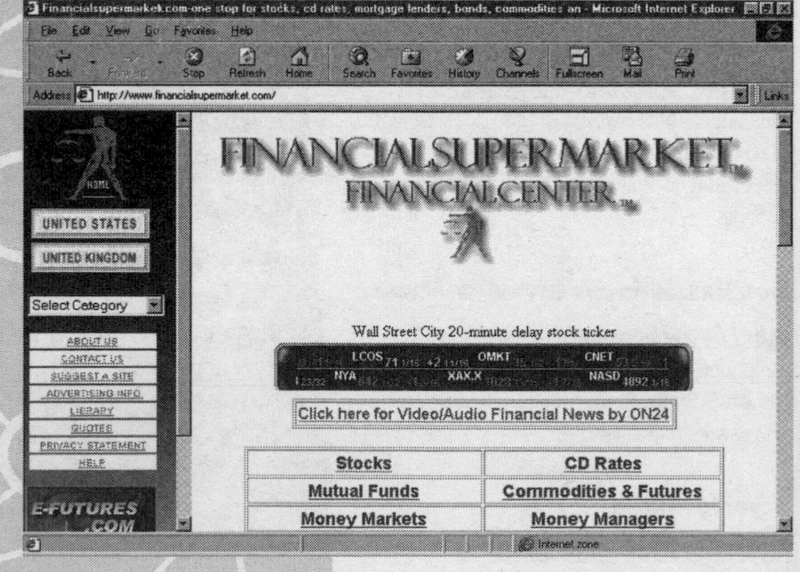

insurance, academic research, mortgage lenders, money markets, and more. Researchers explore the vast amount of information available on the World Wide Web and choose the top sites in each category that is displayed on Financial Supermarket. The summaries provided at this site are based on the researchers' reviews of each individual site.

Economic Net

http://www.economicnet.com/

A database of financial resources including banks, exchanges, news, and more.

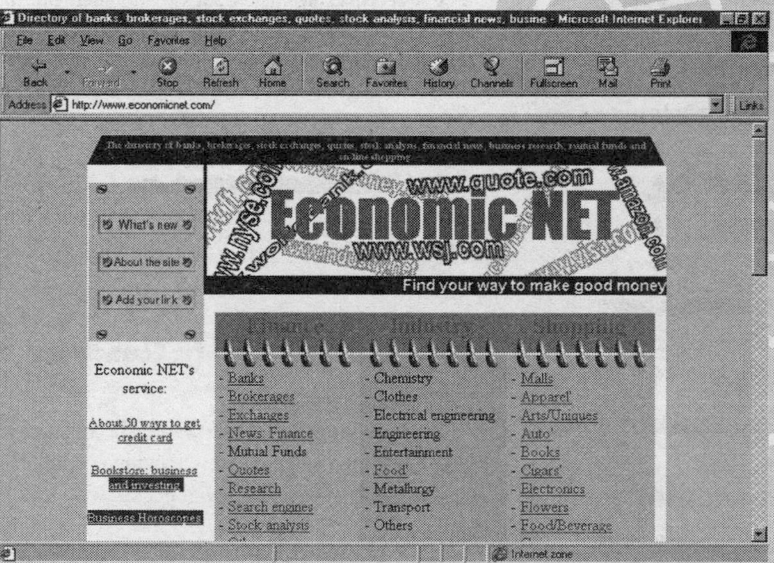

EcEdWeb

http://ecedweb.unomaha.edu/home.htm

The mission of the Economic Education web site is to provide support for economic education in all forms and at all levels—including

K–12 and college. Find curricular materials and useful links.

Microsoft Money
http://moneycentral.msn.com/

Get Quotes
http://www.quotesnow.com/

Planned Giving Resources
http://www.pgresources.com/

Stock Tips
http://www.stocktipster.com/

Instant Coupons
http://www.e-save.com

International Economics Study Center

http://internationalecon.com/
This site provides free on-line text with straightforward explanations of international trade theory and policy analysis. Also includes international finance notes, problem sets, and other special features.

Econolink

http://www.progress.org/econolink/
Check out links to the best web sites that have anything to do with economics. These sites are uniquely categorized into the best sites for content, research, innovation, journalists and students, etc.

Economicsearch.com

http://www.economicsearch.com/
Encounter research links, course tutorials, a job center, and a discussion board for economists and students of economics.

WWW Virtual Library: Economics

http://rfe.wustl.edu/
This lists the many resources on the Internet of interest to academic and practicing economists, and those interested in economics.

Economic History Services

http://www.eh.net/
Features a directory of economic history sites.

Ten Talents Ministries

http://www.tentalents.org/

Ten Talents Charitable Gift Fund is a Christian stewardship ministry which helps individuals in their giving to churches and other charitable organizations. Ten Talents assists Christians in simplifying the task of giving appreciated assets to charity (which makes it possible to increase giving by saving on taxes), as well as offers education for a biblical view of money and finances through their Today Fund. A Vision Fund is also provided for the purpose of setting aside money to be invested and given to charity over the long term as it grows, allowing each person to effectively set up his own "mini foundation" for giving.

Morally Responsible Investing

http://www.ppgmn.com/

This is a financial planning firm that matches up your investments with your values and beliefs. They can let you know if you may be profiting from the areas of abortion, pornography, nonmarriage lifestyles, or anti-family entertainment. Member of the National Association of Christian Financial Consultants.

Sound Mind Investing

http://www.soundmindinvesting.com/

SMI is an easy-to-understand financial newsletter, endorsed by Christian teachers Larry Burkett and Ron Blue, that provides specific investment advice based on biblical principles. The SMI web site has almost seventy articles on money management and investing which you can tailor to your situation.

FIRST AID

This is a section you *need* to browse. Knowing first aid can help you handle a crisis and might help you save a life. When you find yourself with a few minutes to spare, surf through these sites for information and tutorials that may be life changing for someone you love.

First Aid Kit

http://expage.com/page/firstaidkit/

Ever wondered what your first aid kit should consist of? This is the place to get your question answered.

First Aid

http://www.sd6.bc.ca/gss/library/public_html/gssweb/firstaid.htm

Learn about first aid procedures and what to do in such situations, and check out links to all kinds of first aid information.

Skill for Life

http://firstaid.ie.eu.org/

First aid information for a variety of situations.

Active First Aid On-Line

http://www.parasolemt.com.au/

This site outlines the first aid treatment of emergency conditions, including CPR, EAR, medical emergencies, sports injuries, body trauma, and venomous bites and stings.

Rescue 411

http://library.advanced.org/10624

This web site is devoted to raising awareness about first aid and accident prevention. Learn to recognize signs of health emergencies like a heart attack or low blood sugar. Hone your first aid smarts with the interactive game show, "You Bet Your Life!"

First Aid Links

http://www.netpath.net/~cbulmer/firstaid.htm

Select list of first aid links.

Learn CPR

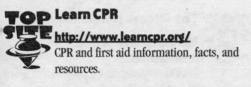

http://www.learncpr.org/

CPR and first aid information, facts, and resources.

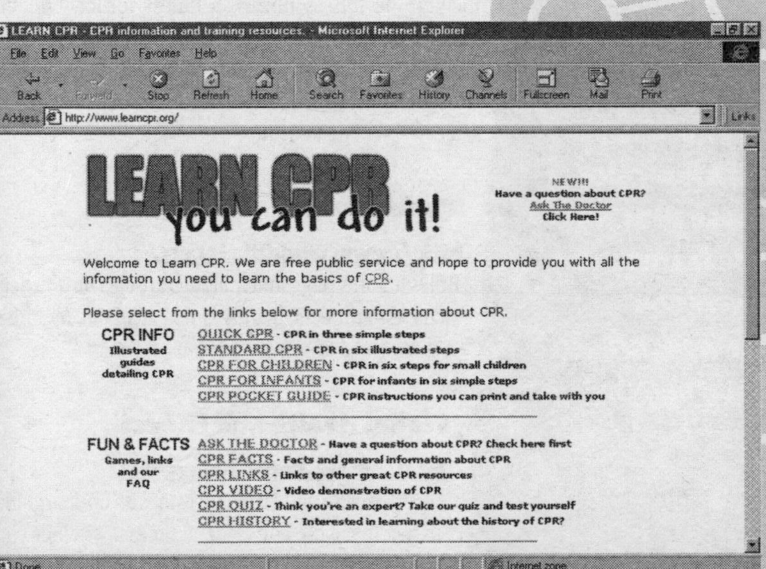

Emergency Cardiovascular Care

http://www.proed.net/ecc/ECC_home.htm

From the American Heart Association, this site is dedicated to providing you with education and information on fighting heart disease and stroke.

FITNESS

Forty-five minutes of mouse clicking does *not* count toward your daily physical fitness routine. The more you sit in front of your PC, the more you may need to burn off a few calories. These sites will help you learn to stay fit and give you creative ways to keep your body healthy.

TOP SITE

The Fitness Jumpsite

http://primusweb.com/fitnesspartner/

The Fitness Jumpsite is a powerhouse full of fitness, health, and nutrition information. Categories include the fitness library, a fitness forum, bulletin boards, specific fitness and training activities, food and nutrition, and more. Use the activity calorie calculator to see how your workout stacks up against other calorie-burning activities.

World Fitness

http://www.worldfitness.org/

Bill Wheton's page that includes articles on a variety of fitness subjects, mainly aimed at adults. Includes a store and a fitness instructor's corner.

Global Health and Fitness

http://www.global-fitness.com/

Global Health and Fitness provides an on-line guide to healthy living and optimal fitness. Whether you are a beginner or advanced, they'll help you avoid the common mistakes that waste your time, teach you techniques for making your routine much more effective, and guide you step-by-step to achieving new results again and again. Features information on fitness exercise and diet programs, personal trainers, weight loss, healthy recipes, strength training, and nutrition supplements.

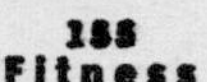

High-Energy Fitness

http://www.highnrg.com/

Specializing in women's fitness, this site offers cutting-edge information on training, nutrition, and sports supplementation. Sections include Meet the Trainer, fitness resources, articles and info, healthy eating, and Ask the Trainer.

HealthWorld On-Line

http://www.healthy.net/Fitness/index.asp

HealthWorld On-Line is an Internet resource on wellness, natural health and alternative medicine information, products, and services. Free Medline search, bookstore, dietary supplements store, Global Health Calendar, forums, and family health features.

Better Homes and Gardens Guide to Fitness and Health

http://www.bhglive.com/health/

Find featured articles, health news, and informative links.

FOOD

In the time it may take you to drive to the grocery store, you can learn some basic nutritional facts, select some well-balanced meals, identify the ingredients you'd need to make them, and arrange to have them shipped directly to you. With discount prices and overnight delivery, more and more people are beginning to do their shopping on-line.

The National Food Safety Database

http://www.foodsafety.org/

This is a multistate agency effort toward a sustainable system of national food safety databases. It seeks to provide a highly informative, efficient, and accurate web site which will provide one-stop shopping for food safety information.

Foodsafe Program

http://foodsafe.ucdavis.edu/

Food safety information on topics from agriculture to seafood from the University of California, Davis.

Cuisine Net Diners Digest

http://www.cuisinenet.com/digest/

CusineNet is a web site for the seriously food-obsessed. They have restaurant listings for many different cities.

The Food Museum

http://www.foodmuseum.com/hughes/main.htm

The Food Museum examines what in the world we eat and how we eat it, where it came from, how it has changed, what its impact is on culture, and what its future may be.

Food Guide

http://www.food-guide.com/
Check out links to recipes, quick meal ideas, cookbooks, chefs, and anything related to food.

GourmetSpot

http://www.gourmetspot.com/
Great food and beverage resources in abundance.

Chef Heaven

http://www.chefheaven.com/
A comprehensive guide to sites about recipes, food, cooking, shopping, health and nutrition, and all things related to food.

Flanagain's FoodNotes

http://www.foodnotes.com/
Links to food sites including recipes, food safety information, restaurants, shopping, and more.

TOP SITE

Buy Your Groceries On-Line

http://www.netgrocer.com/
Why run to the store if you can have it shipped to you? Check out the future of grocery shopping without lines, carts, or hassles.

Where's the Beef?

http://www.farmersmarketonline.com/windmill.htm
Here's you'll find homegrown beef—delivered to your door.

Other Links

http://www.candydirect.com/

http://www.hothothot.com/

http://www.ffgc.com/

http://www.thelobsternet.com/

http://www.cakesonline.net/

http://www.sweettechnology.com/

http://www.wireacake.com/

http://www.chefskitchen.com/

FOREIGN

The web won't let you feel the sand of the Sahara under your feet or let you taste a fresh mountain spring in Tibet, but you can experience the world and its cultures with the click of the mouse in your living room.

TOP SITE

National Geographic Society

http://www.nationalgeographic.com/

A great site with lots of interactive features including downloadable maps, country facts, and geographical resources.

Country Profiles

http://abcnews.go.com/reference/countryprofiles/countryprofiles_index.html

This is a browsable library of nearly every country in the world, meant to enhance news coverage by providing background about a country's history, culture, geography, natural resources, government, politics, economics, and demographics. For each country, you'll also find a color map, its flag, and its national anthem in RealAudio. In addition, you can use the Interactive Atlas, a database of sortable statistics and cultural differences, to compare each county to others in the world and to conduct your own investigations of world geography, demographics, and cultural diversity.

Library of Congress Studies

http://lcweb2.loc.gov/frd/cs/cshome.html

A series of studies on nations that include facts-at-a-glance and comprehensive sections on history, society, and culture.

Safari Web's Travel Tips

http://www.safariweb.com/travel.htm

A list of dos and don'ts for international travel.

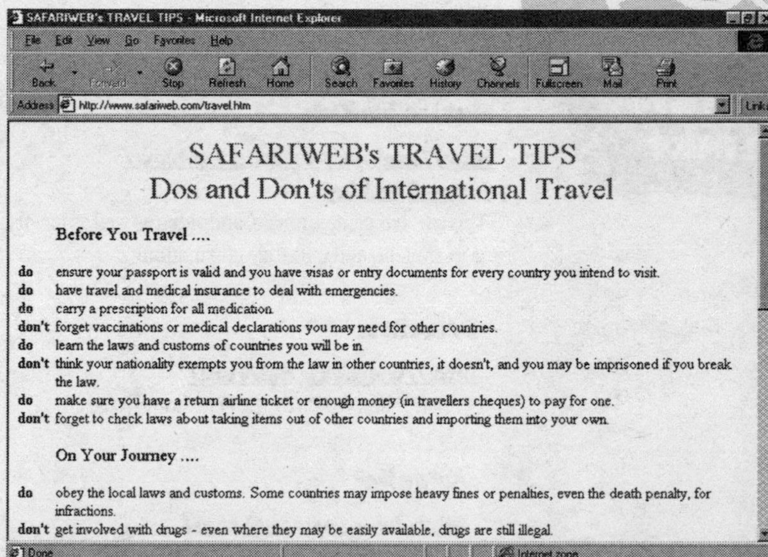

SAFARIWEB's TRAVEL TIPS - Microsoft Internet Explorer

File Edit View Go Favorites Help

Back Forward Stop Refresh Home Search Favorites History Channels Fullscreen Mail Print

Address http://www.safariweb.com/travel.htm Links

SAFARIWEB's TRAVEL TIPS
Dos and Don'ts of International Travel

Before You Travel ....

do ensure your passport is valid and you have visas or entry documents for every country you intend to visit.
do have travel and medical insurance to deal with emergencies.
do carry a prescription for all medication.
don't forget vaccinations or medical declarations you may need for other countries.
do learn the laws and customs of countries you will be in.
don't think your nationality exempts you from the law in other countries, it doesn't, and you may be imprisoned if you break the law.
do make sure you have a return airline ticket or enough money (in travellers cheques) to pay for one.
don't forget to check laws about taking items out of other countries and importing them into your own.

On Your Journey ....

do obey the local laws and customs. Some countries may impose heavy fines or penalties, even the death penalty, for infractions.
don't get involved with drugs - even where they may be easily available, drugs are still illegal.

Done Internet zone

The Smithsonian Center for Folklife and Cultural Heritage

http://www.si.edu/folklife/

The Smithsonian Center for Folklife and Cultural Heritage promotes the understanding and continuity of contemporary grassroots cultures in the United States and abroad. It produces the Smithsonian Folklife Festival, Smithsonian Folkways Recordings, exhibitions, documentary films and videos, symposia, and educational materials.

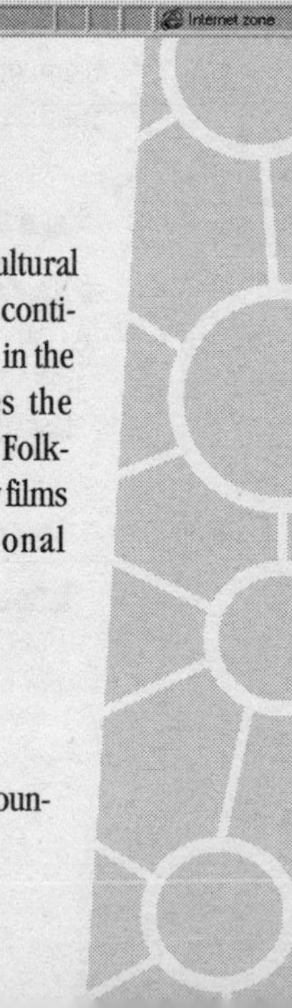

Native Web

http://www.nativeweb.org/

This site provides resources on indigenous countries around the world.

Oyeme!

http://www.oyeme.com/

Oyeme! is a searchable index and portal focused on the Latino community of the United States and Latin America.

Mexico for Kids

http://explora.presidencia.gob.mx/index_kids.html

This site has games, music, and video as well as history, government, and cultural information.

Eurocities

http://www.euw.net/euro/

Provides links to European city home pages.

AsianNet

http://www.asiannet.com/

Find information about and links to business, government, education, arts, and culture for East and Southeast Asia.

Asia Society Links

http://www.asiasociety.org/links/

A searchable, categorized directory of Asia-related links; links are generously annotated with descriptive text.

Everything Africa

http://www.everythingafrica.com/

Provides information about all the African countries.

Index on Africa

http://www.africaindex.africainfo.no/

A site including resource pages for individual countries and daily top stories on Africa. Maintained by the Norwegian Council for Africa.

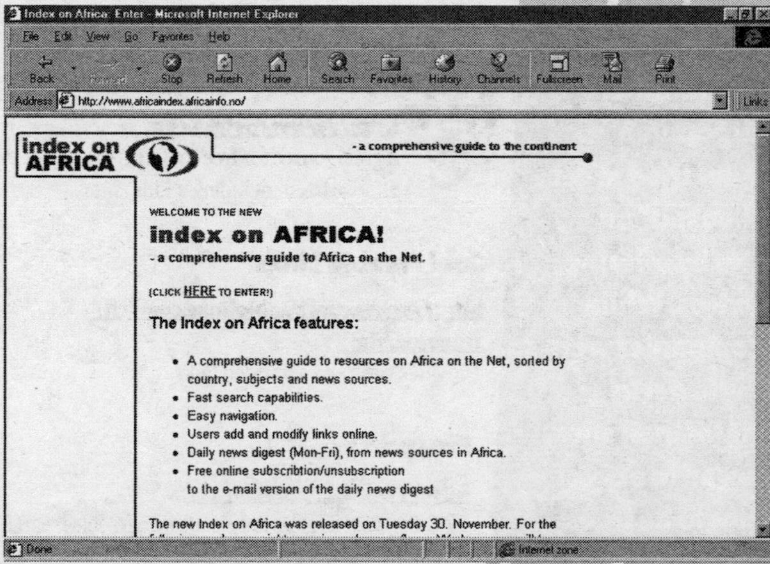

Middle East Internet Pages

http://www.middle-east-pages.com/

This is an index to Middle Eastern web sites.

Arab Internet Directory

http://www.arabview.net/aid/

A heirarchal (category based) Internet search utility for Arab/Arabic related sites.

FREE STUFF

When the Internet became popular, companies tried to get users "hooked" on their sites by offering free services. While many companies were planning to begin charging for their sites, users began to expect most sites to be free. Now many sites help you link up with free products and services available to you—*free*.

MyFree.com

http://www.myfree.com

A great source for free stuff. Has categories to choose from including a kids' site.

Cool Freebie Links

http://www.coolfreebielinks.com/cfl/freebies.htm

Provides reviewed and rated links.

Prospector

http://www.prospector.cz/

Find reviewed freebies links, and use a freebies search engine.

100 Percent Free Stuff

http://100percentfreestuff.com/
http://www.freecontests.com/

Searchable directories including contests, catalogs, magazines, and more.

About.com: Freebies

http://freebies.miningco.com/shopping/freebies/

Provides weekly features covering some aspect of freebies, contests, and free services.

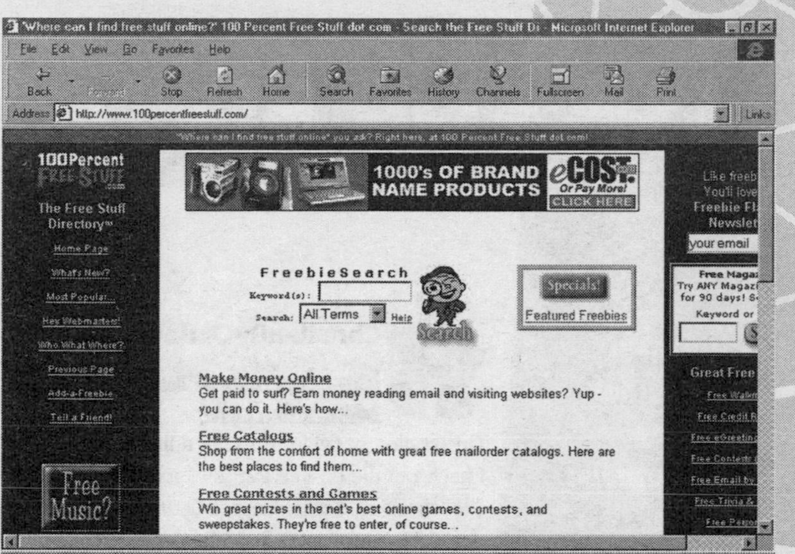

Did You Know?

...that 52 percent of 1998's Internet users lived in the U.S.?

FUN FOR KIDS

Kids pick up navigating the Internet as soon as they learn how to use the mouse. While they'll learn that the Internet is filled with great information, why not show them that the web is also filled with fun? Check out these sites and find the ones best suited for your kids. Some of these sites are so much fun, you may have trouble giving up your chair.

Christianity Online—Kids

http://www.christianityonline.com/community/kids/

This section of CO features fun things to do for kids. Check out the on-line games which include classics like checkers, Tetris, Frogger, Connect the dots, Web Invaders, Hangman, Q-Bert, Missile Commandos, Concentration, and more. Or play sports games like bowling, baseball, air hockey, catch; and new games like Help Horton, Moo Maze, Robix, Snowman, Musical Bottles, etc. Enjoy activities like Paint It and Etch-a-Sketch. This site also offers on-line Bible stories, Bible studies, and chat for kids—but you have to be an AOL user to access it.

A Cool Ministry

http://www.acoolministry.com/

A cool place where kids can learn about Jesus and being a Christian, while having some fun, too. Monthly newsletter, on-line games, jokes, cartoons, free digital cards, Yahoo! Kids' Club, kids' links, and lots more.

Abundant Life Kids

http://members.truepath.com/KIDS/

A Christian web site dedicated to providing a site for kids and parents. On-line games, Bible stories you can read or listen to, and links for both parents and kids. Information on contemporary issues like "Pokémon" are here also.

Apple City Kids

http://applecity.com/Kids/

A family-friendly site with a reading room of stories (some you can listen to on-line), games, and links to fun stuff on the web (including a special category for Christian links).

Christian Links for Kids and Teens

http://www.kids-teens.org/

Links to on-line testimonies, kids' home-pages, devotionals for kids, games, ABCs, fun pages, and more. Find homework help or join a prayer chain. Also features on-line birthday, book, and video club—as well as links to ministries and sites for parents.

Angel Fire Girls

http://angelfiregirls.com/

This is the place for Christian girls between the age of 7-12 to come to share thoughts and ideas about God and life. They have a game page for anyone to use. For members, they feature a monthly newsletter, an I. D. card, pen pal list, message board, and great book club.

Beantown

http://www.calvary.com/beantown/

Beantown is a fun page for kids, with Bibles stories, puzzles, crafts, science experiments with a Biblical perspective, and more! This page is sponsored by Calvary Chapel Monterey Bay and is updated weekly.

Mr. Rogers

http://www.pbs.org/rogers/

The Learning Kingdom

http://www.learningkingdom.com

The Hampster Dance

http://stydie.dv8.org/

Thomas the Tank

http://www.thomasthetankengine.com

Submit a Site

hudson@techie.com

Guideposts for Kids

http://www.gp4k.com/index.shtm

This is the on-line home of a fun, colorful, fantastic, faith-filled magazine. You'll find a safe spot where kids can go and find sound advice, inspiration, and lots of fun. At the phone booth you'll find a toll-free number to call anytime to hear cool stories and songs and Scripture verses. At the art studio you can paint on-line or print out stationery or pictures to color at home. The arcade is the place to go for all kinds of fun games, and the card shop lets you send E-mail postcards to family and friends on-line. All this and more!

Kids for Canaan

http://www.lightedway.org/Kidsite/kids.html

Bible and nature stories, crafts, games, puzzles, quizzes, snacks, safe E-mail penpals, Breakfast with God (worship times) and more for kids.

BigIdea.com

http://www.bigidea.com/

From the makers of Veggie Tales, this site is packed with fun games, stories, and activities. Check out video clips or learn more about upcoming Veggie Tales events.

TOP SITE

Disney Interactive

http://disney.go.com/DisneyInteractive/

Features fun interactive things to do that involve your favorite Disney characters. Play picture puzzle with Tigger, help Buzz Lightyear rescue Woody, create and send an original Simba song, submit a recipe to the Disney Kitchen, and much, much more!

Children's Playroom

http://www.entourages.com/barbs/playroom.htm

This site is a great resource for books you can read on-line—complete with illustrations. Check out the activities section which features links to sites like the Busy bee Coloring Book, Alphabet Made Fun, and Planet Zoom. Also features links to school and non-school web sites, children's ministries, and general kid-fun sites.

LearningPlanet.com

http://www.learningplanet.com/

This site features fun, interactive learning activities and games for kids. You can also sign up to be notified whenever a new activity is added to the site.

Sassy's Place for Kids

http://www.geocities.com/Heartland/Plains/7316/

A safe, fun place for kids on the web. Games, Bible stories, and verses, stories about Sassy's dog, Spanky, coloring pages, preschool section and more. Designed for ages 3 to 11.

Did You Know?

...that by February 2000 275.54 million people worldwide were on-line?
...that 2.45 million people in Africa were on-line?
...that 54.9 million people in Asia/Pacific were on-line?
...that 71.99 million people in Europe were on-line?
...that 1.29 million people in the Middle East were on-line?
...that 136.06 million in Canada and the USA were on-line?
...that 8.7 million people in South America were on-line?

GAMES

At the end of a long day, sometimes you don't feel like doing much. Rather than do some mind-numbing surfing, settle down and play an on-line game. Many of these sites allow you to play against other people all over the world. At Yahoo.com's game site, as many as 50,000 people are playing games at any given time. With numbers like that, you're bound to find someone looking for a quick game.

TOP SITE

Yahoo!Games

http://games.yahoo.com/

Play games on Yahoo! with people all across the Internet. All games are free and require no extra plug-ins. Find board games like backgammon or chess, card games like hearts or bridge, single player games like crosswords or mazes, or other games like MahJong or Word Racer. You can also play fantasy sports games like auto racing, baseball, golf, hockey, or soccer.

Igames Multiplayer Game Communties

http://www.igames.com/

On-line multiplayer gaming site with numerous classic card and board games—including hearts, backgammon, cribbage, spades, and gin rummy.

Games Galore

http://games.edioms.com/

Play Fantasy Futures—a fun Internet trading game. Or play java script games like Match' Em or Picture Puzzle. Or java applet games like Bustout or Mastermind or Peg Solitaire.

Christian Gamers Ring

http://www.geocities.com/cgronline/

Christian Gamers Webring—a fellowship of believers who like to play on-line games. Designed to be a safe place to make a friend. The sites on this ring are, in one way or another, associated to gaming and Christianity. You can find groups dedicated to certain games or styles, and others that are for a broad range.

Christian Games Forum

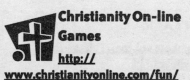

http://www0.delphi.com/christiangames/

For Christian Games enthusiasts—chat, leave messages, and play on-line games (particularly adventure and RPG-type games).

Crosswalk Games

http://games.crosswalk.com/

Play Hangman, Tale twister (like Mad Libs but better!), Closed Captioned (a humorous game with pictures and captions), or java games (arcade-style games).

Christianity On-line Games

http://www.christianityonline.com/fun/

A host of on-line games including classics like checkers, Tetris, Frogger, Connect the Dots, Web Invaders, Hangman, Q-Bert, Missile Commandos, Concentration, and more. Or play sports games like bowling, baseball, air hockey, catch; and new games like Help Horton, Moo Maze, Robix, Snowman, Musical Bottles, etc. You can even enjoy activities like Paint It and Etch-a-Sketch.

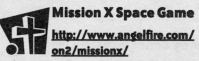

Mission X Space Game

http://www.angelfire.com/on2/missionx/

A Christian on-line space game with many special effects! As commander of the MX Enterprise, you are on a mission to save the world from ultimate disaster!

For Kids

Yahooligans! Games

http://games.yahoo.com/games/yahooligans.html

SuperSite for Kids

http://www.bonus.com/

Humongous Entertainment

http://www.humongous.com/

Christian Kids' Fun Center

http://www.angelfire.com/mt/BibleTruths/KidsFun.html

GENEALOGY

Genealogy work used to involve years and a lot of travel. Even a few years ago, researches would need to visit the National Archives or pay a visit to the Mormon repository in Salt Lake City. Now databases are on-line and researchers can network and compare notes over the Internet. Log on to some of the sites here and search for your surname. You're likely to find some new "cousins."

The USGenWeb Project

http://www.usgenweb.net/

This is the home page for the USGenWeb Project. They are a group of volunteers working together to provide Internet web sites for genealogical research in every county and every state of the United States. This project is noncommercial and fully committed to free access for everyone. Check out the "help for researchers" section to get started doing your own genealogical study.

Ancestor's Attic

http://members.aol.com/Tuffsearch/Genealogylinks.html

Ancestor's Attic has tips, tools, charts, forms, vital records, newspapers, maps, libraries, etc. . . .for beginners and the experienced alike.

Genealogy Tutor

http://members.aol.com/GenTutor

This page is for genealogists, family historians, and persons interested in American history and geography. It offers advice and links to related home pages.

Family Genealogy On-Line

http://www.familygenealogyonline.com/

Check out links to genealogy-related web sites and search tools.

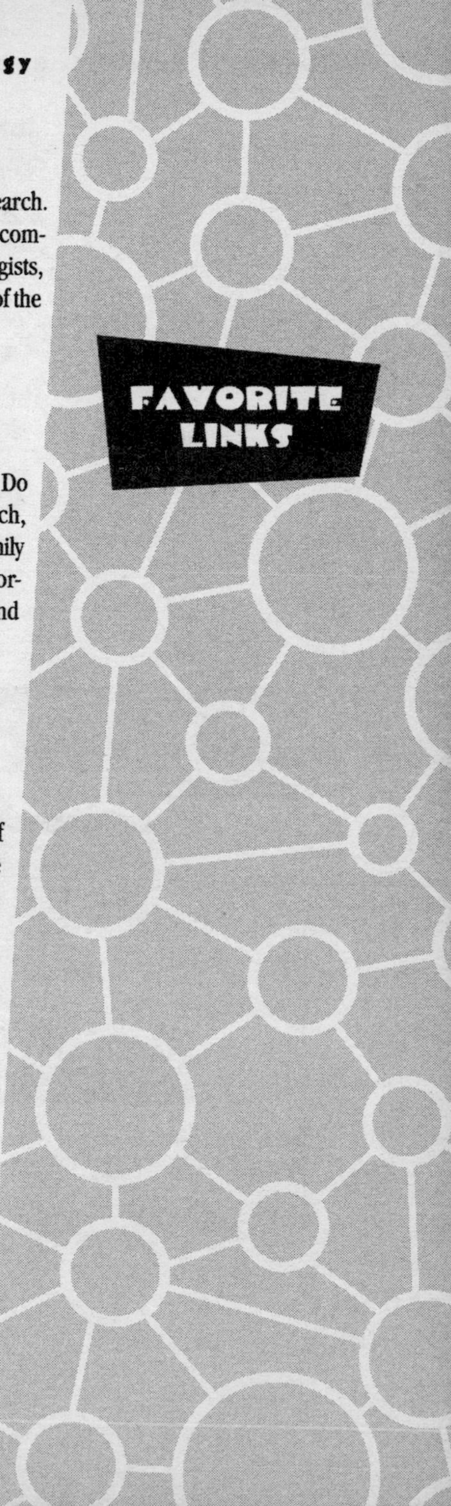

FamilyTreeMaker.com

http://www.familytreemaker.com/

This site is packed with resources for genealogy research. Lots of places to go to find out about your family, a community center to let you interact with other genealogists, and software and help getting started are just some of the many things you'll enjoy at this site.

Genealogy Gateway

http://www.gengateway.com/formula.htm

This web site does searches of over 50,000 records. Do an ancestry search, family search, genealogy search, surname search, or obituary search. Look through family home pages and vital records. Still need more information? This site has guides and links to help you find what you need.

TOP SITE

Family Search Internet Genealogy Service

http://www.familysearch.org/

A project of the Church of Jesus Christ of Latter-Day Saints, this site is known for its extensive database, which contains millions of names. Here you can search the Family History Library's database—which now includes the ability to search for an event or country, find out how to preserve your genealogy, or order family history resources.

Vital Records Information

http://www.vitalrec.com

This page contains information about where to obtain vital records from each state for deaths, births, marriages, and divorces.

Library of Congress Local History and Genealogy Reading Room

http://lcweb.loc.gov/rr/genealogy/

This site hosts one of the world's premier collections of U.S. and foreign genealogical and historical publications.

Census On-Line

http://www.census-online.com/

Find links to census data found on the web.

Web Directory: Cemetery Lists

http://www.interment.net/

An indexed directory of links to web sites with genealogical burial records.

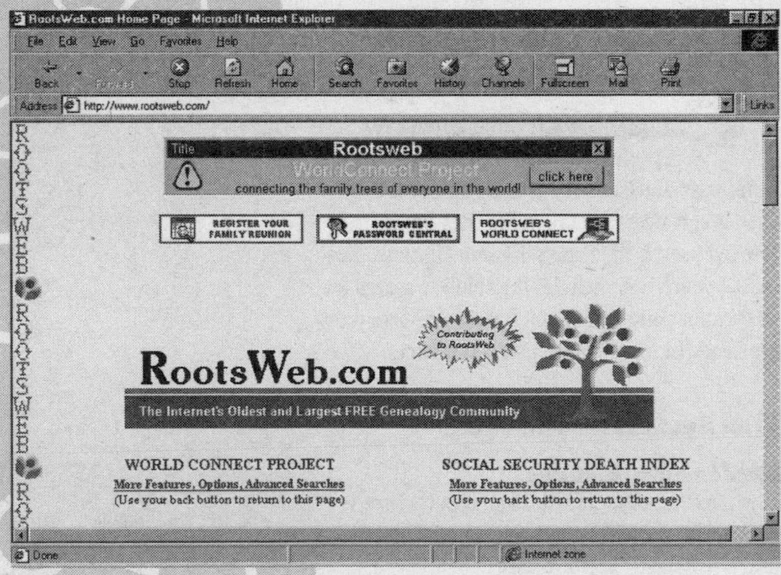

Get to the Roots

http://www.rootsweb.com/

This site is certainly one of the net's largest, free databases.

Land Record Reference Center

http://www.ultranet.com/~deeds/landref.htm
Find information about American land records, including grants, patents, and deeds; surveying terms, Internet resources, and much more.

Documentation and Publications

http://www.dcn.davis.ca.us/~vctinney/sources.htm
This site tells you how to document and publish genealogy and family history, with listings of scholarly Internet tools, resources, and examples.

DID YOU KNOW?

...that in 1963 Douglas Engelbart received a patent on the mouse pointing device for computers?

GEOGRAPHY

Where is Sri Lanka? Why are the Balkans such a spot for conflict? What countries exist where the Soviet Union once stood?

These sites will help you understand the news a little better, locate countries you can't seem to place, or learn more about countries where missionaries you know about live.

Library Map Collection

http://www.lib.utexas.edu/Libs/PCL/Map_collection/Map_collection.html

The Perry-Castañeda Library Map Collection holds more than 230,000 maps covering every area of the world. The collection houses political, topographic, and thematic maps of the world, including continents, regions, countries, states and provinces, nautical, aeronautical maps, survey maps, gazetteers, and much more.

Lycos Geography

http://www.lycoszone.com/dir/geography.html

Get help with your geography homework, research geography topics, and play geography games.

Association of American Geographers

http://www.aag.org/

For ninety-five years, the Association of American Geographers (AAG) has contributed to the advancement of geography. The AAG, a scholarly, nonprofit organization founded in Philadelphia in 1904, advances professional studies in geography and encourages the application of geographic research in education, government, and business. Their site includes information on the association along with related organizations, education and careers in geography, and publications.

National Geographic Society

http://www.nationalgeographic.com/

Web site of the National Geographic Society with as many features as a single issue, such as maps, photography, activities for kids, and shopping.

Virtual Library: Geography

http://geography.pinetree.org/

A directory of links related to geography.

Geography World

http://members.aol.com/bowermanb/101.html

An index of links to geography sites organized by subject areas.

Links to More

http://www.index-site.com/gis.htm

This is an index of geography, Geographic Information Systems, and mapping sites on the Internet.

Pictures of Earth

http://seds.lpl.arizona.edu/billa/tnp/pxearth.html

This is a long listing of satellite pictures for viewing.

Other Links

http://www.cnn.com/WEATHER/worldtime/

http://gulftour.tamu.edu

http://www.uncwil.edu/nurc/aquarius/

http://www.mtnforum.org/

http://www.desertusa.com/life.html

GIFT BUYING

You don't need to fight mall traffic or big crowds when it's time to buy a birthday present or a holiday gift. Buying gifts on-line can be one of the best ways to save time and increase your selection. Just like shopping in a mall, there are many kinds of stores on the Internet.

The best part of all is that rather than spending hours walking from store to store, a few mouse clicks and a few minutes can help you order the perfect gift—often at a discounted price.

Looking for a Specific Gift

http://www.dealtime.com/
http://www.jango.com/
http://www.pricescan.com/

Ever spend all day driving from store to store looking for someone carrying a specific appliance or toy? Or have you spent hours on the phone calling every store in the yellow pages to compare prices? These sites do that work for you by allowing you to comparative shop everything from appliances to video games. Some sites even offer a service to alert you when specific items go on sale. Other options are http://www.bottomdollar.com and http://www.mysimon.com

Virtual Malls

http://www.macys.com/
http://www.bloomingdales.com/
http://www.jcpenney.com/
http://www.nordstrom.com/

The legendary department stores are now on-line. Enjoy them without fighting the mall crowd. Of course, not all virtual malls have brick-and-mortar counterparts. Try shopping at these: http://www.sha-bang.com or http://www.shoponline123.com

Great Deals

http://www.saleseeker.com/

Yet another way to browse and hunt for that great deal. Enter your zip code and you'll get a list of items on sale at stores near you and at Internet stores.

Out of the Ordinary

http://www.send.com/
Tired of giving ties or sweaters? Try this site for a meaningful gift like dinner for two or excellent food products. Need a unique gadget? Try http://www.sharperimage.com/.

When You Need Ideas

http://www.911gifts.com/
http://www.presentpicker.com/
Some sites like these help guide your gift giving. By stepping you through a worksheet you describe the person you're looking for: age, sex, interests, etc. The site responds with appropriate gifts.

Make a List—Check It Twice

http://www.della.com/
This site can take the fretting out of gift giving. It's like having a personal gift registry. You post your interests or specific gifts that you hope to receive. Friends or family members can visit for shopping ideas.

Christian Gifts

http://www.christianityonline.com/
There are many sites that specialize in Christian products: books, Bibles, music, and gifts. Here's one of the many places to pick up an inspirational gift.

Toys

http://www.etoys.com/

http://www.bearst.com/

http://www.disneystore.com/

http://www.buygames.com/

http://www.kbkids.com/

http://www.naturaltoys.com/

http://www.toysrus.com/

http://www.worldofscience.com/

GOD & THEOLOGY

Many Christians fear the Internet because they've heard bad stories about it. Such fear is understandable but unfortunate. The Internet can actually be a good place to *grow* spiritually. Many of these sites can help you grow in your knowledge of God, increase your devotion, and provide ideas for practical application. No, the Internet can't take the place of prayer or church, but you might be able to learn a little more from other Christians around the world.

Christian Classics Ethereal Library

http://www.ccel.org/

A vast library of electronic books selected for edification. Includes many of the greatest Christian books ever written.

Interpretation

http://www.interpretation.org/

Founded in 1947, the ecumenical journal *Interpretation* offers articles on the cutting edge of biblical and theological studies. Its readership includes pastors, scholars, and students.

Fides Quaereus Internetum

http://www.bu.edu/people/bpstone/theology/theology.html

This is a hub for locating serious Christian theological activity on the Internet. Find links to Christian theology pages, newsgroups and chat rooms, Christian theological journals, theological aids and resources, and much more.

FAVORITE LINKS

E-Grace.net

http://www.e-grace.net/

This site contains hundreds of links to Christian theology articles on-line. Just click on a topic in the *Link Index* to view a list of links to articles on that particular Bible doctrine—over forty different topics available. The purpose of this web site ministry is to provide a place for Bible theology study on-line, a place where you can find articles that are sound in doctrine.

Biblical Theology

http://biblicaltheology.webhostme.com/

A resource for those who desire to investigate the relationship of theology to the Bible. The intent of this site is to provide an introduction to theology in a systematic manner. Each section begins with biblical evidence for each doctrine and ends with some theological implications to consider.

Center for Reformed Theology and Apologetics

http://www.reformed.org/

The Center for Reformed Theology and Apologetics (CRTA) is dedicated to providing biblically sound on-line resources for the edification of God's people. Provides debates, articles, and discussions of apologetic methodology. You can read general articles about the Bible and hypertext versions of Reformed books and commentaries. Also includes information on Calvinism, Christianity and Science, education, and Christianity, ecclesiology, eschatology, ethics, historic church documents, sacramentology, and more. Check out links to Bible and other software sites, links to Reformed booksellers and organizations, and Reformed E-mail discussion lists. Also hosts a web-based, topical discussion forum.

Wesley Center for Applied Theology

http://wesley.nnc.edu/

This site includes valuable Christian references not found elsewhere—especially Josepheus's *The Antiquities of the Jews*, an important First Century text. Contains lots of information on a variety of topics including John and Charles Wesley, Wesleyan theology, holiness tradition, Arminianism, and more.

Darkness to Light

http://www.dtl.org/

Explaining and defending the Christian faith from a Reformed-Baptist perspective. Articles on theology and apologetics arranged according to subject.

Reformation Theology

http://www.dallas.net/sovgrace/reformation.html

A guide to the theological underpinnings of the Reformation.

Righteousness

http://members.truepath.com/EdV/

Puritan-influenced articles and links. Biblical studies/messages on nature of salvation. Challenges one to a biblical perspective of today's doctrines and methodologies. Also includes a list of links by topic.

Did You Know?

...that today's average household in the USA contains more computer power than existed in the world before 1965?

Theology on the Web

http://dmapub.dma.org/~thawes/

Geared primarily to college, university, and seminary students and teachers, this site features essays and articles on classical Christianity and theology. Find information under topics like: Creeds and Confessions of Faith, Essays in Theology, and Classical Christianity.

A Christian Think Tank

http://www.webcom.com/~ctt/

This site contains items of Christian apologetics, theology, philosophy, biblical studies, and more. This complex of pages represents one man's Christian journey through 20th-century Western thought. It contains his reflections on philosophy and theology, spirituality and apologetics. These are not abstract opinions, but rather serious, committed, and honest attempts to confront the urgent and contemporary questions of skeptics, of believers, of himself, and of his God.

Mr. D's Notes On Theology

http://www.open.org/~mrdsnts/index.htm

Written by a pastor, this site provides a conservative Christian systematic theology, available for study on-line or as zipped download files. The theology is a practical work divided into small portions. It should be a good reference work even if you disagree with the conclusions

Apostate Cafe

http://www.apostate.com/religion/

A discussion of Christianity, Gnosticism, theology, heresy, and prayer.

Christian Pursuit

http://www.sandalphon.com/

Christian Cultural Studies

http://www.wordbridge.net/ccsp/

theologyandhistory.com

http://www.geocities.com/~jasonvanb/

Theology Forum

http://home.wnm.net/~derekg/forum/

Biblical Theology Discussion Board

http://www.crosslight.org/

Submit a Site

hudson@techie.com

GOVERNMENT

What is the voting record of the people who represent you in Congress? Who's running for office in your town and what is their platform? How can you send a government official an E-mail? These sites help make the government more accessible. Even kids will learn more about how our country works by the sites listed here.

TOP SITE

The Great American Web Site

http://www.uncle-sam.com/

This is a nongovernmental research firm dedicated to providing access to Uncle Sam's voluminous sources of information. From the home page, you can access every branch of government. They provide brief reviews of sites and feature the newest additions (see Weekly Highlights) and their candidates for the best sites throughout Uncle Sam's web.

Federal Gateway

http://fedgate.org/

Federal Gateway is a new web breakthrough that consolidates all government agencies into one Internet site, thereby greatly simplifying the task of acquiring United States federal, state, and local government information—and it's free.

Project Vote Smart

http://www.vote-smart.org/

Project Vote Smart is a national library of factual information on over 13,000 candidates for public office—president, governors, Congress and state legislatures. PVS covers the candidates in five basic areas: backgrounds, issue positions, voting records, campaign finances, and the performance evaluations made on them by over eighty conservative to liberal special interests groups.

Government Sites for Kids

http://www.westga.edu/~library/depts/govdoc/kids.shtml

This page is a listing of U.S. federal government web sites that have been designed for children and youth.

GovSpot

http://www.govspot.com/

A collection of government and civic resources and links.

CIA's Home Page for Kids

http://www.odci.gov/cia/ciakids/index.html

This page describes the role and contribution of intelligence in the modern government. Has a mystery section for kids as well as geography quizzes using data to make decisions about a given country you have picked.

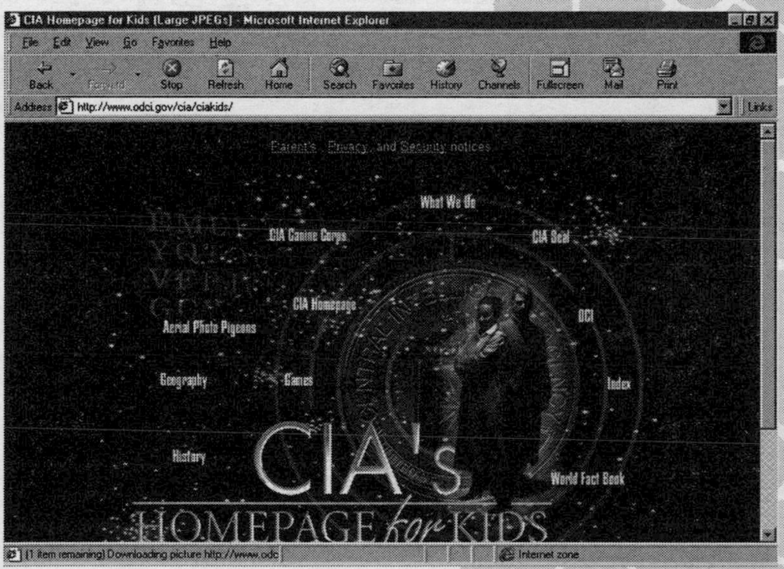

The White House Historical Association

http://www.whitehousehistory.org/whha/pagetwoa.asp

This site is a historical as well as a current tour featuring the White House. There is a kids' section and educational sections for parents and teachers that are great to look at.

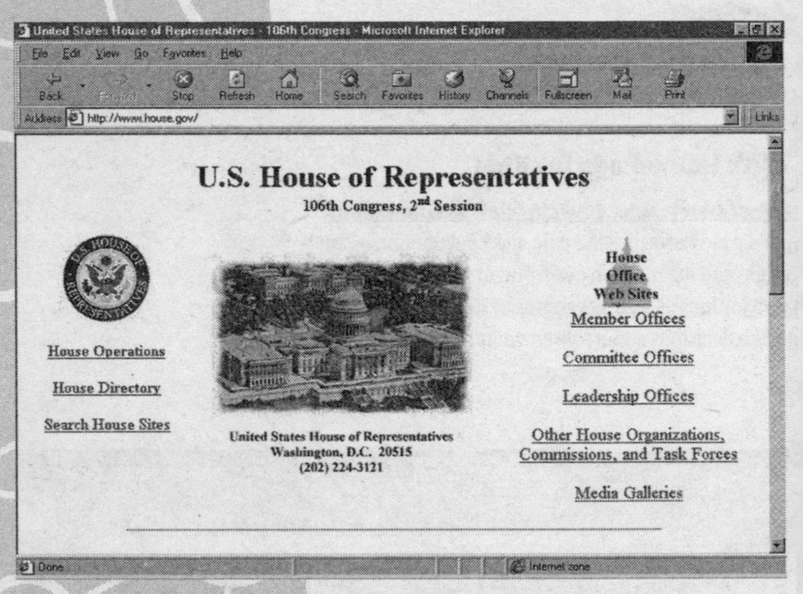

U.S. House of Representatives

http://www.house.gov/

The web site for the U.S. House of Representatives includes committees and the weekly scheduled activity.

U.S. Senate

http://www.senate.gov/

The web site for the U.S. Senate includes committees and the weekly scheduled activities.

Did You Know?

... that by 1999, there were 170 patents issued mentioning the word *Internet*?

Supreme Court Page

http://www2.cybernex.net/~vanalst/supreme.html

A child-friendly site introducing the Supreme Court justices, previous justices, and Supreme Court links.

The Christian Coalition

http://www.cc.org/

The Christian Coalition was founded as a pro-family citizen action organization to impact public policy on a local, state, and national level, to teach Christians effective citizenship, and to promote Christian values in government. At their site, you can find out more about their organization, learn about issues in the news, keep up to date on the current legislation in the House and Senate, and check out the voter education articles.

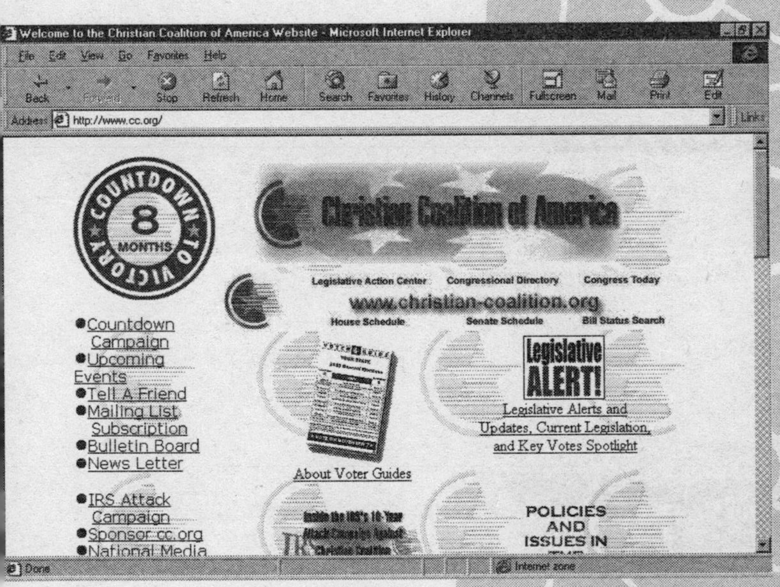

Democracy Web Site

http://
www.fordemocracy.com/

International List of World Courts

http://www.polisci.com/
web/courts.htm

American Presidents

http://
www.americanpresidents.org/

DID YOU KNOW?

...that the U.S. Census Bureau is expected to use the Internet for the 2010 census?

Church and State

http://www.ogi.lcms.org/

An information service of the Office of Government Information of the Lutheran Church—Missouri Synod, providing up-to-date, non-partisan news and analysis of subjects of interest to Christians as they carry out their calling to be faithful citizens in our society.

Christians, Politics, and Government

http://users.churchserve.com/nz/bibpp/

Bible-based axioms about government, politics and public policy for Christians

GRAPHICS

Bring pizazz to your web page, newsletter, program, or bulletin with some new graphics. Many sites offer free graphics. Others charge you a small subscription, or usage fee, for access to their large libraries. Between the free and inexpensive options, you should find what you need for most home uses.

The WhyteHouse

http://www.whytehouse.com/

Check out free web page graphics and javascripts with a Christian theme.

TOP SITE

ArtToday

http://www.arttoday.com/

A large, searchable, categorized set of clip art, photos, fonts, web graphics, and ›unds available on the Internet. Over 150 gigabytes f images. Equal to over 231 CD-ROMs.

Grandstand Graphics

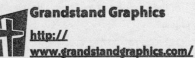

http://www.grandstandgraphics.com/

he images range from cartoon and Bible charac- ›rs to food, people, and animals.

omputer Art

ttp://library.thinkquest.org/3543/

his site was designed to explore the many aspects f computers and art using the Internet as a me- ium. Find lessons, resources, gallery, and ›rum.

bout.com: Clip Art

ttp://webclipart.about.com/internet/ ebclipart/

his site provides resource to backgrounds, tex- ›res, animation, graphics, icons, and more.

Clip Art Review

http://www.webplaces.com/html/clipart.htm
A guide to sites offering free graphic images.

Multimedia and Clip Art

http://www.itec.sfsu.edu/multimedia/multimedia.html
A large collection of multimedia, clip art, and ico resources.

EyeWire

http://www.eyewire.com
These are the people who created the world's fir commercial Type 1 fonts, the world's first stock pho tography on CD, and the world's first vector clip ar EyeWire provides productivity-enhancing visual an audio content, on-line software tools, design re sources, and information for graphic designers an others creating professional-looking graphics EyeWire's product offerings include stock photogra phy, footage, audio, typefaces, illustrations and clip art.

CNET Builder.com

http://www.builder.com/Authoring/Newbies/
This site for beginning web page design instruct you on all the essentials you need to start with.

Project Cool Media

http://www.projectcool.com
A network of web sites sharing the common be lief that anyone can make a great web site if give knowledge, guidance, and inspiration. There something for everyone within, from the first tim web-page maker to the designer with years c experience.

For Kids

http://artforkids.about.com/kids/artforkids/msubcomputerart/.

Coloring Pages

http://www.ivyjoy.com/coloring/onlinelinks.html

http://members.tripod.com/~Nasbwmn/index-7.html

Support for Special Needs

http://www.geocities.com/Heartland/Woods/5387/

Disability Related

http://www.eskimo.com/~jlubin/disabled/graphics/

The Center for Advanced Instructional Media at Yale University

http://info.med.yale.edu/caim/manual

This style manual developed as an outgrowth of Yale's own World Wide Web development projects. This site reflects their attempts to apply some of the lessons learned in twelve years of multimedia software design, graphic interface design, and book design to the new medium of web pages and site design.

GREETING CARDS

The virtual postcard. This fun, new phenomen lets you send an on-line greeting card to a friend. Use them for special occassions, holidays, or just to say, "I've been thinking about you." Blue Mountain Arts is the granddaddy of them all, but there are many other good options, too. There are so many free options, you ought to be able to find one you like.

Bible Cards

http://www.bibleverseart.com/

This site has Christian e-cards that combine Bible verses with beautiful photographs. They also allow you to download Bible-related screen savers and wallpaper.

Christian E-cards

http://www.cjsspecialties.com/

Here's a Christian site that offers free, Christian E-cards. Know someone who needs encouragement with a Christian theme? Browse here.

Big Music Selection

http://www.card4you.com/

While some sites limit your music choice, this site gives you a huge selection of music you can send along with your cute card.

Angel Wink's Heavenly Postcard Shoppe

http://www.geocities.com/heartland/hills/7792/postcardpageindex.html

This site is very complete and has cards for kids as well as adults. The site also hosts voice message cards, which allow you to add another personal touch to your card.

Nature Cards

http://www.e-cards.com?

This site is dedicated to images from nature. While a free service, the web site uses advertising revenue to donate to organizations dedicated to helping protect the environment.

Disney Cards

http://www.postcards.org/

Over 1,000 postcards to choose from, including some with animations from Disney movies.

TOP SITE

Popular E-Cards

http://www.bluemountain.com/

The first well-known site for E-cards remains the most popular. Find cards for any occasion and with almost any theme. Got a sports lover? An animal lover? There's even a section for Christian and inspirational cards. You'll probably find a suitable card for almost anyone.

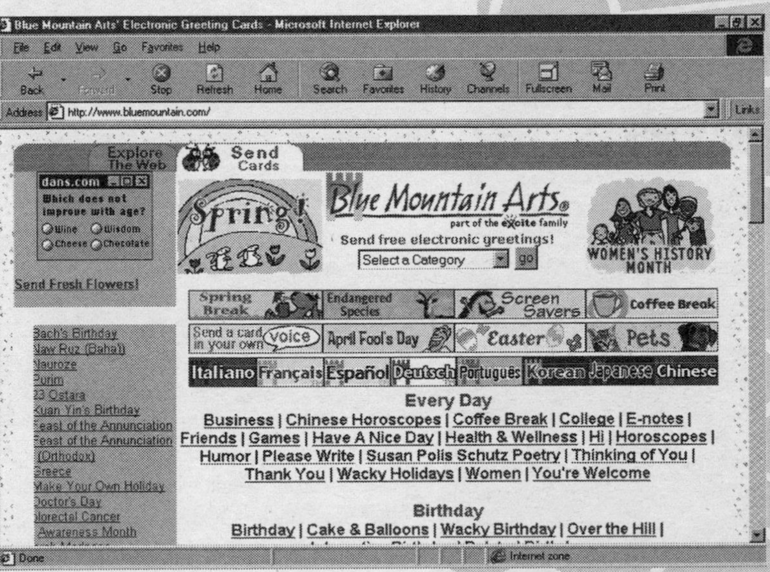

Other Links

http://www.homenfamily.com/cards/cards htm

http://www3.viaweb.com/

http://annieshomepage.com

Hallmark Sites

http://www.hallmark.com/

http://www.shoebox.com/

American Greetings

http://www.americangreetings.com/

Virtual Roses

http://staff.washington.edu/icards/?croses@flowers

Here's a collection of photographs of some award-winning roses. If you can't afford the real thing, and if it's really "the thought that counts," this might help you.

Create Your Own

http://www.cyber-cards.com/

Allows you to send postcards with your own pictures as well as a wide variety of seasonal and scenic pictures.

HEALTH

TOP SITE

Dr. Koop's Community

http://www.drkoop.com/

This site provides health and medical information, including personalized news. Packed with great resources and fun features.

Cooper Institute Resource Center

http://cooperinstitute.org/

This site provides consumers with a set of tools that enables them to define their health objectives and address each issue in an effective and efficient manner. Whether researching an illness on the Internet, negotiating an insurance claim, researching health care legislation or looking for a physician with whom you feel comfortable, this site should be both informative and helpful.

American Medical Association

http://www.ama-assn.org/consumer/gnrl.htm

On-line health information for everyone by the American Medical Association. Multiple sites for a variety of health questions and practices.

HealthOasis

http://www.mayohealth.org/

HealthOasis is the weekly updated Mayo Clinic web site addressing a variety of health issues

When should you be concerned about that lingering cough? What should you do about that new ache you've discovered? What's "normal" for your age? No medical site replaces a timely trip to the doctor, but some of these sites are run by medical professionals. You can get good preventative, medical advice as well as answers to questions that don't merit a trip to the doctor's office.

and concerns to bring you the most relevant information available.

The Health Network

http://www.thehealthnetwork.com/

The Health Network is the one-stop television and Internet site where you'll find the information, support, and motivation you need to make your own decisions about leading a healthy life. Twenty-four hours a day, seven days a week, doctors and other medical experts provide credible, relevant information in a clear, interesting, and easy-to-understand manner.

HealthWeb

http://healthweb.org/

HealthWeb provides links to specific, evaluated information resources on the World Wide Web selected by librarians and information professionals at leading academic medical centers in the Midwest. Selection emphasizes quality information aimed at assisting health care professionals as well as consumers in

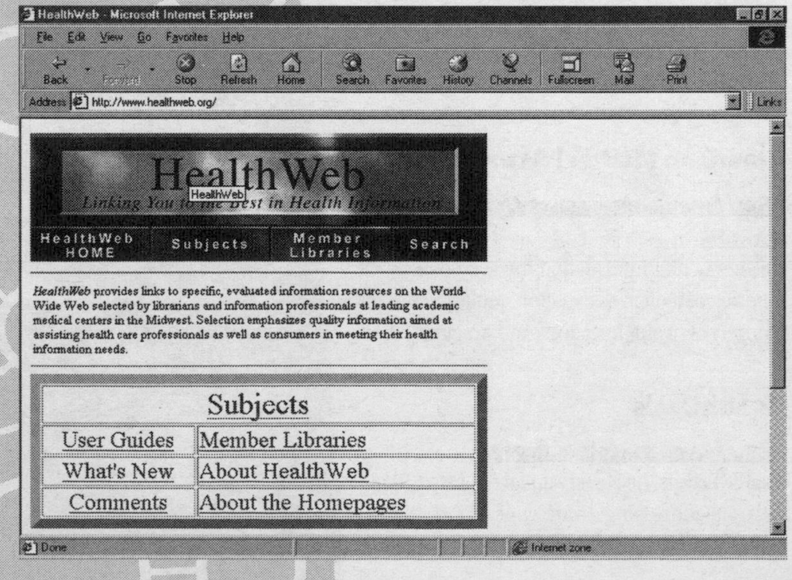

meeting their health information needs. Parental guidance is suggested for some of the topics.

Refdesk

http://www.refdesk.com/health.html#g-i
A well-selected list of web links for national and state health organizations for a particular topic of disease, or more general topics of health and wellness. This is the place to start for surfing health topics. Since this is a comprehensive list, parents should provide guidance; topics covered include sexual disease and dysfunction, nontraditional medical views, and links to sites you may not want your child to visit.

Personal Best

http://www.personalbest.com/
The goal of Personal Best is to help you reach your personal best. Take a few minutes to explore their sample articles and recipes, take a quiz, link up with other health resources, and learn more about their newsletters.

Council on Family Health

http://www.cfhinfo.org/
The Council on Family Health is a nonprofit organization established more than thirty years ago, dedicated to educating consumers about the proper use of nonprescription and prescription medicines, home safety, and personal health. Educational materials available individually or in quantity.

www.health.gov

http://www.health.gov/
List of government sites related to health issues including the General Surgeon's Virtual Office and current projects funded to address keeping us healthy.

Other Links

http://www.avonlink.co.uk/amanda/

http://www.azc.com/client/enn2/hscentral.htm

http://hwcweb.hwc.ca/hpb/lcdc/brch/reprod/sidsjo.html

http://www.phys.com/

Submit a Site

hudson@techie.com

Great Outdoor Recreation Pages

http://www.gorp.com/gorp/health/main.htm

Has information about traveling and staying healthy as well as vacationing in the great outdoors.

FDA Kids' Home Page

http://www.fda.gov/oc/opacom/kids

FDA's kid site from All About Animals to All About Vaccines, and lots of stuff in between.

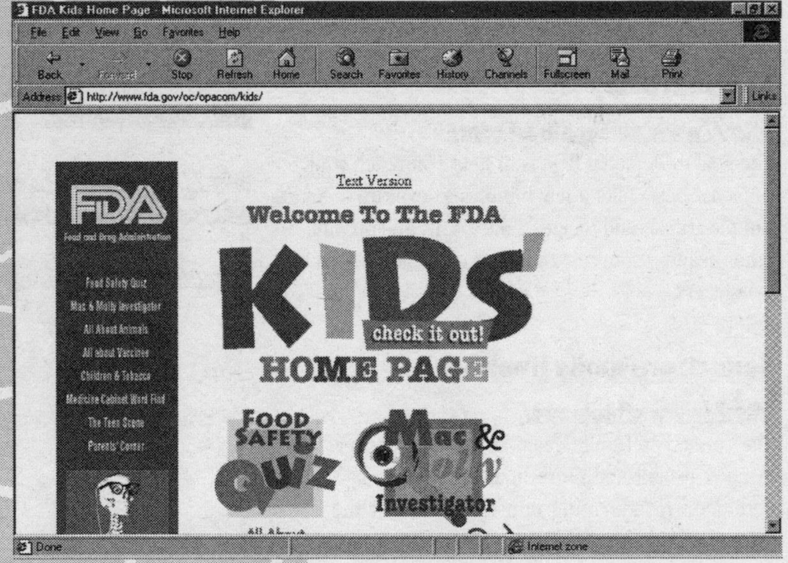

Health Administration

Health Resources and Services Administration

http://www.hrsa.dhhs.gov

The Health Resources and Services Administration (HRSA) directs national health programs, which improve the health of the nation by assuring quality health care to vulnerable and special-needs populations and by promoting appropriate health professions workforce capacity and practice, particularly in primary care and public health. Fact sheets available in the Newsroom.

Bureau of Health Professionals

http://www.hrsa.dhhs.gov/bhpr/program.html

Web site of the Bureau of Health Professionals. The Health Resources and Services Administration provides leadership in education and training, largely through its Bureau of Health Professions administration of Titles VII and VIII of the Public Health Service Act, which strengthens and helps secure the nation's capability to excel in health care, meet ongoing and emerging community needs, and restrain continuing increases in health care expenditures.

Health Care Administration on the WWW

http://www.tsufl.edu/library/8/special/health.htm

Web links page for a variety of health administration agencies, web sites, and research programs in the United States.

Toolbox for Health Managers and Administrators

http://www.pohly.com/admin.shtml

This site contains articles, information, and links to other web sites pertinent to managers and administrators working in health care. You can find information about health economics, medical and insurance legislation, industry news, legal issues, regulatory, compliance, policy, business-planning resources, human resources, careers, terminology, and more.

Children's Hospital
http://vch.vh.org/

Children's Health
http://members.aol.com/Solhouse5/

Chronic Illness, Children,
http://funrsc.fairfield.edu/~jfleitas/contents.html

Diseases in Children
http://www.slackinc.com/child/idc/idchome.htm

KidsDoctor
http://www.kidsdoctor.com/

KidsHealth
http://kidshealth.org/

ParentsPlace
http://www.parentsplace.com/health/

WebMD

http://webmd.com

Arthritis Foundation

http://www.arthritis.org

Fibromyalgia Network

http://www.fmnetnews.com

Partners Against Pain

http://www.partnersagainstpain.com/

Rest Ministries

http://www.restministries.org/

All Health.com

http://www.allhealth.com

HealthCareHR

http://www.healthcarehr.com/

A health care administrator and medical staffing professional's guide to recruitment and administrative resources on the web.

Healthweb—Health Administration

http://www.lib.umich.edu/hw/health.admin.html

Home page for the University of Michigan Health Administration program at the School of Public Health. Has links and sites for all the specialties within the field of health administration.

Health Care

National Health Care for the Homeless Council, Inc.

http://www.nhchc.org/

A membership organization of health care providers working to help bring about reform of the health care system to best serve the needs of people who are homeless.

HealthGrades.com

http://www.healthgrades.com/

This one-of-a-kind Internet service supplies valuable information about the quality of health care provided by individual hospitals, physicians, and health plans in the United States. Provides health care report cards to help you make better decisions about your health care.

Medical Cost and Quality Assistance

http://www.mecqa.com/

This site intends to help visitors evaluate the

cost and quality of health care services. It allows consumers to find and compare dentists, physicians, outpatient facilities, hospitals or insurance companies, as well as listing competitive benchmark pricing by procedure.

Navigating the Health Care System

http://www.eqp.org/

This site is designed to help employees, employers, and the self-employed understand health care issues and the resources of their health care plan and choices.

Midwifery

http://www.acnm.org/

Information on nurse-midwifery care, women's health, prenatal care, childbirth, finding nurse-midwives, education, certification, and questions to ask your prenatal doctor or midwife.

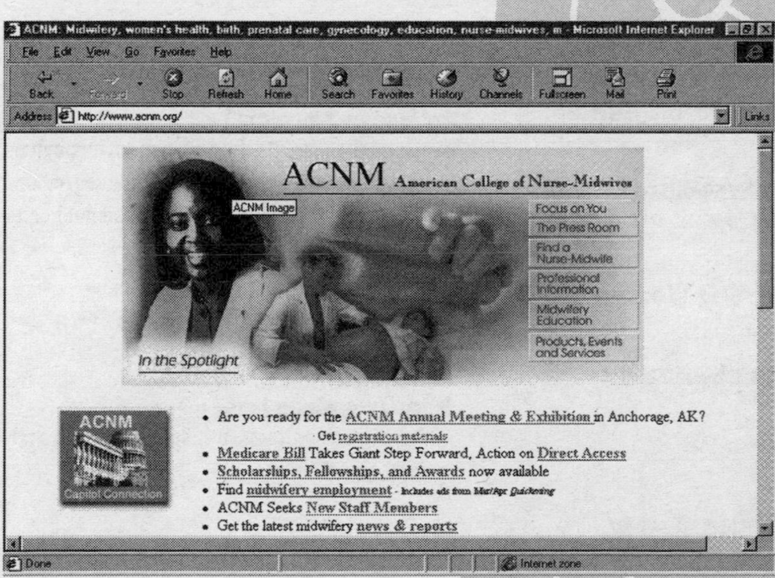

The Obstetrics & Gynecology Network

http://www.obgyn.net/

National Women's Health Information Center

http://www.4woman.gov/

Women's Health Center

http://www.betterhealth.com/womens/

HeartStrong Woman

http://www.heartstrongwoman.com/

HeliosHealth

http://www.helioshealth.com/

Just for Women

http://www.j-f-w.com/

Health Care Information Resources

http://www-hsl.mcmaster.ca/tomflem/top.html
An electronic info source for patients, their families, friends, and health care providers.

Health Care and Healthy Lifestyle Index

http://www.zondlo.com/access/health.htm
An index of sites related to health care.

Mental Health

Mental Health.Com

http://www.mentalhealth.com/
This site's goal is to improve understanding, diagnosis, and treatment of mental illness throughout the world.

Caring for Your Mental Health

http://www.nmha.org/
The National Mental Health Association, through its national office and more than 330 affiliates nationwide, is dedicated to improving the mental health of all individuals.

NAMI (National Alliance for the Mentally Ill) Home Page

http://www.nami.org/
NAMI is a grassroots, self-help, support, and advocacy organization.

HISTORY

The Amazing Bible World History Chart

http://agards.com/bible-timeline/

Easily compare Bible history to world history. Colorful wall chart. Free on-line version.

Christian History Institute

http://www.gospelcom.net/chi/

Christian History Institute is a nonprofit Pennsylvania corporation. Their aim is to make Christian history accessible to the broad public through modern media formats that are visually attractive, communicate effectively, and maintain scholarly integrity. Site includes the feature "What Happened on this Date in Christian History."

Today in History

http://www.440int.com/twtd/today.html

Features a daily summary of news events, famous birthdays, and hit music that happened on this day in history. Presented by 440 International.

This Day in Music History

http://www.partyhats.com/access/currentdate.idc

Find out what happened in the music world today. A history lesson of music news and facts that occurred on this day.

Most people are interested in some sort of history. For some, it's the history of their country; for others, it's biblical history, music history, or the history of their favorite sports team.

Whether you're looking for events that happened in the last few days or the last few thousand years, you're likely to find the topic that interests you.

Women in American History

http://women.eb.com/

Britannica On-Line presents a special multimedia exhibit on women in American history, featuring biographies, interactive time lines, Internet resources, and more.

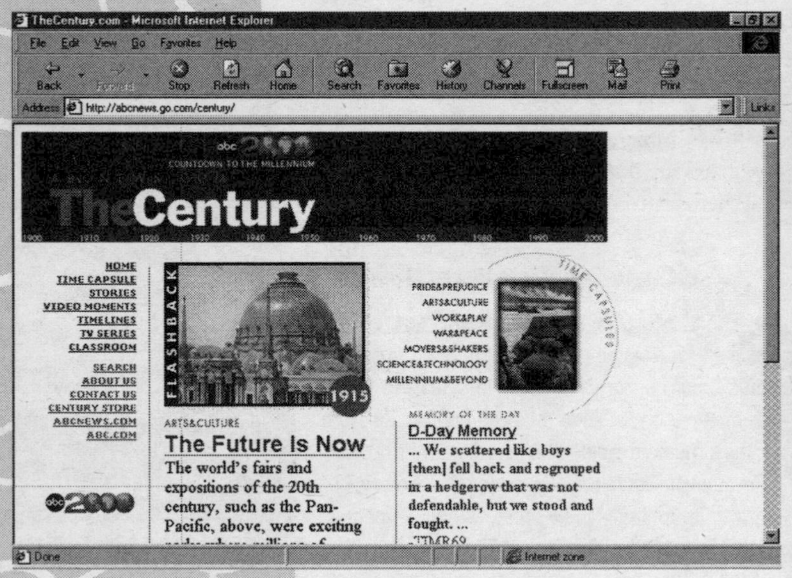

TOP SITE The Twentieth Century

http://www.thecentury.com/

TheCentury.com is part of a landmark ABC News effort to paint a portrait of this incredible century. The Time Capsule is the heart of the site. You can go to this area to record and contribute the recollections, stories, and opinions of the twentieth century that affected you and your family, as well as to read the stories others have posted. TheCentury.com will also bring you the most compelling video and audio moments of the past 100 years, as well as interactive games and activities.

Did You Know?

...that in 1949, forecasting the relentless march of science, *Popular Mechanics* said "Computers in the future may weigh no more than 1.5 tons"?

TheHistoryNet

http://www.thehistorynet.com/

An extensive site with lots of interesting categories. Check out great battles, armies and intrigue, eyewitness accounts, homes and heritage, the picture gallery, and tons more.

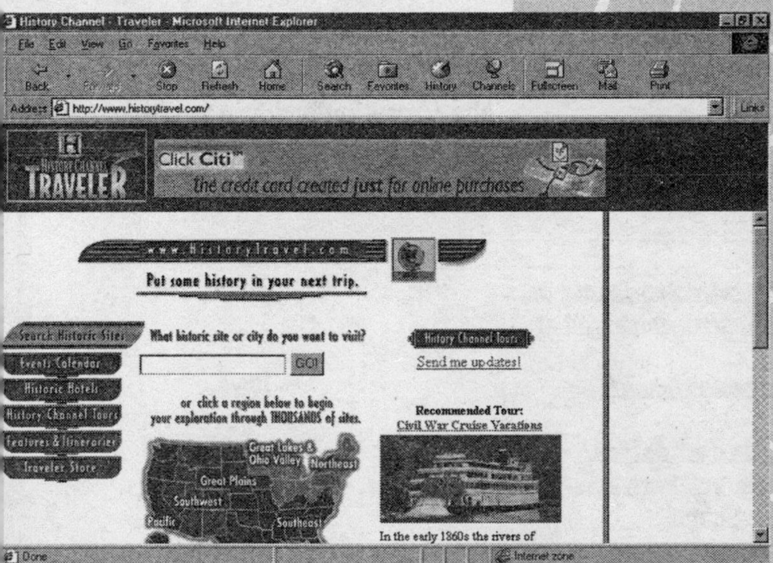

History Traveler

http://www.historytravel.com

This is an on-line guide to historic travel across the country. This page will introduce you to Traveler and show you how to use their guide to find the historic sites, lodging, and events you want to see. Whether you are looking for a packaged tour, planning a family trip, a weekend getaway or a cross-country excursion, Traveler can help you put a little history into your next trip.

Did You Know?

. . . that in 1943 Thomas Watson (while chairman of IBM) said, "I think there is a world market for about five computers"?

HyperHistory On-Line

http://www.hyperhistory.com/online_n2/History_n2/a.html

HyperHistory On-line navigates through 3,000 years of world history with links to important persons of world historical importance; civilization time lines; events and facts; and historical maps.

Gateway to World History

http://www.hartford-hwp.com/gateway/

This is a collection of on-line resources to support the study and teaching of world history and history in general.

Other Links

http://www.freenet.victoria.bc.ca/bchistory.html

http://www.freenet.victoria.bc.ca/women.hist/women.hist.html

http://vvv.com/khan/

http://info.desy.de/gna/interpedia/greek_myth/greek_myth.html

http://www.infi.net/~cksmith/famine/History.html

http://portico.bl.uk/access/treasures/magna-carta.html

http://kuhttp.cc.ukans.edu/history/

http://www.niagara.com/~merrwill

http://www.worldwar1.com

HOBBIES

Collectors. Scrapbookers. Craftmakers. Sewers. Photographers. Bird-watchers.

No matter the hobby, there are probably others who share it with you. Use these sites to learn more and network with those who share a similar pasttime.

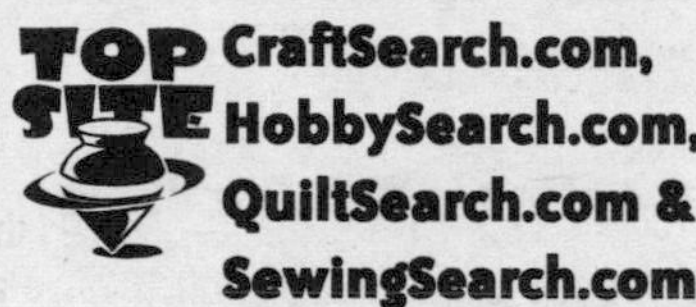

CraftSearch.com, HobbySearch.com, QuiltSearch.com & SewingSearch.com

http://www.craftsearch.com/

Site features Internet search engines for the greater arts, sewing, craft, and hobby markets.

TextileLinks

http://www.textilelinks.com/

A collection of links for spinners, dyers, weavers, knitters, and others involved with textiles.

Knitting Universe

http://www.knittinguniverse.com/nav.taf

This site brings together designs, designers, yarns, shops, authors, books, manufacturers, advertisers, and accessories.

ScrapNetwork.com

http://www.scrapbookideas.com/

Loaded with resources including page layout ideas, scrapbook chat rooms, bulletin boards, and links to scrapbook retail stores.

Scrapbooking Idea Network

http://www.scrapbooking.com/

Here you can discuss creative and safe storage

for your memories, photos, negatives, memorabilia, and textiles in an open forum. Links to a wide variety of suppliers.

CollectorsWeb.com

http://collectorsweb.com/index.shtml

The goal of CollectorsWeb is to provide information and resources to the collecting community. Features a newsletter, articles, web links, and message boards.

Learn About Antiques & Collectibles

http://www.antiques-oronoco.com/

At this site antique furniture, glassware, magazines, postcards, toys, jewelry, china, and much more is explained for the beginning collector. Even features a What Is It Worth? section.

About.com—Kids' Collecting

http://kidscollecting.about.com/kids/kidscollecting/mbody.htm

This site features great resources, explores collections of all kinds, visits collectors across the globe, and helps kids have a lot of fun along the way.

Focus on Photography

http://www.azuswebworks.com/photography/index.html

An intro to photography along with web links. Teaches you about types of photography, camera basics, composition, lighting, history, and more.

Photo Sights

http://www.photosights.com/sightsearch/

A searchable database with links to photography resources, e-zines, and related news.

Did You Know?

...that the last Coast Guard radio navigation station still using Morse code transmitted its last message on March 31, 1995 from Chesapeake, Virginia? Morse first demonstrated his telegraph to Congress in 1884, sending the famous message from Washington, D.C., to Baltimore, Maryland, "What hath God wrought?" Morse's sequence of dots and dashes resembles the modern digital code which forms the basis of modern computer programs.

Ham Radio Guide

http://www.dxzone.com/
Web directory amateur and ham radio guide.

Birder.com

http://www.birder.com/
Is birding your hobby? Check out this site. New photos, quizzes, and bird songs appear almost daily. Rare-bird alerts, scientific discoveries, checklists of birds—it's all here.

SharpWriter.Com

http://www.sharpwriter.com/
A site providing ready reference links for writers.

HOLIDAYS

We shop for gifts to give. We bake with the holidays in mind. We host parties for seasonal events. Here are the sites that will give you some background on each holiday and ideas of how to celebrate them.

Some sites listed here are Christian, others aren't. Keep that in mind when you look specifically at Christian holidays such as Christmas and Easter.

Biblical Holidays

http://biblicalholidays.com/

You'll find this is a great place to visit if you're looking for information about the holidays of the Bible and innovative ideas for celebrating them. This site includes history, ideas, crafts, activities, articles, links, a list group, and tons of information about Christianity's Hebraic heritage.

World's Bank Holidays

http://www.national-holidays.com/

Official list of the world's bank holidays in Asia, Africa, Europe, North America, South America, and the South Pacific. Also gives dates for Catholic, Jewish, Chinese New Year, and other celebrations.

Easter in Cyberspace

http://www.njwebworks.com/easter/

A directory of Christ-centered Easter and Lent web sites. No bunnies—just the Good News.

Web Directory: Virtual Guide to Easter

http://www.the-word.net/links/easter/index.html

Features links to religious and inspirational Easter sites, greeting cards, fun, and games.

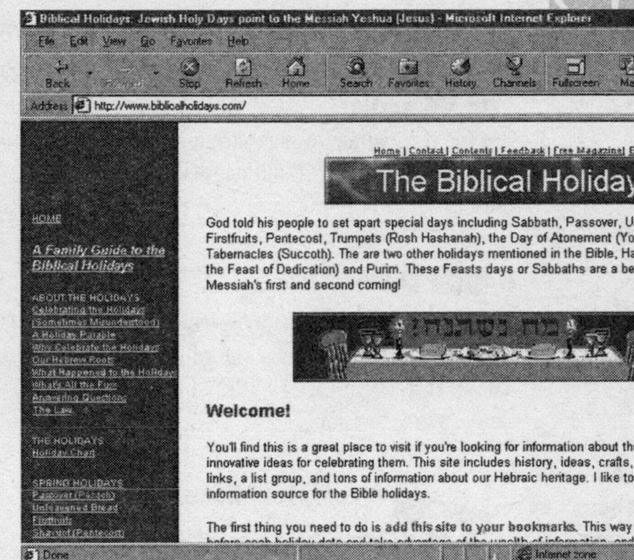

Biblical Holidays: Jewish Holy Days point to the Messiah Yeshua (Jesus) - Microsoft Internet Explorer
File Edit View Go Favorites Help
Back Forward Stop Refresh Home Search Favorites History Channels Fullscreen Mail Print
Address http://www.biblicalholidays.com/
Links
Home | Contact | Contents | Feedback | Free Magazine | E-mail
The Biblical Holidays
HOME
A Family Guide to the Biblical Holidays
God told his people to set apart special days including Sabbath, Passover, Unleavened Bread, Firstfruits, Pentecost, Trumpets (Rosh Hashanah), the Day of Atonement (Yom Kippur), and Tabernacles (Succoth). The are two other holidays mentioned in the Bible, Hanukkah (Chanukah or the Feast of Dedication) and Purim. These Feasts days or Sabbaths are a beautiful picture of the Messiah's first and second coming!
Welcome!
You'll find this is a great place to visit if you're looking for information about the Biblical Holidays and innovative ideas for celebrating them. This site includes history, ideas, crafts, activities, articles, links, a list group, and tons of information about our Hebraic heritage. I like to think of it as the information source for the Bible holidays.
The first thing you need to do is add this site to your bookmarks. This way you can come back
Done
Internet zone

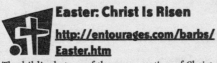

The Joy of Easter

http://members.tripod.com/~AmusedMuse/easter.html

For most people spring is a special time. For Christians, it is extraspecial because we celebrate the resurrection of Christ at Easter. But for many people, Easter and spring are celebrated for other reasons. This site presents all the meaning and traditions associated with Easter. Ever wondered about some of the "pagan rituals" associated with Easter and where they came from? What about the social and cultural traditions? This site will help answer some of those questions.

Easter: Christ Is Risen

http://entourages.com/barbs/Easter.htm

The biblical story of the resurrection of Christ, links to Easter readings, places to visit, information, and more.

Other Links

http://members.aol.com/erthangl44/xmascrafts.html

http://members.aol.com/mrsspyboy/seasonal.htm

http://www.geocities.com/Athens/Troy/9087/

http://www.holidayfestival.com/

http://dlaweb.com/holidayclipart/

http://www.holidayfestival.com/

He is Risen

http://www.execpc.com/~tmuth/easter/

Here you can journey through Scripture, art, music, and essays which reflect on the miracle of the resurrection of Jesus.

Hoppy Easter

http://www.holidays.net/easter/

Here are some fun holiday things for you and your family. This site has Easter stories, animations to watch, and pictures to color.

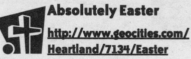

Absolutely Easter

http://www.geocities.com/Heartland/7134/Easter

Easter site with information on Easter, Christ, rabbits, chocolate, and games. Paper crafts, games, and fun.

Memorial Day

http://www.rootsweb.com/~nyseneca/memorial.htm

Learn how this holiday came to be celebrated as we know it today.

Memorial Day Resource Guide

http://members.aol.com/vetsofamer/memday.htm

Links and downloads related to the Memorial Day holiday.

Celebrate the Fourth of July

http://www.netm.com/4th/index.htm

Fourth of July facts including firework safety, the national anthem, the Declaration of

Independence, and other items that celebrate the birthday of the United States of America.

Celebrating of All Saints' Day

http://www.faculty.fairfield.edu/faculty/jmac/se/allsaint.htm
This site describes the history and meaning of the feast of All Hallows' Day.

Thanksgiving Sites

The Thanksgiving Tradition

http://eagle.cc.ukans.edu/~keb/thanksgiving.html
Learn more about the roots of our Thanksgiving Day holiday. Includes Lincoln's Thanksgiving Proclamation.

Thanksgiving Directory

http://www.virtualquincy.com/quincy/holiday/thanks.html
A directory listing of over forty-five Thanksgiving web sites on the WWW.

Thanksgiving Art

http://edtech.kennesaw.edu/web/thanksgi.html
A listing of Thanksgiving links in categories like research/informational links, on-line activities, off-line lesson plans and activities, and Thanksgiving clip art.

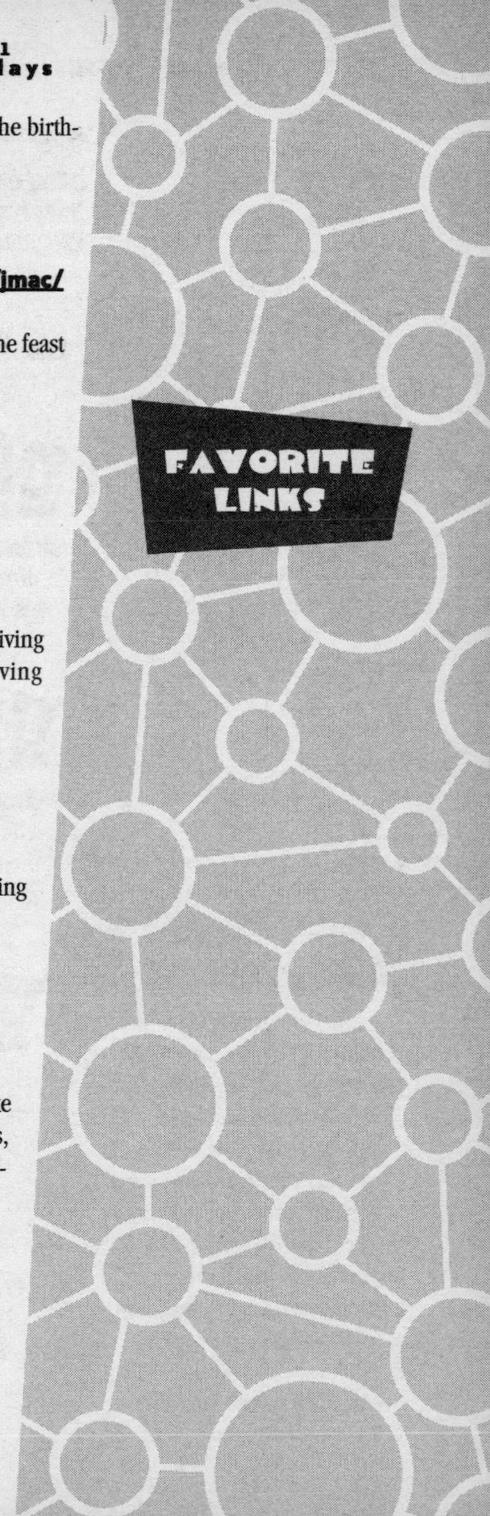

Aristotle's Thanksgiving on the Web

http://www.aristotle.net/thanksgiving/links.html

Celebrate Thanksgiving, food, beauty, fun, and more on Aristotle's Thanksgiving Day web page.

Christmas

Web Directory: Christmas in Cyber space

http://www.njwebworks.net/christmas/

A directory of Christ-centered Christmas and Advent sites. No Santas and no Frosty.

Cyberspace Place Christmas Backgrounds

http://www.cyberspaceplace.com/christmasindex.html

A beautifully developed graphic web site with special themes for the holidays. As long as you follow their guidelines, you may download the graphics for free.

Christmas Eternal

http://members.carol.net/~asmsmsks/xristmas.htm

This site looks at the meaning and history behind Christmas customs and symbols from a traditional Christian perspective.

Search for the Meaning of Christmas

http://techdirect.com/christmas/

This site invites you to join in sharing Christmas tradition. It also reminds you that it is never too late to start a family tradition.

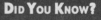

DID YOU KNOW?

...that the average adult blinks between 12 and 20 times per minute? The function of blinking, of course, is to lubricate the eye. However, we are wired to blink less when looking at a compelling target. This is part of the reason that people who use computers for hours on end tend to experience eyestrain—they usually blink as little as 5 times per minute.

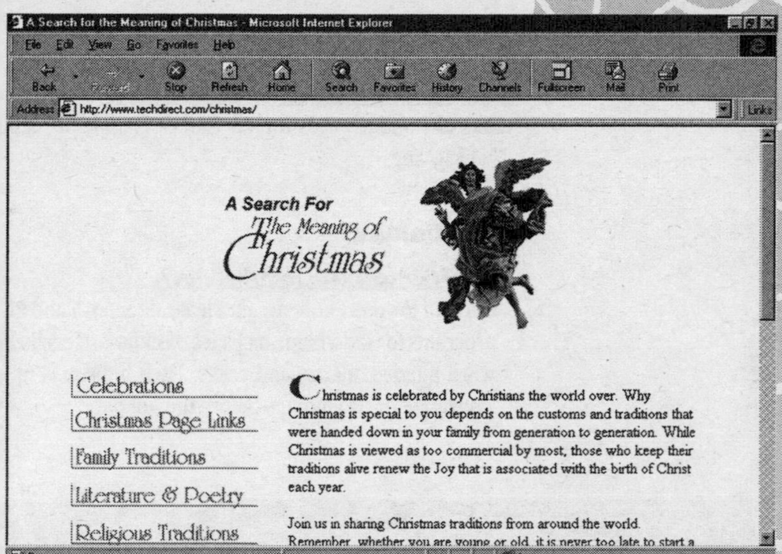

A Search for the Meaning of Christmas - Microsoft Internet Explorer
File Edit View Go Favorites Help
Back Forward Stop Refresh Home Search Favorites History Channels Fullscreen Mail Print
Address http://www.techdirect.com/christmas/
Links
A Search For
The Meaning of
Christmas
Celebrations
Christmas Page Links
Family Traditions
Literature & Poetry
Religious Traditions
Christmas is celebrated by Christians the world over. Why Christmas is special to you depends on the customs and traditions that were handed down in your family from generation to generation. While Christmas is viewed as too commercial by most, those who keep their traditions alive renew the Joy that is associated with the birth of Christ each year.
Join us in sharing Christmas traditions from around the world.
Done
Internet zone

Twelve Days of Christmas

http://www.bayside.net/npo/RLDS/12days/

Site connects the verses of the popular carol with biblical sources and references.

Christmas in the Holy Land

http://www.jesus2000.com/christmas.htm

Every year on the 24th of December, Christians from all over the world gather in Bethlehem to celebrate the birthday of Jesus Christ. This site lets you view video clips of this special time.

Claus.com

http://www.claus.com/

Award-winning Santa Claus site for parents and kids. Play games in Elf School. Print your Honorary Elf Diploma. Christmas recipes. Choose and name your Elf Buddy. E-mail Santa Claus. There's lots to do.

Did You Know?

. . . that on a typical day, your name is transmitted between computers five times?

Holiday Pages

http://www.library.ucsb.edu/holidays/

Links to holiday pages for Christmas, Hanukkah, and Thanksgiving.

Kids Domain

http://kidsdomain.com/holiday/

Fun stuff for every holiday: gift ideas, Macintosh and PC programs for kids, coloring pages, holiday art, original word puzzles, mazes, and crafts. Each holiday is updated one or two months before the holiday.

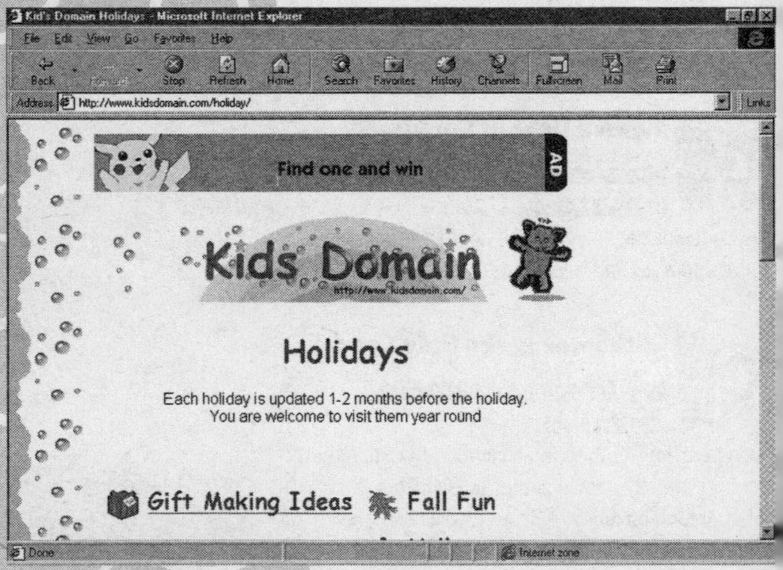

The Holiday Page

http://wilstar.com/holidays/

All the holidays, all the time. Check out the history, traditions, and customs of America's holidays. Also find holiday word search puzzles, send someone a holiday greeting, or download the holiday countdown feature.

Holidays and Festivals

http://persweb.direct.ca/ikhan/links/linkholidays.html

A directory of links for over twenty different holidays.

Four Holidays

http://4holidays.4anything.com/

Learn about nearly every holiday under the sun. Discover tradition, recipes, gift ideas, and more. Site also features information on unusual holidays.

Did You Know?

...that people who are computer science majors, or who really love to delve deep into computers, tend to usually play an instrument? It's believed to have something to do with the pattern recognition and processing area in the brain.

HOME & GARDEN

Some of the magazines with the greatest circulation help readers keep a better home or garden. It's not surprising then, to find so much related information on-line.

Log on to read articles, trade ideas, or even shop for the items you need for home improvements.

Sound Home

http://www.soundhome.com/

A comprehensive source of information regarding home construction, home remodeling, and home maintenance. A service of Sound Home Inspections, Inc.

The New Homemaker

http://www.newhomemaker.com

The New Homemaker (TNH) provides the practical advice and resources that will further the rebirth of the household arts. TNH is unabashedly nontraditional. They prefer cloth diapers to paper, breast milk to formula, natural to chemical, thrift to convenience, equality to submission; they make their biases clear from the get-go. Whether or not you agree with their perspective, this site is full of interesting ideas for the home.

Country Sampler on the Web

http://www.sampler.com/decideas/decideas.html

This "how-to" decorating magazine comes online to show you just how easy it is to create a uniquely decorated home. Each month, you'll find beautiful and affordable new projects, helpful decorating hints, their TV listings, and highlights from their current magazine. Get a head start on your decorating success, satisfaction, and savings with a visit to this site.

Martha Stewart

http://www.marthastewart.com/

This web site offers a unique integration of Martha Stewart's television program, radio show, newspaper column, and magazines. Additionally, they have recently launched seven distinct channels on their site, each devoted to one of their core content areas—home, cooking and entertaining, gardening, crafts, holidays, and weddings.

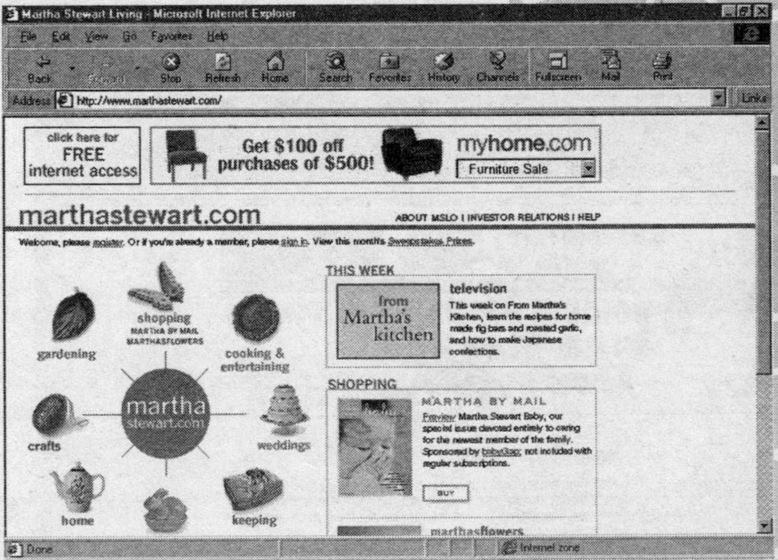

Better Homes and Gardens

http://www.bhg.com/homeimp/

From a name you already know and trust to bring you the best in home and garden information, the *Better Homes and Gardens* web site will answer all your questions—even the ones you didn't know you had.

DID YOU KNOW?

...that women age 50 and over spend the more hours a month on-line than any other demographic group?

ARMiller's Home and Garden Links

http://www.nmt.edu/~armiller/homegar.htm
Directory for home and garden sites.

Home & Garden Television

http://www.hgtv.com/
Home & Garden Television is the only network devoted to providing comprehensive information to inspire the home enthusiast. Here you'll get top tips from some of America's best homebuilders, remodelers, decorators, interior designers, gardeners, craft experts, and lifestyle hosts.

Submit a Site
hudson@techie.com

GardenSeek

http://www.gardenseek.com/
A directory of nationwide gardening resources.

Garden Planet

http://www.worldleader.com/garden/
Features lots of on-line gardening links.

Nursery Links

http://www.nurseryman.com/index.html

Dedicated to helping you find nursery-related sites.

Garden of Praise

http://gardenofpraise.com/garden.htm

The creators of this site believe that the gardener works with God to grow something beautiful for all to see, and to cause His name to be glorified among the believers. Come get gardening tips from a fellow believer.

Home & Hearth

http://homehearth.virtualave.net/

This page features recipes, information about cooking, quilting, gardening, and other interesting hobbies.

Other Links

http://dsc.discovery.com/dscdaytime/greatchefs/greatchefs.html

http://www.wwrecipes.com/

http://www.housebeautiful.com/

http://www10.garden.com/index.html

http://www.sewing.org/

http://www.living.com/

HOME PAGES

Building Tools

Comprehensive Counter

http://www.superstats.com/

If you want thorough counter statistics, this is a good option. With free and paid versions, this service will let you know who's referring your site, where surfers are coming from, and even give you some other interesting information—like what size screen your users have.

Basic Counter

http://www.xoom.com/

If you just want to know some basic info, this is a simple counter. The free version does come with banner advertising.

Cute FTP

http://www.tripod.com/

Cute FTP is free for home users and helps you quickly upload your site to your host.

HTML Editor

http://www.microsoft.com/

In order to create and post your page, you'll need an HTML editor. Microsoft offers a free version of Front Page Express as part of Microsoft Internet Explorer 5.0.

Free Guest Book, Boards, and Polls

http://www.freeguestbooks.com/

You don't need to know a lot of programming to host a guest book, message board, or poll. This site is free.

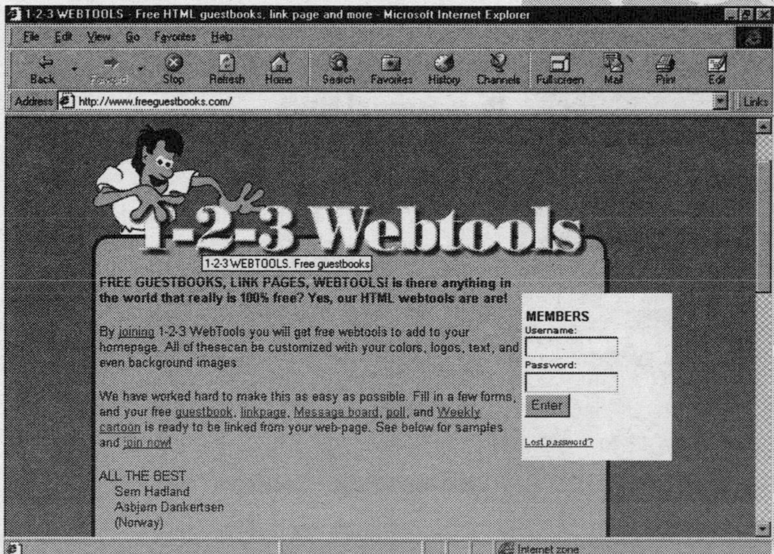

Free Hosts

http://www.tripod.com/

http://www.xoom.com/

You can turn many places to host your web page free of charge. If you're in business for yourself, or have extra cash, you can consider buying a domain. Otherwise, find a site that will host your page for free.

Buying a Domain

http://www.register.com/

This site will allow you to see if the domain you want is already taken. If it is, you can often look up who owns it. If not, you can buy it.

Did You Know?

. . .that there are an estimated 760 U.S. households joining the Internet per hour?

HOMESCHOOLING

It's never been a better time to be a homeschooler. The Internet delivers the "age of information" to your home classroom. No matter the subject of study, good information is available on-line. These sites are geared toward homseschoolers or those just interested in it. They will help you keep up on laws and curriculums as well as give practical teaching and learning tips.

Where in the Web and Other Homeschool Stuff

http://www.geocities.com/Athens/Aegean/3446/

This site features homeschooling advice, tips, and links for busy homeschooling moms. Here you will find links categorized by subject and grade level. Subject links have been given a brief commentary as to what helpful things are at that site so you will know beforehand if you want to spend your valuable time following the link.

Homeschool Central

http://homeschoolcentral.com/

A collection of links in a variety of categories like new homeschoolers, state resources (state sites and laws), study resources, homeschool sites, and organizations. Also features an on-line bookstore and a search option.

TOP SITE

Christian Education Links and Resources

http://www.tcmnet.com/~cc/edu/edulinks.html

Christian and general educational resources, early childhood education, home schooling, and miscellaneous resources.

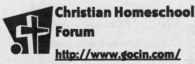

Christian Home Educators Electronic Convention

http://www.cheec.com/

This electronic convention is set up like a real convention. It provides on-line audio/video seminars on homeschooling topics and a curriculum hall with vendors—from A Beka to Usborne!

Home School Internet Resource Center

http://www.rsts.net/home/

Your home school mall and infomart. This award-winning site provides extensive homeschooling resources—including educational links, curriculum fair, free software downloads, colleges, chat line, home-school E-pals, help for learning disabilities, and much more. Check out the audio/video section or order from the on-line catalog.

Christian Homeschool Forum

http://www.gocin.com/homeschool/

Members from the Christian Interactive Network's Christian Homeschool Forum share support and encouragement for those interested in homeschooling. Find out how to get started homeschooling, check out book suggestions and reviews, read articles on a variety of topics, and benefit from the tips and inspirations.

Bible-Based Homeschool Information

http://www.homeschoolinformation.com/

This site includes hundreds of pages including frequently asked questions, helpful homeschool articles, ideas to help you utilize the Internet, freeware links, education philosophies, lesson ideas, list of homeschool catalogs, magazines, links, resources, list groups, educational software, message boards, newsgroups, and tons more!

Home School World

http://www.home-school.com/

The official site of *Practical Homeschooling* magazine and *The Big Book of Home Learning*. See the Home Life Catalog. Find articles, organizations, events, and shopping. Also check out the legal defense of homeschooling, K-12 book reviews, and daily devotions.

The Wisdom Tree

http://www.angelfire.com/fl/loveyy/freehomeschool.html

Homeschooling family helps, educational freebies, educational store, toys.

Biblical Foundations for Christian Homeschooling

http://pages.prodigy.com/christianhmsc/home.htm

Christian homeschoolers with a home page dedicated to encouraging other families who have made the choice to teach and train their children at home. Each month, they'll provide a link to a "New Site of the Month," a web home page that will be a blessing to you and your children. In addition, you'll find new monthly updates with you and your family in mind. You are invited to enjoy their collection of original homeschooling essays and outlines, including "A Philosophy of Christian Education."

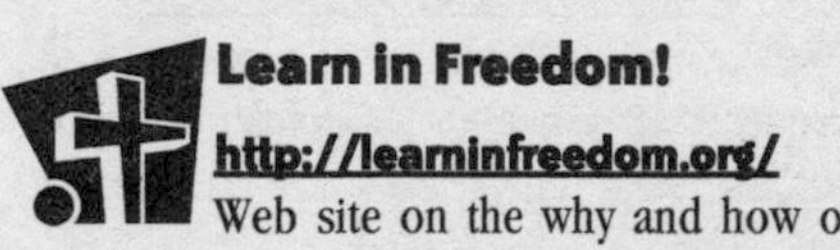

Learn in Freedom!

http://learninfreedom.org/

Web site on the why and how of

...that over 40 percent of 9–17 year olds say the Internet has improved their attitude to attending school?

homeschooling by Christian homeschooling dad, with links to a large homeschooling bibliography and many other Christian homeschooling sites, as well as original research essays on homeschooling history, college admissions for homeschoolers, homeschooling growth, and the harmful effects of socialization in school. A good place for skeptical relatives.

Successful Home Schooling

http://one.ctelcom.net/koinonia/HmSch.htm
Features informative articles for those inquiring about homeschooling, for new homeschoolers, and even for experienced home schoolers. Learn about socialization, the law, curriculum, the first year, teaching teens, learning styles, personalities, attention spans, and more from a mom who homeschooled for sixteen years.

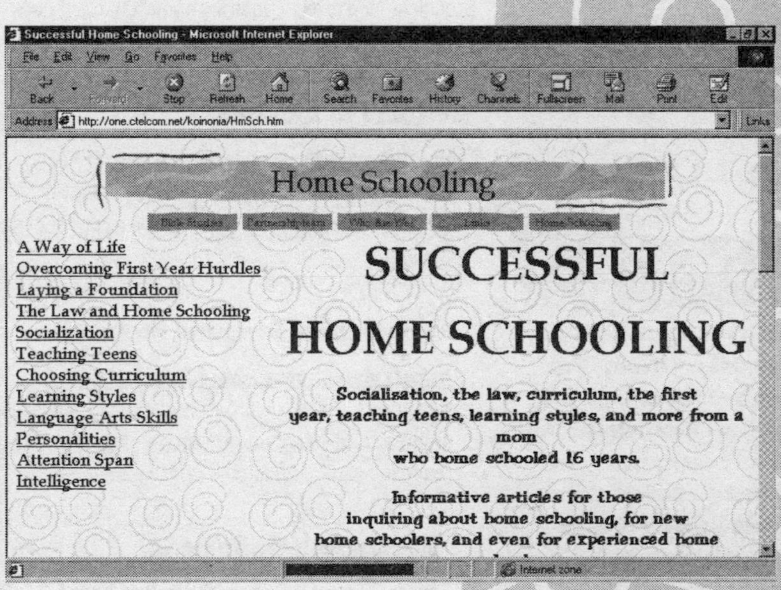

Homeschooling On A Shoestring

http://www.geocities.com/Athens/4663/

The purpose of this page is to make available to the reader ways of cutting costs while homeschooling. It is hoped that the reader will be enabled to save money while maintaining a high quality of education. Some homeschoolers love bargains, others try to cut costs out of necessity. Regardless of why, their goal is to help you do the best you can to save money. Includes links to craft sites, freebies on the web, free fun, free kids' stuff, etc.

How To Homeschool Newsletter On-Line

http://www.howtonews.com/

A quarterly on-line newsletter featuring articles, resource recommendations, FAQs, catalog highlights for Best Picks, and direct E-mail for homeschooling questions.

At Home In America

http://www.athomeinamerica.com/

A free newspaper on homeschooling. Read it online, get your free print copy, and have a copy sent to a friend!

Home School Discount Store

http://www.homeschooldiscount.com/

Save up to 40 percent on educational software, homeschool curriculum, computer games, science kits, and educational board games.

BookmobileOnline.com

http://www.bookmobileonline.com/

We buy and sell new and used homeschool books and materials. Since 1989 we have served over 100,000 homeschool families. Check Book-

Did You Know?

...that if you adjust a monitor in the Northern Hemisphere its colors will be wrong if you plug it into a computer in the Southern Hemisphere? The Earth's magnetic field pulls the electron beams hitting the cathode-ray tube in computer monitors. Every computer monitor has to be calibrated relative to its position in the earth's magnetic field.

mobileOnline.com first. Also get free textbook news from their most popular publishers.

Books4HomeSchool

http://www.books4homeschool.com/

Your source for Christian homeschool books. This free resource lists K–12 grade books in all major subject areas featuring book reviews by homeschooling families. At this site, you will also find a church history project, polls, over 225 homeschool web site links, a Curriculum Discussion Group and much more. Also features a legislative alert with legislative news of importance to Christian homeschoolers.

The Homeschool Book Swap

http://www.homeschoolbookswap.com/

This site is dedicated to providing a friendly place to find New and pre-owned educational materials at the best prices. Great site to sell your homeschooling items. All welcome. No fees. Earn free books just for browsing.

DID YOU KNOW?

...that one out of every three teenagers uses the Internet to make new friendships?
...and that one out of four teenagers uses the Internet to maintain existing friendships?
...and that half of all teens said they use the Internet for casual relationships and interaction through chat rooms?

HUMOR

Comedian Jay Leno reads over 400 jokes a day to prepare for the *Tonight Show*. While you may not have a stand-up career, you can use these sites to keep stride with Jay. These sites will give you the laugh you need.

Kool for Kids

http://www.needham.org.uk/kids.htm

Good clean jokes for kids ten and under. You can also link to Bible quizzes and Bible search sections.

Squigly's Playhouse

http://www.squiglysplayhouse.com/

Squigly's Playhouse is a fun and safe place for kids to play and learn. You'll find lots of things to do here—including a jokes and riddles section.

kidsjokes.com/

http://www.kidsjokes.com

Find jokes, knock-knocks, riddles, puzzles, and more. You can also send an E-greeting card from here.

Scatty.com

http://www.scatty.com/

A joke site for kids and all the family. Check out animal jokes, knock-knock jokes, sports jokes, silly jokes, and lots more.

Kim's Chuckle-A-Day

http://www.geocities.com/~chuckleaday/

Here you'll find clean jokes suitable for all ages.

Funny-Bone

http://funny-bone.spunge.org/

Features free, clean humor for all ages and a free daily mailing.

Laugh-Lines

http://www.laugh-lines.com/index.shtml

A weekly free and clean humor web site and E-bulletin. A happy place for clean-minded people and a safe place for kids of all ages.

My Humor

http://www.myhumor.org/

Site contains jokes and funny stuff suitable for all ages. Their goal is to prove that humor can be clean *and* funny at the same time. Lots of different categories to check out—from puns to cartoons.

Fun

http://www.healthmetro.com/consumer/confun.html

Laugh Break

http://www.bottco.com/Schoolsite/Laughs.html

Fun with Science

http://www.celestia.com/alpha/SRP/MA96/Html/KidsHumor.html

Submit a Site

hudson@techie.com

INTERNATIONAL

As the gap between countries in the first and third worlds grows, the work of these international organizations becomes more important.

Many of these sites represent organizations giving humanitarian assistance, aiding development, keeping peace, or sharing the gospel.

World Relief

http://www.worldrelief.org/

This organization is all about helping th hurting. World Relief addresses the physical and spiri tual needs of those it serves. Read world-relief new and find out what this organization is doing and ho you can be involved.

Great Commission Air

http:// www.greatcommissionair.org/

This organization's goal is to provide safe and effi cient air transport for Christian missions and hu manitarian relief in small aircraft that are capable o using short, rough airstrips and carrying up to one thousand-pound loads at a time.

Choice Humanitarian

http://www.choice.humanitarian.org/

Choice Humanitarian is a nonprofit, volunteer o ganization comprised of people like you who fee a sense of commitment to help indigenous peopl of the developing world. Choice Humanitaria specializes in manpower, materials, appropriat technology, and education.

World Vision

http://www.wvi.org/

World Vision has six objectives: transformational development that is community-based and sustainable, focused especially on the needs of children; emergency relief that assists people afflicted by conflict or disaster; promotion of justice that seeks to change unjust structures affecting the poor among whom they work; strategic initiatives that serve the church in the fulfillment of its mission; public awareness that leads to informed understanding, giving, involvement, and prayer; and witness to Jesus Christ by life, deed, word, and sign that encourages people to respond to the gospel. At their site, you can select a country and see what World Vision is doing around the world. Also check out the latest headlines and features.

Project HOPE

http://www.projhope.org/

Project HOPE alleviates suffering, saves lives, and helps communities attain lasting improvements in health care. By providing health education, health policy research, and humanitarian assistance, HOPE is helping people around the world to live longer, healthier lives. HOPE (Health Opportunities for People Everywhere) was originally known for the *S.S. Hope,* the world's first peacetime hospital ship, which had its maiden voyage in 1960.

ReliefWeb

http://www.reliefweb.int/w/rwb.nsf

ReliefWeb is an electronic clearinghouse for those needing timely information on humanitarian emergencies and natural disasters—designed specifically to help the humanitarian community improve its response to emergencies.

Miscellaneous

http://www.123world.com/

http://www.willamette.edu/law/longlib/forint.htm

International Politics

http://polisci.nelson.com/introip.html

Yale

http://www.library.yale.edu/govdocs/gdchome.html

Government Missions

http://www3.itu.int/MISSIONS/US/

The International Committee of the Red Cross

http://www.icrc.org/eng/

The International Committee of the Red Cross (ICRC) is an impartial, neutral, and independent organization whose exclusively humanitarian mission is to protect the lives and dignity of victims of war and internal violence and to provide them with assistance. It directs and coordinates the international relief activities conducted by the movement in situations of conflict, and endeavors to prevent suffering by promoting and strengthening humanitarian law and universal humanitarian principles. Site features include news, operations by country, issues and topics, information on international humanitarian law, publications, photo gallery, and links.

The Red Cross

http://www.redcross.org

The American Red Cross, a humanitarian organization led by volunteers and guided by its Congressional Charter and the Fundamental

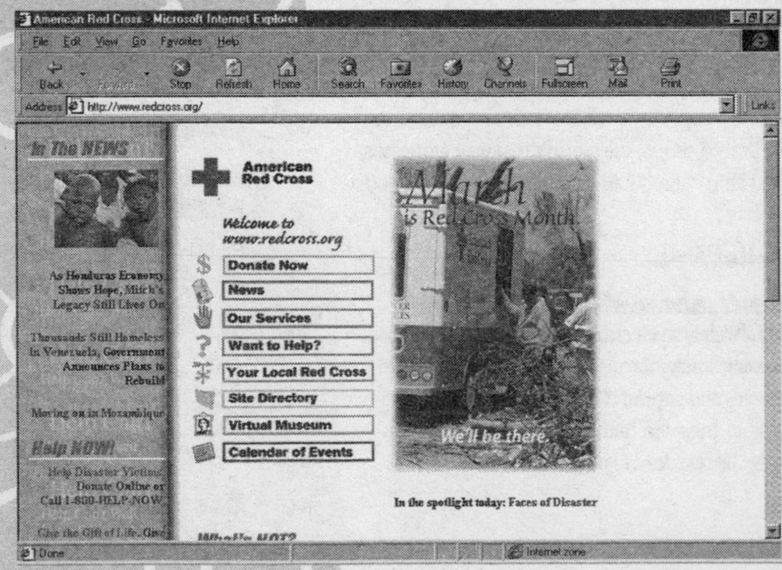

Principles of the International Red Cross Movement, will provide relief to victims of disasters and help people prevent, prepare for, and respond to emergencies. At their site, you can find out more about the organization and the many services it provides, find out ways to get involved and help, or visit the virtual museum.

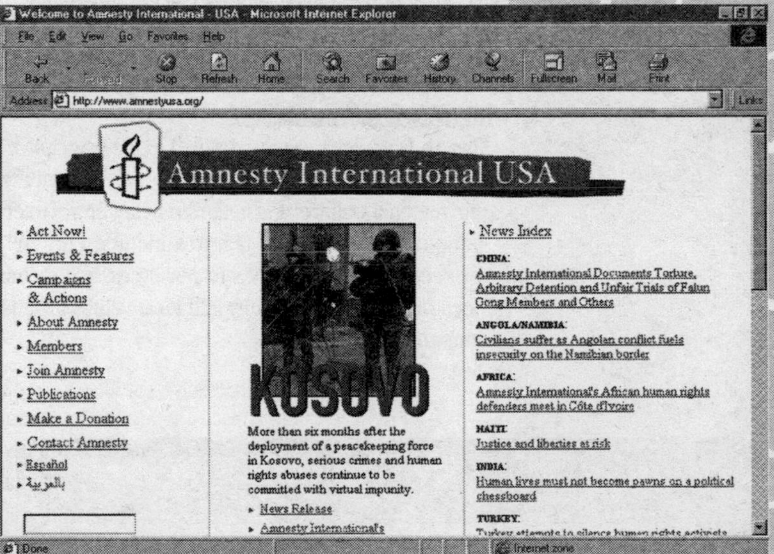

Amnesty International USA

http://www.amnestyusa.org/

Amnesty International is a Nobel-Prize-winning grassroots activist organization. They are dedicated to promoting and defending the rights of prisoners around the world. At their site you can find out more about this organization and check out current news, campaigns, actions, events, and features.

Did You Know?

...that 27 percent of adults in the U.K. use the Internet?

Rotary Foundation

http://www.rotary.org/foundation/

This is a not-for-profit corporation that supports the efforts of Rotary International to achieve world understanding and peace through international humanitarian, educational, and cultural exchange programs. Check out this site to find out more about Rotary International.

Kiwanis International

http://www.kiwanis.org/

Kiwanis is an organization devoted to the principle of service; to the advancement of individual, community, and national welfare; and to the strengthening of international goodwill. Site features include club and projects information, links to resources, and a club locator to help you identify and locate clubs around the world.

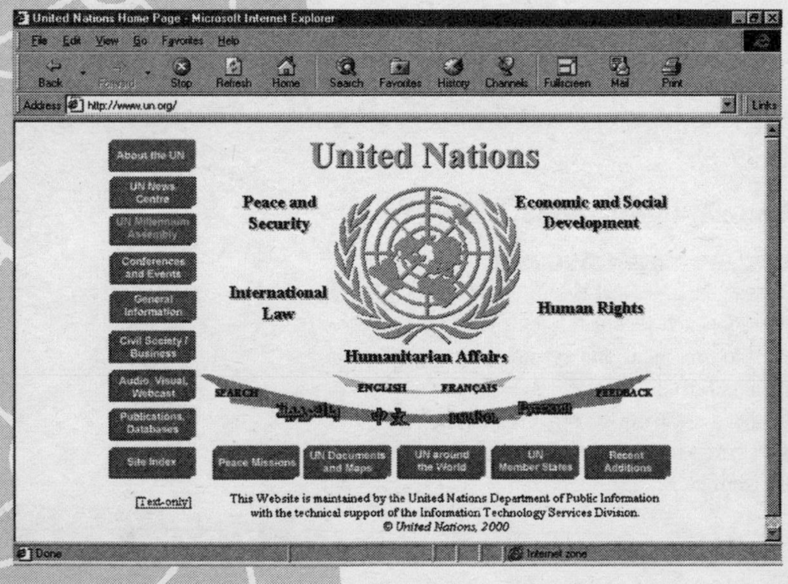

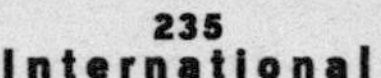

United Nations

http://www.un.org/

This site's features include daily news updates, pictorial history, documents and maps, information on peace missions, audio and visual web casts, links to publications and databases, and descriptions of U.N. departments and offices.

Web Directory: Union of International Associations (UIA)

http://www.uia.org/

A resource for learning more about intergovernmental organizations (IGOs) and international nongovernmental organizations (NGOs).

World Trade Organization (WTO)

http://www.wto.org/

This organization regulates trade and tariffs worldwide. Formed as successor to the General Agreement on Tariffs and Trade (GATT). Find out more about the organization and about world trade at this web site.

INTERNET 101

Newcomers to the net (aka, "Newbies") often have questions. Rather than take a class, the best way for most people to learn is through some hands-on courses available on-line. Log-on to some of these sites and you'll be surfing like a pro in no time at all.

Internet 101

http://www2.famvid.com/i101

Internet 101 was created for those who want to know just the basics. This guide will provide you with enough knowledge to have fun on the Internet, yet will not bore you with too many details.

Beginners Central

http://www.northernwebs.com/bc

An on-line tutorial covering the basics of web surfing.

Navigating the World Wide Web

http://www.imaginarylandscape.com/helpweb/www/www.html

This guide is intended to help people who are just getting started on the Internet learn their way around. Think of it as a friendly service station that gives out free road maps.

Life on the Internet Beginner's Guide

http://www.screen.com/start/guide/default.htm

This page is an index to various sections dedicated to the basics of the Internet. Inside eachsection, you'll find links to the latest version of Internet software, guides for additional background, resource lists, and search tools—thousands and thousands of destinations.

Learn the Net

http://www.learnthenet.com/english/index.html

This is a web site dedicated to helping you save time and money when roaming through cyberspace.

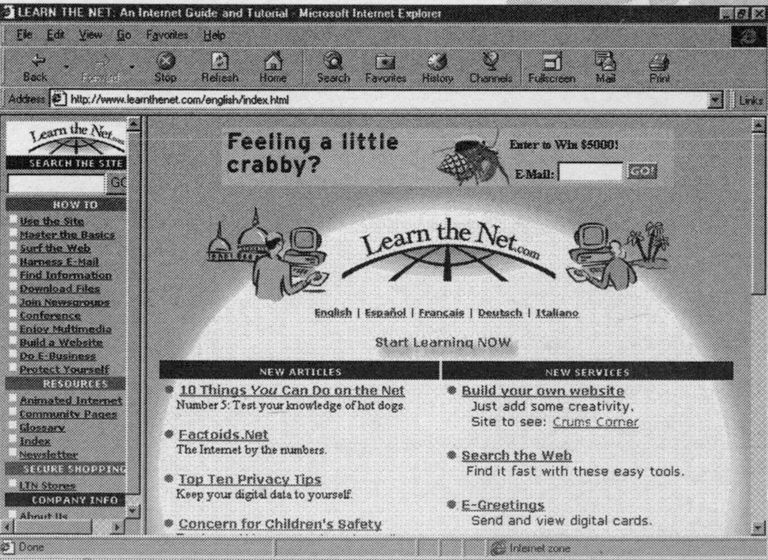

Kaleidoscapes' Kids' Cool Animation

http://www.kaleidoscapes.com/kc_intro.html

Geared towards kids, this site features an Animation Tutorial using the GIF Animator to help you learn about animation on the Internet. Also included are links to art and animation software. The Web Reference section offers tutorials on creating 3D art and animations.

Did You Know?

...that the *Fort Worth Star Telegram* reviews 50 web sites a week?

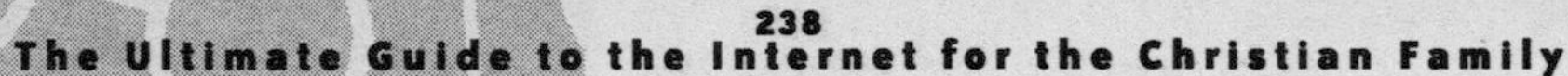

FAVORITE LINKS

Newbie University

http://www.newbie-u.com/

The goal of this site is to "help newbies become knowbies." This site will give you the basics on chatting, newsgroups, and ftp transfer.

INTERNET BROADCASTS

ChristianRock.Net

http://www.christianrock.net/

This is a 24-hour Internet-based Christian rock radio station.

SolidGospel.com

http://www.solidgospel.com/

Your home for southern gospel on the net. Check out the song of the day, the interactive news, photo gallery, and—of course—find and listen to your favorite artist.

Gospel Train

http://www.gospeltrain.com/

With a vast library from the beginning of the recording industry up to the present day, the Gospel Train will take you for a musical journey on the main line and the many branches of the soul gospel experience. This site brings you authentic soul and gospel music.

Family Radio

http://www.familyradio.com/

This is a nonprofit, nondenominational, educational organization dedicated to obeying our Lord's command to preach the gospel to every creature. At their site you can listen live, check out the RealAudio library, get station listings and program guides, and much more.

Your AM/FM radio offers you a broad, but limited, selection of music and talk. The Internet, however, has no limit. Do you have a favorite radio program in another state? You can probably find a station carrying it live. More and more sites are offering radio and TV-style broadcasts that will improve and expand as the Internet grows. Most convenient of all, many programs on the Internet are available for on-demand downloading.

Oneplace.com

http://www.oneplace.com/

This site is loaded with information and resources for the Christian community. Features live Christian radio from across the country. Just pick a station and enjoy!

Involved Christian Radio Network

http://www.icrn.com/

This is your on-line source for the best in Christian broadcasting. You can listen to over fifty radio-based broadcast ministries.

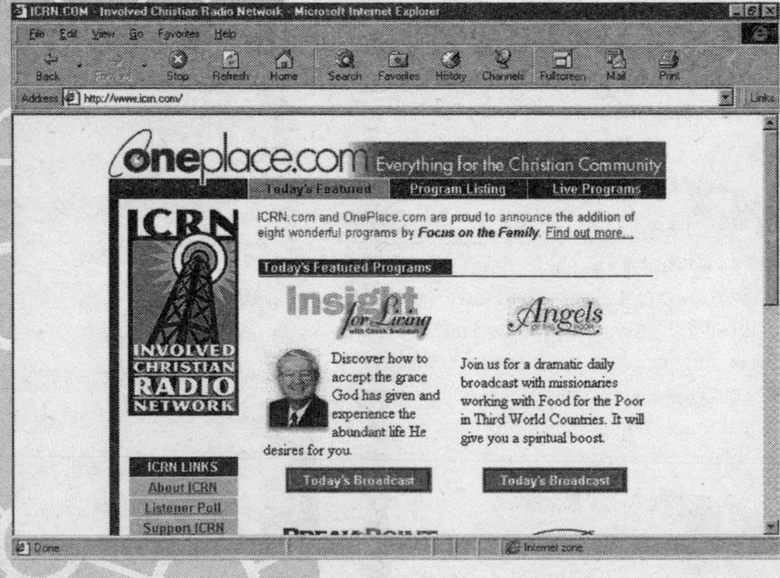

Yahoo! Broadcast

http://www.broadcast.com/

Yahoos links' page to Internet broadcasts under a variety of topics including music, sports, news, spirituality, entertainment, and children's. Parental guidance is strongly suggested because the categories are very broad.

Live Radio

http://www.broadcastsports.com/

http://espn.go.com/liveradiotv/

http://www.1on1sports.com/

http://www.kir.org/radio.htm

http://disney.go.com/RadioDisney/

Submit a Site

hudson@techie.com

ISSUES & CAUSES

Christians are often vocal proponents of certain social causes (i.e., pro-life or euthanasia). These sites help you team up with others who share your concern and convictions as well as help you make social action a little easier.

International Union of Gospel Missions

http://www.iugm.org/

Founded in 1913, IUGM's 270-member rescue missions provide over 30 million meals and 12 million nights of lodging each year to the homeless and needy.

Volunteers of America

http://www.voa.org/

Volunteers of America is a national, nonprofit, spiritually based organization providing local human service programs and the opportunity for individual and community involvement.

Ultimate Pro-Life Resource List

http://www.prolifeinfo.org/

An extensive directory of right-to-life resources on the Internet.

InterLIFE

http://www.interlife.org/

A one-stop resource for information on life issues. Categories include activist resources, euthanasia, family and adoption resources, Holocaust resources, life-related court cases, news, information on Planned Parenthood, pro-life resources, and the dark side of the web.

Euthanasia

http://www.mcgill.pvt.k12.al.us/jerryd/cm/euthan.htm

Links to Internet information on euthanasia, with special emphasis on Roman Catholic perspectives.

International Coalition for Religious Freedom

http://www.religiousfreedom.com/

This site features a country-by-country analysis of the state of religious freedom, a monthly newsletter, and other articles.

The Injustice Line

http://www.injusticeline.com/

Check out true reports of injustice in the U.S. and elsewhere plus extensive links to other civil rights sites.

World Campaign

http://www.worldcampaign.net/

This is a media campaign to create global awareness and action on population, hunger, environment, poverty, disease, war, human rights, and personal growth.

E-The People

http://www.e-thepeople.com/affiliates/national/

Among many other things, this site allows users to send an E-mailed or faxed letter or a petition to over thousands of federal, state, and local officials. It is a nonpartisan site that works with over 150 on-line newspapers, television stations, and Internet portals to help bring government closer to the people.

Hunger Relief

http://www.secondharvest.org/

Homeless

http://4homeless.hypermart.net/soup_kitchens.html

Endangered Animals

http://www.amnh.org/exhibitions/endangered/index.html

http://cyberfair.gsn.org/tenan/index.html

Environment

http://www.learner.org/exhibits/garbage/intro.html

Recycling

http://www.dnr.state.oh.us/odnr/recycling/news/reports.html

http://www.gardenweb.com/faq/data/tips/1998035837007261.html

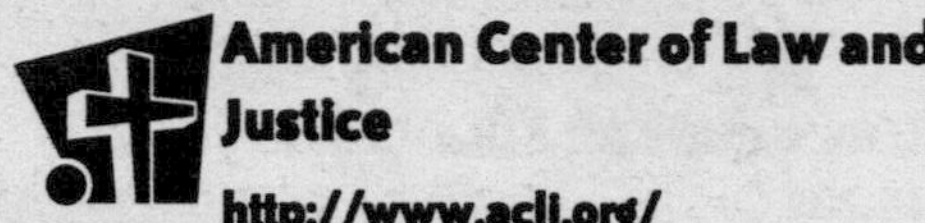

American Center of Law and Justice

http://www.aclj.org/

American Center of Law and Justice is dedicated to defending the rights of the believer in Jesus Christ, such as prayer in the classroom and religious rights of students in the schools. Parental guidance needed because of the nature of the problems handled by this site.

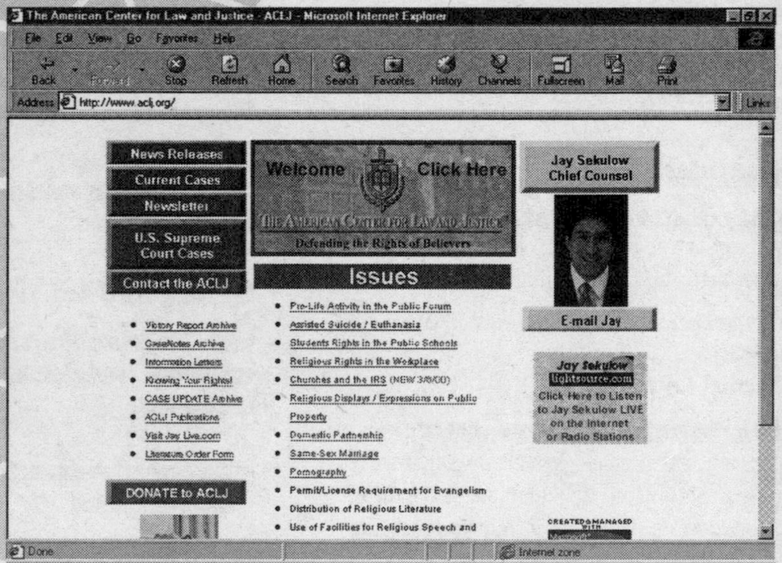

Did You Know?

. . .that computer crime costs more than 10 billion dollars per year?

LODGING

On-Line Reservations

http://www.travelbase.com/

Lodging.com and NITC Travelbase provide on-line hotel reservations for over 30,000 hotels, motels, bed and breakfasts, and resorts across the U.S.

TravelWeb

http://www.travelweb.com/

TravelWeb's on-line database offering variety of lodging options includes hotel reservations, motel, and resort reservations. TravelWeb also includes flight information.

The National Lodging Directory

http://www.guests.com/

A directory of hotels, motels, bed and breakfasts, and vacation rental property across the United States.

Internet Lodging Directory

http://www.usa-lodging.com/

USA lodging directory of motels, hotels, bed and breakfasts, specializing in budget and economy accomodations throughout the United States.

Accommodation Search Engine

http://ase.net/

This guide will help you find a hotel, bed and

The net makes it easy to find a bed and breakfast near your hometown or a few states away. Using the net will help make your vacation plans a little easier. Try narrowing down your site search, too, by the region or state you want to visit. There are thousands of small sites waiting to be discovered such as http://www.kensrents.com/.

breakfast, or resort from thousands of hotels, lodges, inns, bed and breakfasts, resorts, and accommodation web pages.

Yahoo! Lodging

http://lodging.yahoo.com/

Use the powerful Yahoo search engine and network to find a place near your destination. No luck? Try http://www.lycos.com/travel to use the Lycos search engine.

Rocky Mountain Hideaways

http://www.kensrents.com/

Here's your chance to vacation in the Rockies. Spend a relaxing week in a tiny valley town in the middle of the Rocky Mountains. Breathtaking views with mountains on all sides.

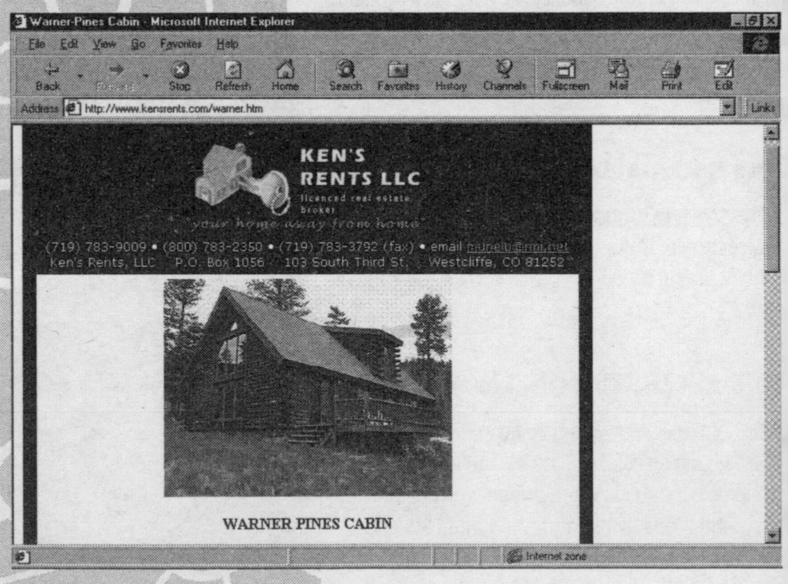

Christian Bed and Breakfast

http://www.icbbn.com/icbbn.html

The International Christian Bed and Breakfast Network (ICBBN) is a private hospitality network designed for Christians to enjoy fellowship with one another and to provide lodging at affordable prices. Members travel across the country or around the world. The way it works is simple: You and your household become members by completing the ICBBN Application Form. You offer to host other members in your home when it is convenient for you. When you travel and wish to stay with fellow members, you simply choose your accommodation sites from the Membership Directories.

SonLight Travel.com

http://julieat.tripod.com/

This is a full service Christian travel site featuring on-line reservations for airlines, hotels, car rentals, and great special deals. They specialize in family and group travel, saving travelers up to 65 percent.

Chains

http://www.holidayinn.com/

http://www.marriott.com/

http://www.hyatt.com/

http://www.bestwestern.com/

http://www.bedandbreakfast.com/

http://www.motel6.com/

LONG TERM CARE

Caring for a loved one is difficult, often underappreciated work. These sites will help give you the support you need, offer new ideas, and help you learn more about the illness being suffered by the loved one you are caring for.

These sites can remind you that you are not alone in your effort and that similar work is shared by thousands of people around the world.

Elder Care

http://www.ec-online.net/

ElderCare On-Line is a beacon for people caring for aging loved ones. Whether you are caring for a spouse, parent, relative, or neighbor, this site provides an online community where supportive peers and professionals help you improve the quality of life for you and your elder.

Cancer Care

http://cancerzone.findhere.org/

A links page for all types of information on cancer, caregiving, and the latest in research information.

Keeping in Touch

http://www.nfcacares.org/

The National Family Caregiver's Association strives to minimize the disparity between a caregiver's quality of life and that of mainstream Americans.

Support Needed?

http://www.caregiving.com/

Caregiving On-Line offers you access to the support, information, and resources you need when you care for an aging relative. The web site is an offshoot of *Caregiving* newsletter, a monthly print publication.

Family Caregiver Alliance

http://www.caregiver.org/

Welcome to the web site for Family Caregiver Alliance, the premier support organization for caregivers. Here you'll find specialized information on Alzheimer's disease, stroke, traumatic brain injury, Parkinson's disease, ALS, and other disorders and long term care concerns. This site has wonderful features for families, caregivers, professionals, policymakers, and the media.

Faithful Friends Nursing Home Ministry

http://www.faithfulfriends.org/

A Christian ministry serving the residents of nursing homes and the groups that visit them. Many on-line resources, references, and links are available.

Selecting Help

http://www.careguide.net/careguide.cgi/eldercare/ecthink/ecthink.htm%21

Agency Help

http://www.hfd.cdphe.state.co.us/.%5Cstatic%5Chha.htm

Choosing a Facility

http://coltrane.thirdage.com/family/caregiving/factsheets/assisted/questions.html

Provider Help

http://www.hcam.org/choosing.html

MAGAZINES

Magazines are convenient. You can keep a copy in your briefcase, read while on the bus, catch up while at the doctor's office, or enjoy them with a cup of coffee.

There are times you don't need that convenience, which makes it nice that most big magazines also exist on-line. These sites allow you to look up a story, browse past issues, as well as write letters to the editor.

If there's a magazine you used to receive, or one that you would like to try, you can often enjoy it free on-line.

Big Pages Magazine Links

http://www.bigpages.com/links/magazines.html

Find select links to magazines in a variety of categories. Check out the number one magazine for finance, food and cooking, or parenting. If you don't like that one, then you can check out the number two magazine! Lists up to five selections for each of twenty-six categories.

ZineVine

http://www.zinevine.com/

A jump list of magazines on the web dealing with computers.

Business Week

http://www.businessweek.com/

Provides complete contents of current issue, both domestic and international editions, plus BW Daily Briefing, BW Enterprise for small business, and more. Requires paid subscription for full access.

Education Week

http://www.edweek.org/

A place to go on the World Wide Web for people interested in education reform, schools, and the policies that guide them.

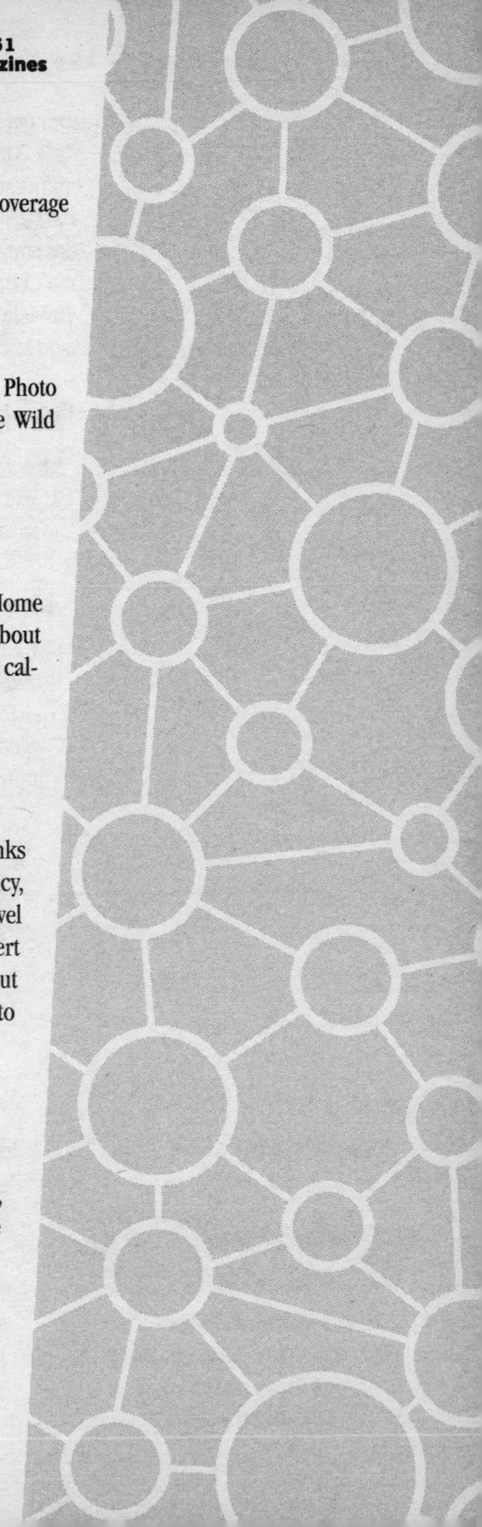

CNN/SI

http://www.cnnsi.com/
Get up-to-the minute, comprehensive sports coverage from CNN and *Sports Illustrated*.

Backpacker Magazine

http://www.backpacker.com/
Site includes Gear Finder, Daily News, Forums, Photo Gallery, Weekend Wilderness Guide, anyplace Wild TV, and more.

Outside On-Line

http://www.outsidemag.com/
An interactive, electronic outdoor community. Home of *Outside* magazine, Check out expert info about outdoor and adventure activities, an extensive calendar of events, and discussions.

Travel & Leisure

http://www.pathfinder.com/travel/TL/
Loaded with travel information and articles. Links to travel sites and destinations, maps, currency, and weather. Check out the travel diary, hot travel tips, and news. Join a chat or ask the travel expert a question. Utilize travel planners and find out about hot deals. You can even find out where to book your trip.

Shoestring Travel

http://www.stratpub.com/
An e-zine including hotel, restaurant, airfare, and recreation information for inexpensive travel.

Taunton Press Publishers

http://www.taunton.com/
If you are looking for expert, how-to advice

from people who've been there before, this is the right place. The Taunton Press goes straight to today's master craftspeople—carpenters and cabinetmakers, gardeners and chefs, designers of fashion and furniture—to get the tips and techniques you need to guarantee success. Their magazines include Fine Woodworking, Fine Homebuilding, Threads, Fine Gardening, Fine Cooking, and Kitchen Gardener.

Natural Land

http://www.naturalland.com/
A resource for healthy living, gardening, cooking, fitness, nutrition, and more.

Martha Stewart Living

http://www.marthastewart.com/
Official site of Martha Stewart. Come get information, advice, ideas, and tips on gardening, crafts, home, weddings, holidays, cooking and entertaining, and more.

TOP SITE

Better Homes and Gardens

http://www.betterhomesandgardens.com/
The place for cooking, recipes, gardening, decorating, home repair and remodeling, and more. Also features a just-for-kids section.

People Magazine

http://www.people.com/
An entertainment magazine with articles on celebrities as well as fun and games.

Entertainment Weekly

http://www.ew.com/ew/aol/
Features daily news, reviews, games and columns about the latest in movies, TV, books, video, music, and multimedia.

DID YOU KNOW?

...that President Clinton mentioned the Internet in the 2000 Statue of the Union address six times?

Christian Magazines

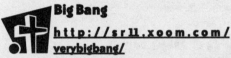

Christianity Today Publications

http://www.christianityonline.com/

Link to any of Christianity Today's publications: *Christianity Today, Books & Culture, Campus Life, Christian Parenting Today, Christian History, Christian Reader, CO Magazine, Leadership, Marriage Partnership, Men of Integrity, Today's Christian Woman, Virtue,* and *Your Church*. At this site you can read current issues of these magazines, search for articles on various topics from these publications, or find out about subscriptions or free trial hard copies of these magazines.

Big Bang

http://sr11.xoom.com/verybigbang/

An alternative Christian youth e-zine.

Christian Youth News

http://www.christianteens.net/cyn/

A magazine for teens that features articles on the issues that are important to today's teens as well as interviews with Christian artists, album reviews, and more.

Christian Computing

http://www.gospelcom.net/ccmag/

This magazine reviews software, hardware, and application for Christian-related computer issues. Subscribe to the magazine, read the current issue on-line, listen live, or check out the downloads and other resources.

Other Christian Magazines

Christian Digest

http://www.christiandigest.com/

Christian Home and School

http://www.gospelcom.net/csi/chs/

Guideposts

http://www.guideposts.org/

Interpretation

http://www.interpretation.org/

World on the Web

http://www.worldmag.com/world/home.asp

Need to be somewhere, but don't have directions? Want to know how many miles to a certain city? Want to be able to give someone detailed directions or a map to your home? These maps are one better than your road atlas since they give you actual door-to-door directions.

Thomas Bros. Maps

http://www.thomas.com/

This site offers maps that are highly accurate, content rich, easy to use, and visually appealing. Thomas's maps are developed with a simple, basic concept of a street atlas with a page and grid layout keyed to a street index system in the atlas.

Maps.com

http://www.maps.com/

Begin your journey at Maps.com. Find maps at the tips of your fingers. Feel free to buy from the on-line store, check out the tools they offer, or get special deals by joining the Maps.com club. Search for downloadable digital maps, paper maps, travel accessories, atlases, and more.

Map Town

http://www.maptown.com/

Map Town is your source for maps, travel guides, and travel information for the world. They have over 23,000 products from maps to aviation charts to travel guides to globes to GPS units to voltage adapters and money belts. This site covers every country in the world with maps and travel guides and also has an information page on every country covering population, economy, politics, geography, and military facts. An on-line map for each country is also available.

MapBlast

http://www.mapblast.com/mblast/index.mb

Need specific directions to a certain destination? Enter the starting and ending address and you'll receive a map within seconds with written and visual directions of how to get there. This site is very detailed and gives step-by-step driving directions as well as maps to be created, printed, published, or E-mailed.

Universal Map On-Line

http://www.universalmap.com/

Looking for a map of your state, region, or hometown? Universal Map is one of the largest publishers of geography and travel-related information in the United States. This site is proud to offer one of the most extensive lines of local road map titles available. Search the database for the travel destination of your choice.

Place Maps

http://www.tgimaps.com/place/

You'll be lost without a PlaceMap of your hometown and one for every city you visit as well. These quality, laminate-style maps illustrate major buildings, points of interest, attractions, and other landmarks together with the major roads needed to get there. While traditional maps show every little street, they don't show where things are and how to easily get there.

National Map Center

http://www.mapsworld.com/

Mapsworld.com offers thousands of maps for you to download 24 hours a day. Users can login to Mapsworld.com and find just the right map for their needs. In a matter of minutes, you can download the map of your choice and put it to use in magazines, print, broadcast,

Directions

http://www.mapquest.com/

Railroad Maps

http://memory.loc.gov/ammem/gmdhtml/rrhtml/rrhome.html

Fishing

http://www.eastcape.org/FishMap/Map.html

Mountain Maps

http://www.mtop.com/MTop/front.html

Orienteering

http://www.the-spa.com/tony.maniscalco/tryo.htm

http://www.us.orienteering.org/

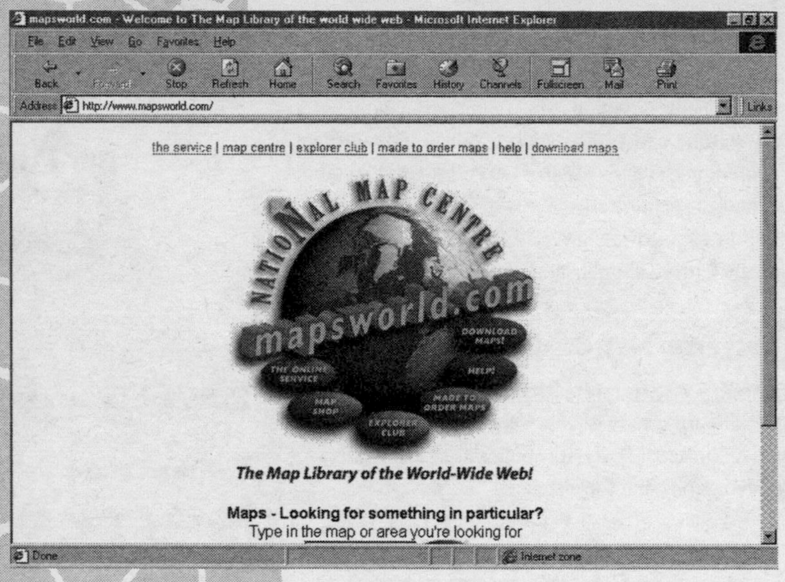

multimedia, web, and CD Roms by following the simple instructions provided.

International Map Trade Association

http://www.maptrade.org/

Welcome to the world of maps. IMTA members are the companies that create and sell the maps, atlases, globes, and map-related products you use. Find a map specialty retailer anywhere in the world. Link to publishers and retailers on the web. Find information on maps, geography, and mapping technology.

Old Maps and Prints

http://home.flash.net/~omp1548/

Old Maps and Prints is in its twenty-fourth year in the trade, in which they have found clients and colleagues throughout the world. Maps of North America, the United States, and its states and regions, selected for their historical interest, quality, and value, are this site's specialty.

Cultural Maps

http://xroads.virginia.edu/~MAP/map_hp.html

Cultural Maps is dedicated to the graphical presentation of nongraphical information—the immediate goal is to build a digital American historical atlas.

World History Maps

http://www.hyperhistory.com/online_n2/History_n2/a.html

HyperHistory On-Line navigates through 3,000 years of world history with links to important persons of world historical importance; civilization time lines; events and facts; and historical maps.

MATHEMATICS

Does $A^2 + B^2$ always equal C^2?
Studying math can be difficult and discouraging. No matter what level you're learning, there's always more to grasp. These sites can help be the tutor you need. If you're a teacher or homeschooling parent, these sites can help you with lesson plans and creative learning activities.

MathWork

http://www.coastlink.com/users/sbryce/mathwork/

This web page will allow you to create and print math worksheets for children learning simple arithmetic (addition, subtraction, multiplication, and division). You choose the complexity level, and problems are randomly generated.

TOP SITE

Interactive Assessment Worksheets

http://www.geocities.com/Heartland/Ranch/2200/assess.htm

Math problems, with alternate problem-solving strategies and printable worksheets.

Interactive Mathematics Miscellany and Puzzles

http://www.cut-the-knot.com/

Math puzzles and interactive education with a lot of math information for teachers, students, and parents.

Mathematical Quotation Server

http://math.furman.edu/~mwoodard/mquot.html

"Life is good for only two things, discovering mathematics and teaching mathematics"—Siméon Poisson. Want more? Check this site out.

Homework Doctor

http://www.tagnet.org/homework

This site exists to help Christian middle and high school students with their math, science, English, French, religion, and all other subjects. View categorized links, submit your questions, chat, use translation tools, or search an encyclopedia.

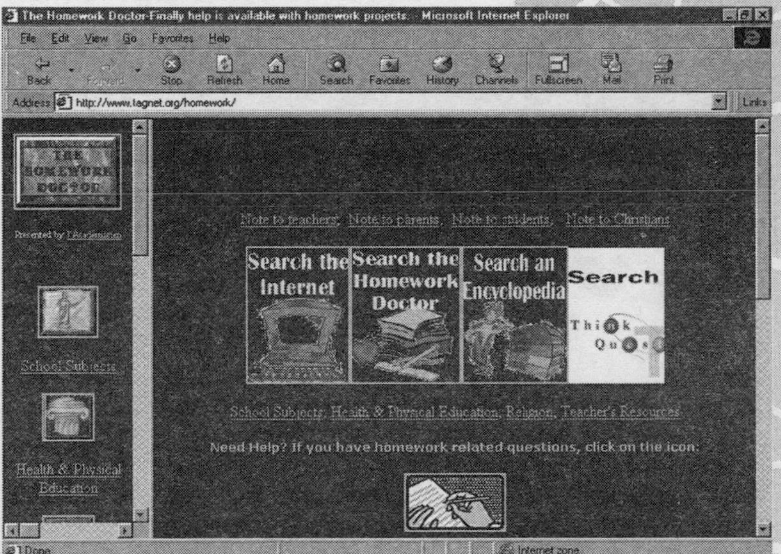

Welcome to the Math League

http://www.mathleague.com/

Math Leagues, Inc. provides students with fun and educational math contests, problem books, and math educational software. Site might be of special interest to homeschoolers.

The Math Forum Internet Mathematics Library

http://forum.swarthmore.edu/library/

The Internet Math Library is our best resource for teachers, students, and parents looking

Did You Know?

. . .that it would take every man, woman, and child in the United States 125 years working nonstop with handheld calculators to perform the 1 trillion calculations which the Intel supercomputer can do in one second?

for web sites across the Internet on math topics. Sites are gathered from our own explorations and submissions from users.

InfoUse's PlaneMath

http://www.planemath.com/

PlaneMath is on-line activities about math and aeronautices. Accessible to all students interested in fourth- through seventh-grade-level math.

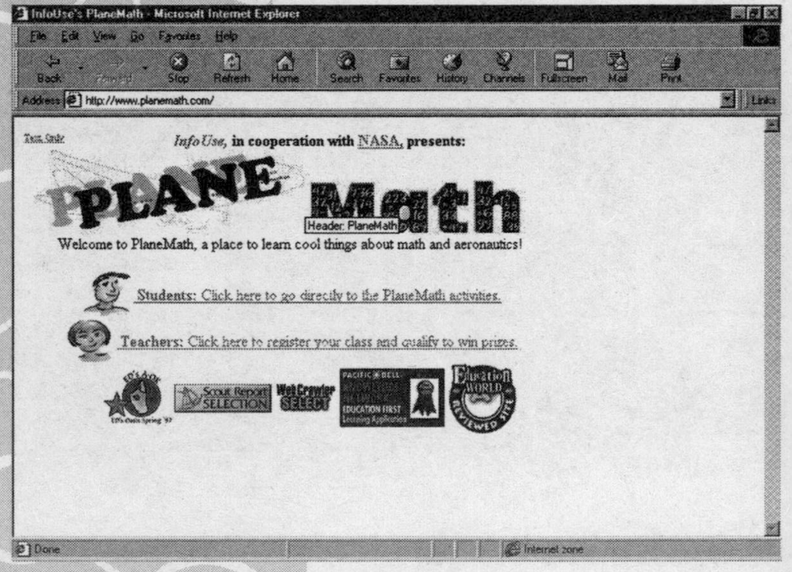

S.O.S. Math

http://www.math.utep.edu/sosmath

S.O.S. Mathematics is the web site where you can work with materials to help you do your homework, prepare for a test, or get ready for class. The material presented reviews the most important results, techniques, and formulas.

Did You Know?

. . .that the average Internet user will spend 63 million seconds, or 23.5 months, on the Internet in their lifetime, and that 9.5 of those months will be spent using E-mail?

The Math Forum: Student Center

http://forum.swarthmore.edu/students/

Student Center at the Math Forum provides resources for students to talk to others about math and find resources to explore math using the Internet. It also has links for fun math learning: virtual field trips and web sites built for and by students.

Other Links

http://www.math.uiuc.edu/Algebraic-Number-Theory

gopher://ericir.syr.edu:70/11/Lesson/NewLesson/Math/

http://www.seresc.k12.nh.us/www/alvirne.html

http://www.math.utah.edu/ed/resources/resources.html

http://bourke.gen.nz/paul.html

http://www.nctm.org/journals/jrme/jrme-home.htm

http://www.cam.org/~aselby/lesson.html

http://forum.swarthmore.edu/mathsites

http://MathCentral.uregina.ca/

MEN'S HEALTH

Men face physical problems that are embarrassing for some to discuss: prostate problems, baldness, or even stress management. Use these sites to ask and learn in the privacy of your home. Once you feel you have a better grasp on your situation, or begin to recognize warning signs, consult your doctor.

TOP SITE

The Network

http://www.menshealthnetwork.org/

The Men's Health Network (MHN) was created to address the growing men's health crisis. The goals of the MHN are to save men's lives by reducing the premature mortality of men and boys, to increase the physical and mental health of men so that they can live fuller and happier lives, and to significantly reduce the cycles of violence and addiction that afflict so many men. The extensive links page requires parental guidance because of the wide variety of issues in men's health it covers. Very informative site for this emerging concern.

Common Problems Averted

http://medic.med.uth.tmc.edu/ptnt/00000391.htm

A fact sheets from the University of Texas—Houston Medical School about the common men's health concerns. Includes practical suggestions for improving lifestyles and screening for health risks.

Men's Health Center

http://www.healthy.net/menshealth/

Find articles and information that deal specifically with men's health issues.

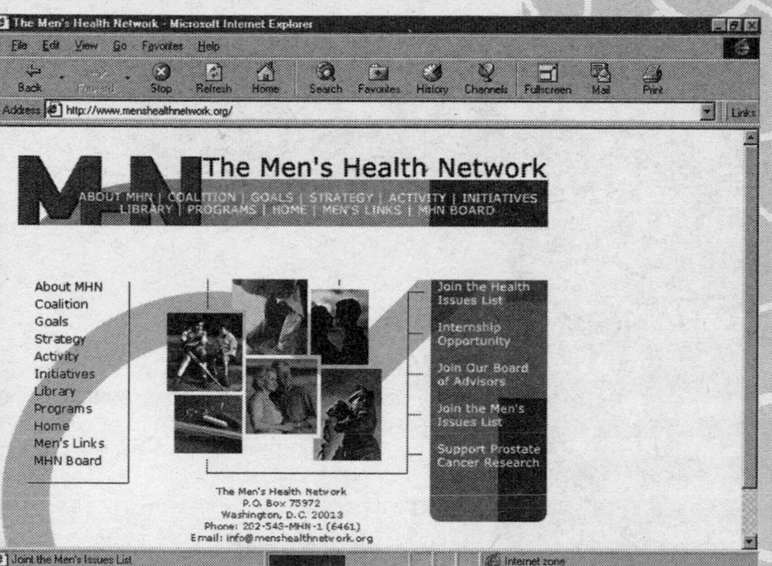

Men's Health Issues

http://medic.med.uth.tmc.edu/ptnt/00000391.htm

This site includes information about exercise, fat and cholesterol, and prostatic cancer screening.

Men's Library

http://www.vix.com/pub/men/health/health.html

The World Wide Web Virtual Library site for men's health issues. Find links under categories like diet, mental health, commercial sites, health legislation, and more.

PlanetRx.com—Men's Health

http://www.planetrx.com/ecenter/men.html

Get the latest health news and read related articles, shop for the products you need, and find drug information, all right here. Also features men's health message board and live chat.

Did You Know?

...that 38 percent of online purchasers are female, while 62 percent are males?

MILITARY

When sons and daughters used to go into the military, parents and friends would often wait weeks at a time to hear news from or about them. During war-times, loved ones would read the paper to try to recognize the names of those en-gaged in battle.

Today, the Internet makes communication instant. A soldier in the Persian Gulf can E-mail home in seconds. News about military engagements cross the newswire quickly.

Air Force

http://www.af.mil/

The official site of the air force. If you want to join, o just browse, it is all here.

Army

http://www.army.mil/

The official site of the army. News articles are on th home page with lots of choices for other information

Navy

http://www.navy.mil/

Official site of the navy. Check out their picture gal lery and find the picture of a jet breaking the soun barrier.

Marine Corps

http://www.usmc.mil/

Official site of the Marine Corp. Check out thei picture gallery.

Coast Guard

http://www.uscg.mil/welcome.html

Official site of the Coast Guard. There is a boatin safety site that includes all the important info yo need to know if you own and operate a boat.

National Guard

http://www.ngb.dtic.mil/

This web site provides virtual, on-demand information about the National Guard Bureau, the Army National Guard, the Air National Guard, and National Guard-sponsored organizations and events.

Surgeon General

http://www.surgeongeneral.gov/sgoffice.htm

The virtual office of the Surgeon General, who is the head of another, noncombat military force, the United States Public Health Service. This site has a kids' page, too.

The Pentegon

http://www.defenselink.mil/pubs/pentagon/

This site offers a virtual tour of the Pentagon, headquarters of the Department of Defense for the U.S. government. Tour information and map are included for planning a trip to the building.

POW/MIA

http://www.dtic.mil/dpmo

Welcome to the home page of the Defense POW/Missing Personnel. The information assembled on the following pages is to assist readers in understanding the U.S. government effort to achieve the fullest possible accounting of our missing in action—from all wars.

West Point

http://www.usma.edu/

Home page of the U.S. military academy for the army, West Point. Information about admissions, events and attractions, and visiting the academy are included.

Wars of the 20th Century

http://www.geocities.com/Athens/Academy/6617/wars.html

For Students

http://www.cfcsc.dnd.ca/links/milhist/20.html

Military Reunions

http://terracasa.com/checkpoint/index.html

Military Families

http://www.kraftmilitary.com/

Military Support Network

http://www.maingate.com/

Tour a Missel Site

http://www.xvt.com/users/kevink/silo/

Naval Academy

http://www.nadn.navy.mil

Home page for the Naval Academy. Includes admission and information about the Academy's programs, campus, and a virtual tour is available.

Coast Guard Academy

http://www.cga.edu

Besides admission information, this branch of the military maintains the USCGA *Barque Eagel,* America's Tall Ship. Be sure to check it out at this web site.

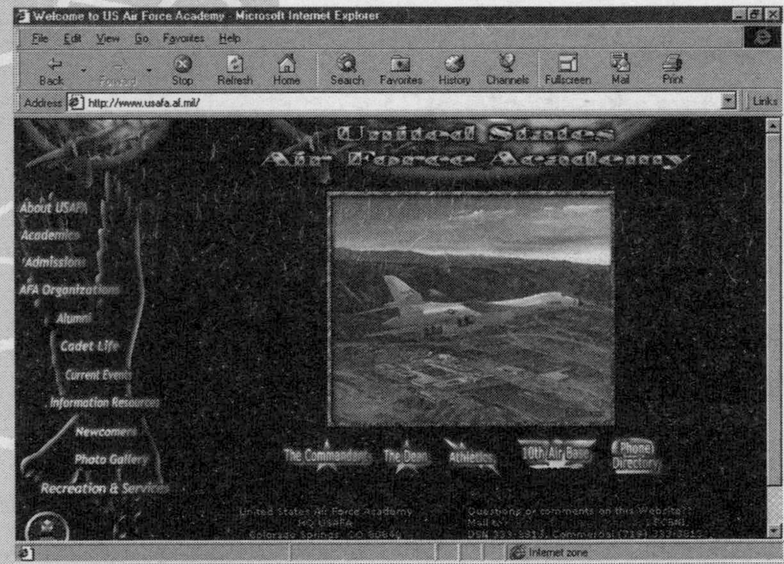

Air Force Academy

http://www.usafa.af.mil

Includes admission and program information. Be sure to linger on the home page and watch the changing pictures of various air force planes in action.

Merchant Marine Academy

http://www.usmma.edu

Web page of the Merchant Marine Academy, a part of the Department of Transportation. The academy has liaisons with all the military branches, and offers a unique education that combines education in maritime transportation industry and the military.

Medal of Honor

http://www.homeofheroes.com

This new museum is under construction in Pueblo, Colorado. You can take a virtual tour of all three floors and learn about our country's heros who have been awarded the military Medals of Honor.

Christian Military Fellowship

http://www.cmf.com/

CMF is a worldwide, nondenominational fellowship of Christians in and associated with the United States Armed Forces.

Officers' Christian Fellowship

http://www.ocfusa.org/

OCF is a ministry of Christian military officers providing prayer, Bible studies, conferences, contacts, visits, publications, and retreat centers to military personnel and their families.

Surftown

http://www.militaryministry.com/

Military Ministry Network is a civilian-based, interactive cyber ministry designed exclusively to meet the daily needs of military personnel for godly living in the military.

MISSIONS

The world is a wide web of people needing the gospel. These sites will help connect you with mission agencies as well as formal and informal mission opportunities. These sites can help you discover your mission field—whether it's around the block or around the world.

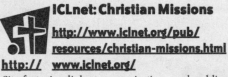

Antioch Missionary Links

http://www.fallis.org/antioch/index2.shtml

This site features a reviewed and rated listing of missionary web sites. AML has a twofold purpose: First, to link people to missionaries who are using the web. Second, to help missionaries build web sites that will educate, edify, and challenge believers to be part of the works God is doing.

ICLnet: Christian Missions

http://www.iclnet.org/pub/resources/christian-missions.html

http://www.iclnet.org/

Site featuring links to organizations and publications related to missions.

Mission Opportunities Database

http://www.globalmission.org/go.htm

An index of Christian mission information, centered around an opportunity/employment database of many agencies. Includes a feature that lets you look for short-term missions opportunities.

FAVORITE LINKS

Everypeople.net

http://www.everypeople.net/

EveryPeople.net is designed 1) to be a dynamic portal to the best of the World Wide Web's missions information and 2) to be able to automatically take on the major appearance features of web sites which make it a part of their content. Features at this site include prayer resources and information about worldwide missions. You can view video clips or check out music and books that relate to missions. Link to sites where you can read on-line biographies of missionaries. Or check out the wide variety of links to missions agencies, maps, church resources, and information sources.

Missionboard.com

http://www.missionboard.com/index.cfm

Missionboard.com is a catalyst for communication among Christian missions, churches, and individuals. You can research missions all over the world, find a home church, raise interest and support in your project or ministry, and keep up with the day-to-day activities of mission projects and churches all over the world.

Christian Missions Page

http://www.sim.org/

Hosted by the Society for International Ministries, this site includes a wide variety of informational articles, discussion areas, links, and other resources. Find out more about SIM through articles, RealAudio news briefs, or an SIM video that you can watch on-line. Or link to other Christian missions sites or use the "Great Commission Search Engine" to search over 190 mission web sites. Get information on mission events, world Christian resources, prayer requests, and more. Also includes a fun game with prizes.

MOVIES

Many Christians believe they can't trust the movie reviews on TV or in the newspaper because the critics' values are not the same as theirs. Some parents are hesitant to take the recommendations of coworkers or friends because they feel their viewing standards might differ. These sites list all potentially objectional material, give a plot synopisis, and let you pick out movies that match *your* standards.

Family Style

http://www.familystyle.com/

Each movie in the Movie Guide has been reviewed and the content in the areas of profanity, nudity, sex, violence, and drugs/alcohol noted. No attempt has been made in these reviews to judge the quality or artistic merit of the movies. The reviews supplement the MPAA rating system by giving you specific information about why each movie was rated PG, PG-13, R, or NC-17.

Teach with Movies

http://www.teachwithmovies.org

Learning Guides to each recommended film describe the benefits of the movie, possible problems, and helpful background. Discussion questions, bridges to reading, projects, and links to the Internet are also provided. Films with gratuitous violence, explicit sex, or other offensive scenes are not recommended by TWM.

Christian Perspective

http://www.christiananswers.net/spotlight

Rates movies in terms of offensivenesss to a Christian perspective; the highest rating is 5, the lowest is 1.

Movie Show Times

http://www.filmfrenzy.com/
http://showtimes.hollywood.com/
http://www.moviefone.com/

These three sites tell you show times for all movies for the area codes entered in their location finder site. Review and various "stats" are also available, such as the top ten movies at the box office this week, etc. Parental guidance may be needed for some movies since all releases are listed.

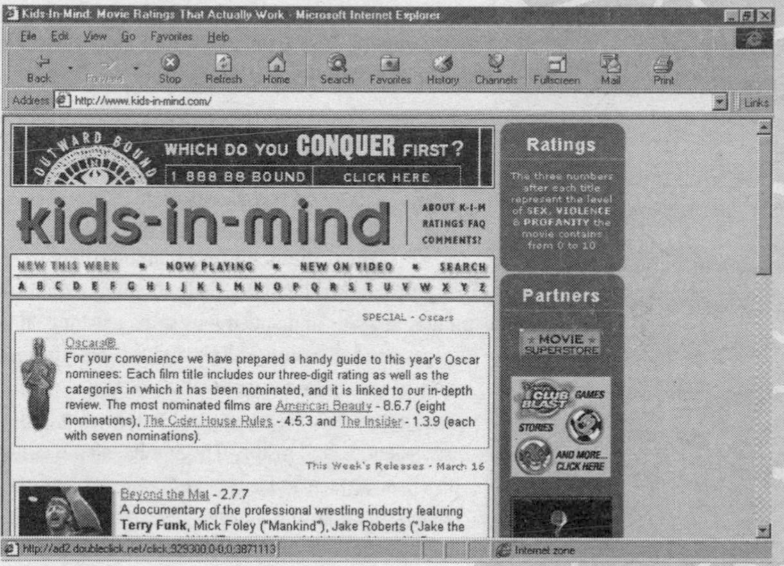

TOP SITE Keep Kids in Mind

http://www.kids-in-mind.com/

Kids-In-Mind reviews the potentially objectionable material contained in movies. The areas of sex, violence, and profanity are rated with a numbering system. This site simply lists material that parents may not want their kids to watch or hear. Then parents can decide whether a movie is OK for their own kids, according to their own standards.

DID YOU KNOW?

...that the devices that make up computer memory in a 64 megabyte computer chip are so small that up to 10,000 devices could fit in the diameter of a human hair?

MUSEUMS, GALLERIES, CENTERS

If you grew up near a major city, you probably went on many field trips to museums. Year after year, you may have traveled to the same museum, looking at the same exhibits. But have you ever been to the Smithsonian? The Louvre? The Sistine Chapel? Some of the great museums of the world are availabe for an on-line tour. Note to parents: The same level of parental guidance is needed browsing these sites as in browsing the halls of a physical museum.

Web Art

http://www.mowa.org/enter.html
The Museum of Web Art is a new and innovative site with a special kids' section that is great!

TOP SITE

The Smithsonian

http://www.si.edu/index_old_browser.htm
The Institution is as an independent trust instrumentality of the United States holding some 140 million artifacts and specimens in its trust for "the increase and diffusion of knowledge." The Institution is also a center for research dedicated to public education, national service, and scholarship in the arts, sciences, and history. The Smithsonian is composed of sixteen museums and galleries and the National Zoo and numerous research facilities in the United States and abroad. Browse their departments menu; they are developing exhibits exclusively for on-line users.

National Zoo

http://www.si.edu/natzoo/
The National Zoo has live web cameras located throughout the animal exhibits. This site takes you to the menu for watching the animals.

Design Museum

http://www.si.edu/ndm/

Cooper-Hewitt, National Design Museum, and the Smithsonian Institution invite you to experience how design affects every aspect of your daily life. The National Design Museum investigates the uses, structures, effects, and meanings of these products of design and their roles as forces for communication and change in our daily lives. Interactive exhibits for children are available; check their programs site.

The Metropolitan Museum in New York

http://www.metmuseum.org/education/index.asp

The Explore and Learn page at the Metropolitan Museum of Art in New York is full of interactive exhibits for kids of all ages.

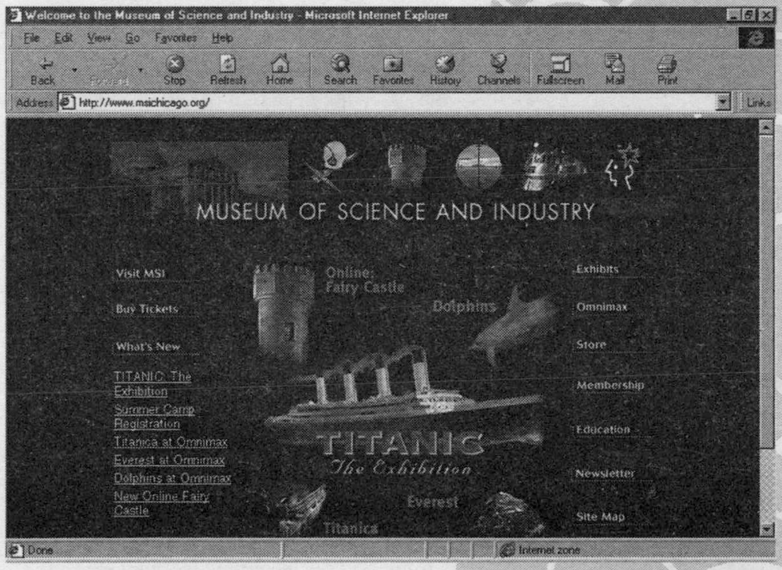

The Virtual Bible Museum

http://www.bibletreasure.com/

Vatican Museums

http://www.christusrex.org/www1/vaticano/0-Musei.html

Art Safari

http://www.moma.org/docs/menu/index.htm

Go to Educational Resources on the Art Safari site and really enjoy yourself with the kids, exploring several interactive and creative programs that teach design at the same time.

Science and Industry

http://www.msichicago.org

The Museum of Science and Industry in Chicago is the first museum in the world to develop hands-on exhibits. The site has on-line exhibitions for the viewer and information about the museum's offerings.

Field Museum

http://www.fmnh.org/exhibits/online_exhib.htm

The Field Museum of Natural History in Chicago has a great choice of on-line exhibits.

University of Southern California

http://digimuse.usc.edu/front.htm

Drawing on the resources of USC's faculty in engineering, communication, and museum studies, this site is developing an on-line museum, with neither walls nor guards, globally accessible 24 hours a day. Visitors to the art museum will be able to view two-dimensional images and utilize remote telerobotic devices equipped with video cameras to view three-dimensional works and participate interactively, in real time, in art performances and installations.

NASA

http://pds.jpl.nasa.gov/planets

This is a collection of many of the best images from NASA's planetary exploration program.

Submit a Site

hudson@techie.com

Space Museum

http://www.zianet.com/space/index.html

Home page for the Space Center in Alamogordo, New Mexico, this site has lots to choose from that goes beyond space. Check out their Antarctica exhibit called the Polar Connection.

Air and Space

http://www.nasm.edu

The Smithsonian Institution's National Air and Space Museum (NASM) maintains the largest collection of historic air and spacecraft in the world. Click on Exhibitions for a variety of on-line tours.

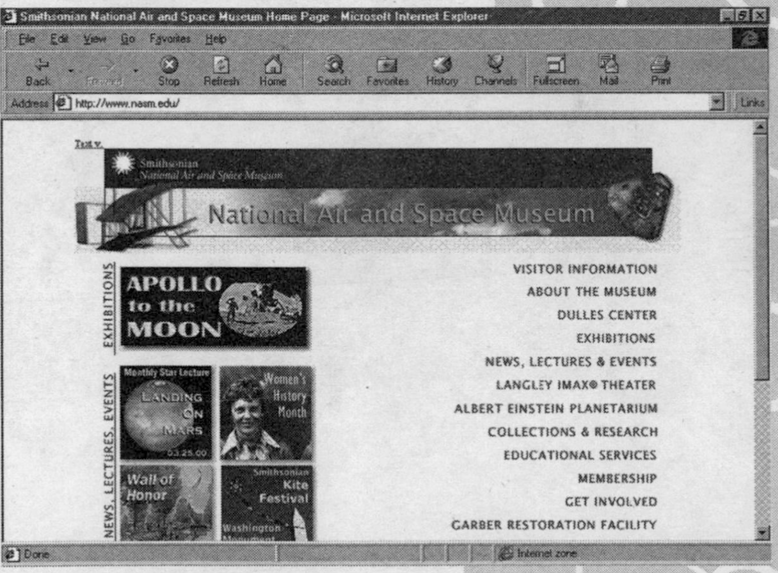

Art Resources

http://wwar.com

World Wide Arts Resources offers the definitive, interactive gateway to all exemplars of qualitative arts information and culture on the Internet.

On-Line Museums

http://www.icom.org/vlmp/

These pages provide an eclectic collection of WWW services connected with museums, galleries, and archives. This is a directory to virtual museums in the world. Check out the children's section for links to museums.

The Louvre

http://www.louvre.fr/louvrea.htm

The web site of the Louvre Museum in Paris gives you a virtual tour as well as a tour of each of its seven galleries.

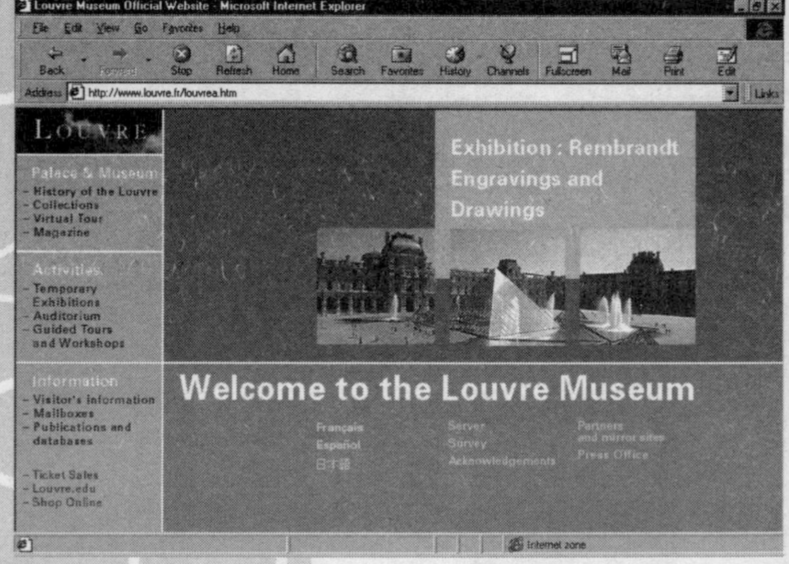

The Sistine Chapel

http://www.christusrex.org/www1/sistine/0-Ceiling.html

The Sistine Chapel has its own virtual museum with multiple views of the masterpiece.

National Art Gallery

http://www.nga.gov/onlinetours/onlinetr.htm
The National Art Gallery in Washington, D.C. has a number of virtual tours, including architecture and current exhibitions.

Fine Arts Museum

http://www.famsf.org/
The home page for the Fine Arts Museum of San Francisco, with a super Art Imagebase that lets you examine in detail hundreds of artworks. Tours that have ended are available for review, as well as previews of ones coming up. This is a terrific site!

The Hermitage

http://www.hermitage.ru/
The web site of the Hermitage Museum in Russia, located in the winter palace of the czar, offers an excellent digital collection of its exhibits. The English language is an option and makes browsing much easier.

FAVORITE LINKS

DID YOU KNOW?

...that five million tourists a year visit the Louvre Museum in Paris, but more than double that number visit the Louvre on the Internet? It's one of the favored destinations on the World Wide Web.

MUSIC

The Internet allows you to go broader than your radio dial ever could. Use http://www.netradio.com for the broadest category of music you'll ever find. Other sites let you behind the scenes to learn more about the musical style, artists, and composers of your choice.

TOP SITE

Net Radio

http://www.netradio.com/

NetRadio.com's vision is to become the Internet's leading fully integrated entertainment and marketing platform for media and media-related products and services. The company's unique expertise lies in developing and delivering interactive multimedia content. Its ability to recommend and deliver music products to its audience is unsurpassed. You can chose to listen or learn about different types of music, including kids' music. You can buy music from this site, too.

Music History

http://www.fmnh.org/sounds/index.htm

An on-line exhibit from the Field Museum of Natural History in Chicago, play one of the Field Museum's musical instruments through the magic of digital technology.

Unusual Instruments

http://www.mhs.mendocino.k12.ca.us/MenComNet/Business/Retail/Larknet/larkhp.html

Lark In The Morning now offers over 6,000 musical items: instruments from many cultures, antique instruments, instructional books, repertoire books, videos, cassettes, and CDs. Here you will find a wealth of information on unusual musical instruments.

African-American Music and Culture

http://www.indiana.edu/~aaamc/

The Archives of African-American Music and Culture (AAAMC) supports the research of scholars, students, and the general public from around the world by providing access to oral histories, photographs, musical and print manuscripts, audio and video recordings, and educational broadcast programs, among other holdings. The AAAMC provides reference services in person and by telephone, mail, and the World Wide Web for the general public and for researchers throughout the world. Inventories are available for some collections at a minimal fee.

Latin-American Music

http://www.music.indiana.edu/som/lamc/info/geninfo.html

The Latin-American Music Center (LAMC) provides information about Latin-American music repertoire, particularly the scores, recordings, and books available in the collection at Indiana University. It also provides valuable information for contacting composers, performers, scholars, and institutions related to Latin-American music. The archives contain biographies of composers, notes on their works, and press material. Provides reference services in person and by telephone, mail, and the World Wide Web for the general public and for researchers throughout the world. Inventories are available for some collections at a minimal fee.

If It's Not Baroque...

http://baroque-music.com/frames/frames.shtml

A great source for everything related to Baroque music. Covers composers, instruments, recordings, and articles.

Other Links

http://stimpy.music.ua.edu/features/addresses.html

http://www.ucs.mun.ca/~cmea

http://www.culturefinder.com/basicsq.htm

http://www.classical.net

http://classicalmus.com/composers/haydn.html

http://weber.u.washington.edu/~sbode/music/french2.html

http://www.sju.edu/~bs065903/gershwin/homepage.htm

http://weber.u.washington.edu/~sbode/music/german1.html

http://classicalmus.com/composers/puccini.html

Country Music

http://www.countryweekly.com/

An on-line magazine for country music which includes a history of country music, tour schedules, and articles on current artists.

CCM

http://www.ccmcom.com/

Christian Contempary Music magazine is on-line with a digital version of their magazine and links to listen to Christian music.

Gospel Music

http://gospelmusic.sogospelnews.com

The Gospel Music Webring is a ring of gospel music artists, musicians, songwriters, and just plain lovers of gospel music. It is designed to give those with like interests a way to link their web pages with others of the same interest.

Black Gospel Music

http://afgen.com/gospel.html

Site offers articles, information, books, and CDs from Tommy Dorsey to Bobby Jones.

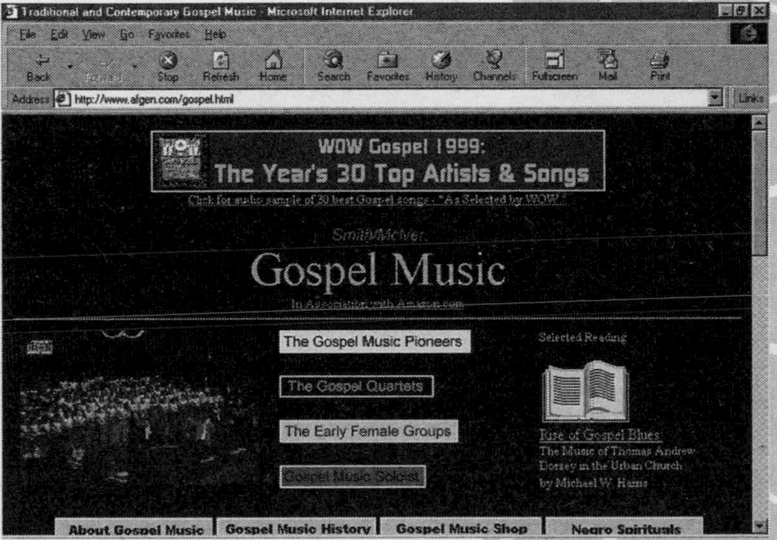

Jazz

http://www.pk.edu.pl/~pmj/jazzlinks

The site for the greatest amount of jazz links on the web. Good variety of subjects for this popular genre.

American Music Center

http://www.amc.net/links/index.html

The American Music Center links page to all types of music genre. Covers the whole gamut of music types and organizations.

Did You Know?

...that on-line listeners are called "streamies"?

PHARMACY

Many people already fill their prescriptions by mail. If you don't need a prescription filled right away, filling it through the mail with a discount company can save you money. Net pharmacies are the next generation of these mail-order pharmacies. Fill your prescription on-line and have it shipped to you. Many sites will let you purchase non-prescription items, too.

FDA

http://www.fda.gov/

The Food and Drug Administration touches the lives of virtually every American every day. The FDA ensures that the food we eat is safe and wholesome, the cosmetics we use won't hurt us, the medicines and medical devices we use are safe and effective, and that radiation-emitting products (such as microwave ovens) won't harm us. The FDA also ensures that all of these products are labeled truthfully with the information that people need to use them properly. Be sure to visit their feature, "Buying Medical Products On-Line."

Rx List

http://rxlist.com/

The information provided on this site is not intended as a substitute for seeking professional medical advice. This site will help you supplement the advice provided by your physician. The RxList database consists primarily of products currently on the U.S. market or close to approval.

Info Needed?

http://www.pharmweb.net/

The sheer volume of material now available on the Internet can make the search for specific and reliable information difficult and frustrating. PharmWeb provides high-quality information about international professional organizations to patients and health professionals using the latest Internet technology. PharmWeb is a well-developed and structured site which has been designed to be fully interactive.

TOP SITE

On-Line Drugstore

http://www.drugstore.com/Default.asp

Drugstore.com is a leading on-line drugstore, a retail store, and information site for health, beauty, wellness, personal care, and pharmacy products. Drugstore.com tries to provide a convenient, private, and informative shopping experience.

More Links

http://www.pharmacy.org/

The Virtual Library links you to pharmacy sites of all types. Probably a good place to start if you are interested in other specific pharmacy topics.

Drug List

http://health.yahoo.com/health/drugs_tree/medication_or_drug/

Eckerd

http://eckerd.com/

Walgreens

http://www.walgreens.com/

PlanetRx

Htpp://www.planetrx.com/

Submit a Site

hudson@techie.com

RADIO

At http://www.netradio.com/, you can listen to one of 120 preprogrammed radio stations. At http://www.icrn.com/, you can listen to daily broadcasts from one of 75 favorite Christian radio shows.

Not satisfied yet? Find hundreds of other radio options from around the world—all just a few clicks away.

TopRadio.com

http://www.topradio.com/

Links to radio stations worldwide. Add your favorite radio station home page and contribute to the format listings. Find stations which air Rush Limbaugh and Paul Harvey News.

TV RadioWorld

http://www.tvradioworld.com/

This is an information directory dealing with the radio and television broadcasting industry worldwide. Features include listings to local radio stations on the web, local television stations on the web, in-depth listings of local television broadcast stations throughout North and South America, including contact information. Also find a growing list of links to sites that deal with the broadcasting industry.

MIT List of Radio Stations on the Internet

http://wmbr.mit.edu/stations/list.html

An alphabetical list of links to over 1,000 radio stations in the U.S. and around the world.

RadioStation.com

http://www.radiostation.com/

Search the FCC's AM and FM radio station technical database, get daily news updates from the FCC, or search the Broadcast Station Location

Page for AM, FM, and TV stations in the area of your choice.

christianradio.com

http://www.christianradio.com/index.asp

This site provides links to Christian radio stations, programs, music artists, radio ministries, and more.

Involved Christian Radio Network

http://www.icrn.com/

Provides current Christian audio broadcasts featuring almost every well-known Christian radio program broadcast daily in the United States. Many shows are archived for the last thirty broadcasts.

Did You Know?

...that PC use in American homes has surpassed the 50 percent mark, and 90 percent of PC users are now on-line?

Old -Time Radio

http://kismit.ne.mediaone.net/otr/oldtime.html

http://www.old-time.com/

http://members.aol.com/tooneyjake/otr.htm

Listening Patterns

http://www.abacon.com/folkerts/survey8.html

TOP SITE

Netradio.com

http://www.netradio.com/

The site connects music enthusiasts with fifteen interactive music communities ranging from jazz, vintage rock, and country to Christian, gospel, and classical. Listeners can see the title and artist of every song as it plays and find information about music and artists. Users simply click at anytime to seamlessly purchase what they're hearing from an inventory of more than 250,000 music titles and 1 million sound samples at NetRadio.com's on-line music store.

Radio Days

http://www.otr.com/index.shtml

Old-time radio site featuring audio clips of radio from the 1920s to the 1950s.

Reel Top 40 Radio Repository

http://www.reelradio.com/

This site contains a collection of RealAudio files featuring the golden era of Top 40 radio—complete with authentic analog.

Radio Directory

http://www.radiodirectory.com/

Radio Directory is an index of radio-related Internet resources designed for the radio professional.

REAL ESTATE

Reals

http://www.reals.com/

A comprehensive real estate and mortgage lender directory by state.

Realty Times Realty Locator

http://www.realtylocator.com/

The RealtyLocator has 100,000 real estate links nationwide for home searches, agents and offices, apartment rentals, realtor associations, new home builders, lenders and mortgage brokers, apartments for rent, and much more. Also includes links to real estate headline news.

International Real Estate Digest

http://www.ired.com/

Real estate and property-related directory of web sites. Links are rated to guide users to better, more informative sites. News and features for the industry, buyers, and sellers.

All Real Estate Ads

http://www.mswebmasters.com/land/

An interactive ad system listing property and real estate of all kinds for sale: homes, ranches, farms, businesses, grasslands, orchards, resorts, condos, and time-shares.

Buying or selling a home can be a lot easier than it was a few years ago.

In today's market, you can comparatively shop for houses and mortgages without ever coming face-to-face with an agent or broker.

Once you find the house you're looking for, fill out an on-line loan application and lenders will compete for your mortgage by offering you the best possible mortgages.

National Agencies

http://www.remax.com/

http://www.century21.com/

http://www.coldwellbanker.com/Coverpage.asp

http://www.prudentialrealty.com/

Mortgages

http://www.mortgagebid.com

Internet-real-estate.com

http://www.internet-real-estate.com/

View real estate listings on-line and use the web to help sell your home and property. A good marketing solution for "for sale by owner" properties.

The RealtyList

http://www.realtylist.com/

Listings of real estate and properties for sale by homeowners and agents from around the world. From farmland in Kansas to an island in the South Pacific, find every kind of property imagineable.

ListingLink

http://listinglink.com/

On-line for over four years, ListingLink is one of the nation's oldest and largest on-line real estate resources. Hundreds of thousands of photo listings with agent and office profiles. Listings are searchable by property type, region/city, price, and amenities, and the site can provide a photo and description of the property and a link to map and driving directions. Users can contact the listing office or agent directly.

America's Most Referred Real Estate Agents

http://www.amrr.com/

Find a realtor, order a relocation package, get buying or selling tips, and check out the real estate glossary.

Realty.com

http://www.realty.com/

Find a variety of real estate resources at this site. Get advice on things like locating a realtor and home improvements, researching neighborhoods and financial options, and find out how to sell your home.

OneStopRealty

http://www.onestoprealty.com/

A one-stop shop for your real estate needs. Everything from finding a house to selecting a mortgage to buying insurance.

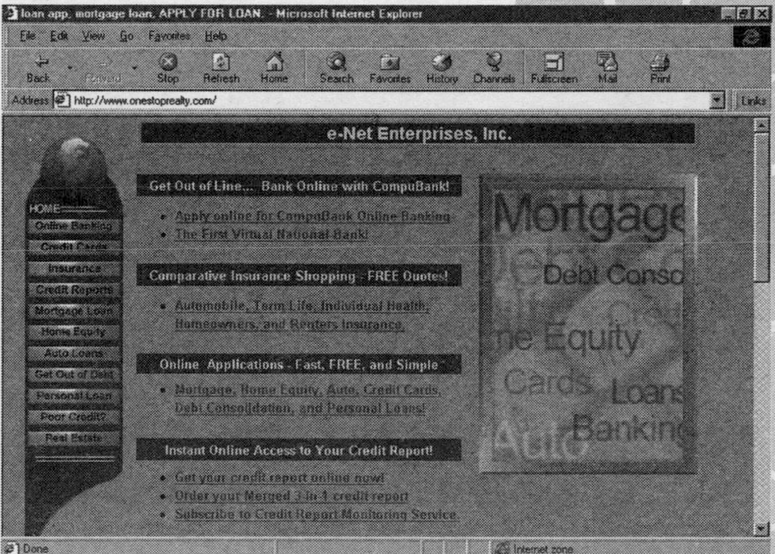

Century 21 Real Estate Corporation

http://www.century21.com/

This site gives consumers access to the Century 21 system's web site, where they can find offices, property listings, and corporate and industry-specific information.

Realty World

http://www.realtyworld.com/

Realty World is a real estate firm whose site offers on-line listings across the country, community information, and real estate news and market trends. Take a virtual tour and see a home in 3-D.

Did You Know?

...that the Internet will probably become a fixture in our normal lives, quite possibly as common a household utility as the telephone?

RealtyResearch

http://www.realtyresearch.com/

Information and data for real estate investment research. Featured are links to city info, including ratings, school, and crime data. Also review demographics, financial markets, economic indicators, rates, news, realty resources for property listings, and much more.

LoopNet

http://www.loopnet.com/

LoopNet is the largest commercial real estate listing service on the Internet. Commercial properties for sale and for lease can be added to and searched for on LoopNet for free. Also take advantage of their buyer/seller matching service, an on-line marketing and targeted delivery service, and an on-line financing service offering direct access to the industry's leading lenders, along with a range of customized services for partnering organizations.

Commercial Real Estate Network

http://www.ccim.com/

The CCIM Commercial Real Estate Network web site is dedicated to facilitating networking and information-sharing between their members and the public. Check out this site if you're interested in commercial real estate.

The Dealmakers@Property.com

http://www.property.com/

Providing insight and information on all aspects of commercial real estate dealmaking and networking, this site includes such things as links to newsgroups, referral services, a tenant search, and a weekly newsletter.

REFERENCE

When you were in grade school, you probably were given a tour of your school library and you probably learned the Dewey decimal system. You were introduced to the reference section and admonished that reference books *had to stay* in the reference section and could not be checked out. Encyclopedia sets alone, costing hundreds of dollars, were one of the library's most valuable collections. On-line, encyclopedias are free, dictionaries are fully searchable, and most other references are more accessible then ever before.

What's That Word?

http://www.onelook.com/

The best place to look up a word or term in an Internet dictionary or glossary. Free search access to a frequently updated database of words, terms, names, and acronyms.

Kids' Research

http://kids.ot.com/surfin/reference.html

Kid's Corner is a search engine for kids! If you can't find what you're looking for here, try http://www.yahooligans.com for Yahoo! for kids.

More Kids' Research

http://coins0.coin.missouri.edu/reference/kids.html

Kids' reference search and links page from Cornell University. There are multiple sites for all types of interests, including topics from cooking to dinosaurs.

Most Popular

http://www.virtualfreesites.com/frankvad/reference.kids.html

Links on this site contain over 2,500 of the most popular information reference locations and tools on the web. The site includes maps, facts, calculators, dictionaries, directories, chat, travel, health, languages, sports, calendars, jobs, weather, music, autos, humor—plus many many more helpful tools to assist you.

Enclyclopedias

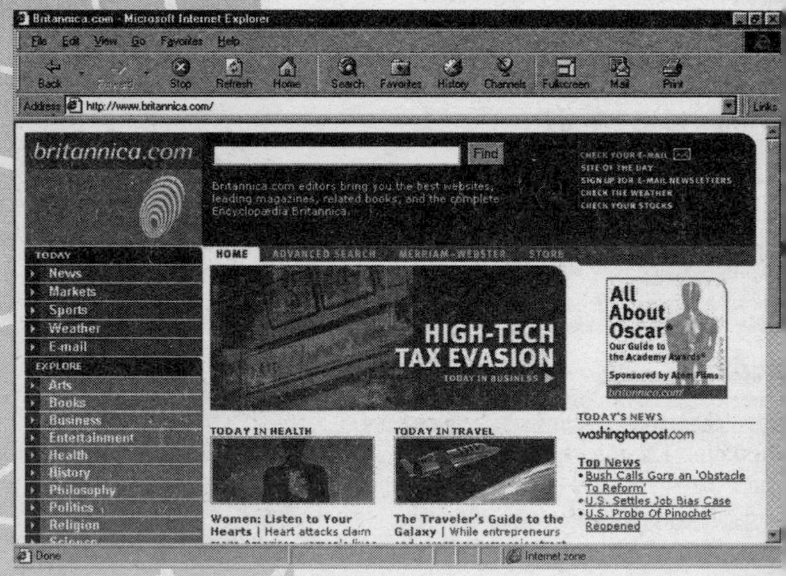

TOP SITE

Britannica On-Line

http://www.britannica.com/

Britannica.com editors bring you the best web sites, leading magazines, related books, and the complete *Encyclopaedia Britannica*. Go to advanced search and select the encyclopedia for the reference information.

Grolier

http://gme.grolier.com/

The *Grolier Multimedia Encyclopedia On-Line* is an affordable, authoritative reference solution that turns any Internet connection into a powerful information resource. It is the complete digital

Did You Know?

...that the Human Genome Project, a 15-year research effort to chemically identify the genes on human chromosomes, is "hosted" by the Internet? Scientists working on the project put gene-sequencing information on the net, allowing access to other scientists throughout the world.

ibrary for the twenty-first century. There is a fee to use he site's on-line information, and a free trial is available.

World Book

http://www.worldbookonline.com/

Updated regularly by *World Book* editors, this site features thousands of articles, maps, pictures, sounds, and video that are delivered to you over the web. *World Book*'s reference resources are supported by Behind the Headlines articles, calendar-based features, and the Learning Zone of extra teacher- and student-related resources.There is a fee and a thirty-day free trial as an option.

Columbia Encyclopedia

http://www.encyclopedia.com/

This site conveniently places an extraordinary amount of information at your fingertips. More than 14,000 articles from the *Concise Columbia Electronic Encyclopedia, Third Edition* have been assembled to provide free, quick, and useful information on almost any topic.

Research It

http://www.itools.com/research-it/

A collection of on-line research tools. Search dictionaries, translate words, find quotations, and more.

Club Net Reference

http://www.cncentral.com/ref.html

Links and reviews of reference sites on the net.

The Internet Public Library

http://www.ipl.org/

The Internet Public Library is the first public library of the Internet and a great hub of

Technical Museum

http://www.thetech.org/exhibits_events/online/

Great Buildings

http://www.greatbuildings.com/

Unusual Net Museums

http://www.wooden-nickel.net/museum/

How It Works

http://www.howstuffworks.com/

information on the web. It is serviced by librarians wh are committed to providing free and valuable services t the Internet community in the greatest tradition of publi libraries. Special attention is given to information fo teens and youth.

Dictionaries

Merriam-Webster On-Line

http://www.m-w.com/

Look up words in the on-line dictionary and thesauru: then check out fun extras like the daily Word Gam the Word for the Wise, and Word Central just for kid:

OneLook Dictionaries

http://www.onelook.com/

Links to over 600 dictionaries, including specialize subject ones. Enter your word and let this searc engine find you the definition.

Dictionaries

http://www.yourdictionary.com/
http://www.libraryspot.com/dictionaries.htm
http://www.lib.uwaterloo.ca/dictionaries.html
http://www.kidofun.com/Links/dictionary.htm
http://www.sapphireswan.com/webguide/wg/dictionary.htm

Links to Internet dictionaries.

LibrarySpot

http://www.libraryspot.com/

This is a virtual library resource center for ed cators and students, librarians and their patron families, businesses, and just about anyone exploring the web for valuable research information. The site was designed to break through the information overload of the web to bring the best library and reference sites together with insightful editorials in one convenient, user-friendly spot.

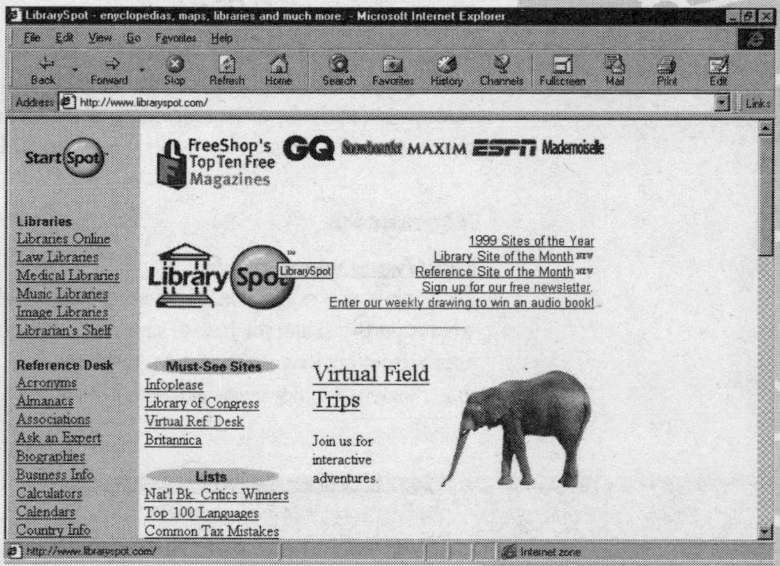

World Wide Web Virtual Library: Subject Cataloge

http://www.vlib.org/

The VL is the oldest catalog of the web. Unlike commercial catalogs, it is run by a loose confederation of volunteers, who compile pages of key links for particular areas in which they are experts; even though it isn't the biggest index of the web, the VL pages are widely recognized as being among the highest-quality guides to particular sections of the web.

eHow

http://www.ehow.com/home/home.asp

This site offers thousands of staff-written, reviewed, and edited step-by-step project solutions within fourteen activity categories, whether it's finding out how to change the oil in a car, make Cajun hot sauce, negotiate a raise, or even throw a knuckleball. Coupled with simple instructions, eHow.com offers printable shopping lists and direct links and directions to relevant shopping opportunities on each topic, so users can order the goods or services necessary to complete their tasks. Users are encouraged to contribute their own how-tos to the site, share tips and tricks for various topic entries, and participate in on-line chats.

Weeno.com

http://www.weeno.com/

Everyone is an "expert" on some topic. Come see what experts just like you have to say on a variety of topics from cooking and health to travel and hobbies. Share your knowledge and learn from others.

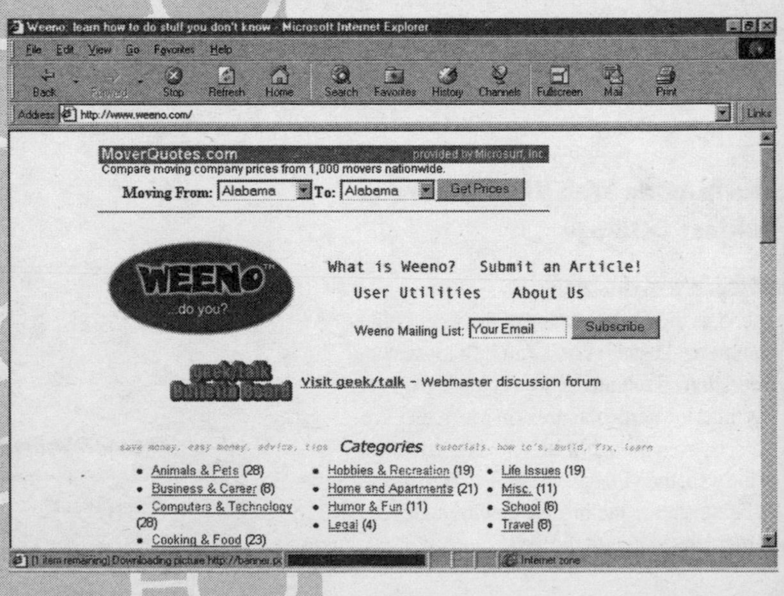

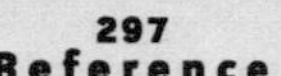

Christian Resource

http://www.ccel.org/

Many classic Christian works are available on-line. Surf over to the Christian Classics Ethereal Library to find many works, including those of: Augustine, Baxter, Calvin, Dante, Graham, Luther, Milton, Nee, Orr, Schaff, Watts. You'll even find classic literature online from great authors like Chesterton and Dostoevsky.

Did You Know?

...that in the U.S., people play on their home computers more in the East and work more on them in the South and West?

RELATIONSHIPS

Most of us are in many relationships. We're parents, children, friends, co-workers, and neighbors. Whenever people relate, there can be stressful conflicts that emerge. These sites help you identify and work on troubled areas, as well as give advice for improving your relationships. Even the healthiest relationships can be made stronger—and there are sites that can help you do that.

Relationships and Parenting

http://www.atthefence.com/

Find answers to tough relationship questions. New articles every month, new letters every week. Read questions and answers on file, or submit a personal question for an on-line answer.

Marriage Builders

http://www.marriagebuilders.com/

In this site, you will be introduced to ways to overcome marital conflicts and restore love. Read articles, join in the discussion forum, check out the question-and-answer column, visit the counseling center, and search for information on a variety of topics.

Ron Hutchcraft Ministries

http://www.gospelcom.net/rhm/

Provides practical answers to real-life issues. This site contains helpful information about issues that affect your life the most: relationships, family, parenting, stress, sex, and more.

FamilyLife

http://www.familylife.com/

A division of Campus Crusade for Christ, FamilyLife provides practical, biblical tools to strengthen marriage and family relationships.

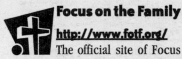

Focus on the Family

http://www.fotf.org/

The official site of Focus on the Family offers practical advice on marriage and raising children.

Gary Smalley's Marriage and Family Ministry

http://www.garysmalley.com/

This site's mission is to provide counseling, seminars, books, video and cassette tapes, and small-group curriculum on the topics of marriage and parenting.

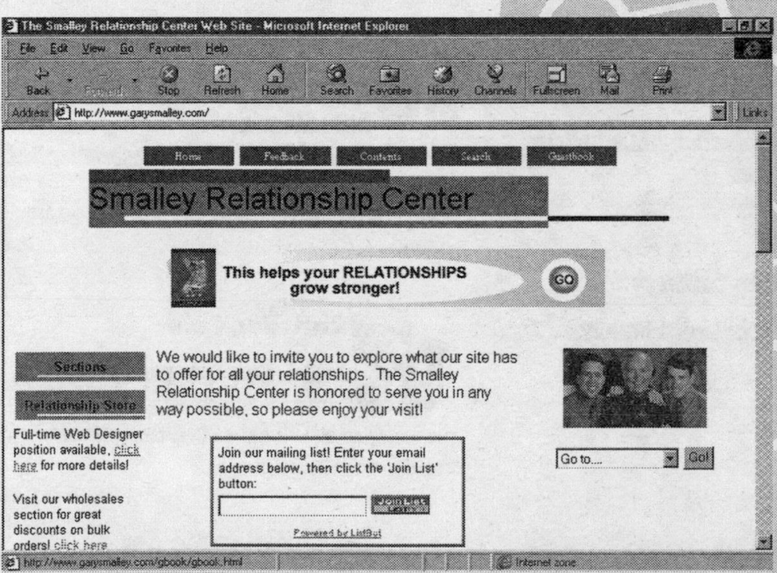

Tel-a-Teen

http://www.tel-a-teen.org/

If you're a teenager with a problem relationship, this site is a good place for you. Chat with trained peers and find a listening ear.

Today's Family Life

http://www.tfl.org/

A ministry dedicated to the prevention and restoration of broken relationships through radio programs, counseling and educational centers, seminars, and other resources.

WholeFamily Center

http://www.wholefamily.com/

The WholeFamily Center is an award-winning interactive site geared to everyone in every family. The site features an on-line magazine, as well as separate marriage, parenting, and teen centers.

Christian Courtship Resources

http://www-personal.monash.edu.au/~nate/christianity/courtship/

Links to resources on Christian courtship as well as original articles.

Christian Cafe

http://thechristiancafe.com/

Christian singles looking for love, romance, friends, fellowship, pen-pals, partners, and relationships in a virtual café.

Christian Singles Worldwide

http://www.christiansingles.com/

This site is dedicated to worldwide Christian singles who love the Lord Jesus Christ and are looking to walk with Him. Through this site, thousands of Christians can correspond with other Christians.

Academic Study

http://www.isspr.org/

Enriching Your Family

http://www.ianr.unl.edu/ianr/fcs/efr.htm

Christian Youth

http://www.tel-a-teen.org

Submit a Site

hudson@techie.com

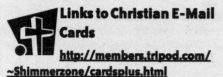

Christian Pen Pals for Kids, Teens, and Adults

http://www.christpages.net/singlechristians/

The Christian Pen Pals and Singles site is a free ads board for those seeking friendship, relationships, love, romance, or pen pals. Special sections for children, teens, and young adults.

Links to Christian E-Mail Cards

http://members.tripod.com/~Shimmerzone/cardsplus.html

It's hard to find free Christian-focused all-occasion electronic greeting cards to send on the Internet. This page has links to many sources of biblically based E-mail cards to send to anyone you care about.

RESTAURANTS

Sure, you can look up restaurants in the yellow pages, but yellow pages don't offer reviews, menu samples, or ratings.

Once on-line, however, you can select a restaurant, make reservations, and get driving directions.

With a resource like this, it will be easy to expand your list of favorite restaurants.

Yahoo! Restaurants

http://restaurants.yahoo.com/

Yahoo! Restaurants is your guide to information, reviews, and services for restaurants throughout the U.S.

Restaurants America

http://www.restaurantsamerica.com/

A listing of menus and restaurant guides from fine restaurants across America.

The Restaurant Home Pages

http://www.restaurant-pages.com/

Links to web sites from restaurants across the country and around the world. View information about their cuisine, locations, services, entertainment, reviews, take-out menus, products, and more. Search for restaurants in a particular region or search the site's database for restaurants by name, location, cuisine, price of a dinner, or by chef.

NetDiners Area Restaurant Guides

http://www.dine.com/

Check out reviews for restaurants in cities all over the world from visitors just like you.

411 Dining

http://www.411dining.com/

Search for a restaurant by city or by type of

cuisine. Links to help you get restaurant discount coupons, find a recipe, or purchase gifts. Also find information on specialty food outlets.

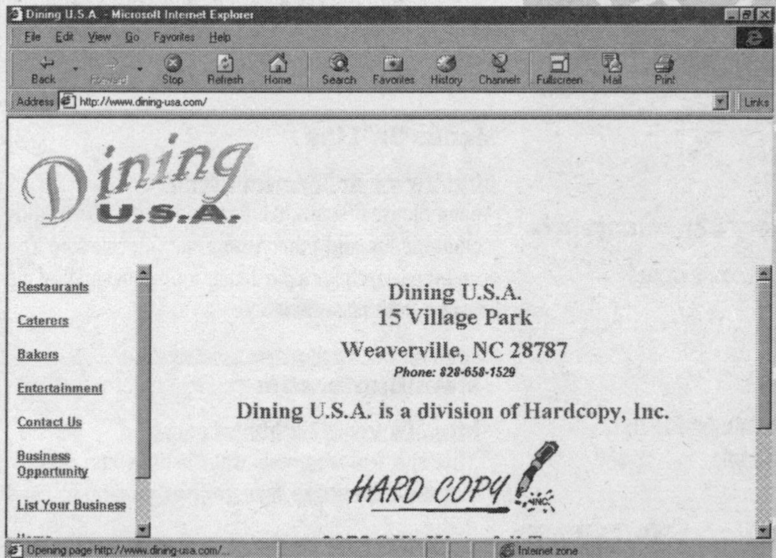

Restaurant Row Dining Guide

http://www.restaurantrow.com/

Search this restaurant guide by location, food type, ambiance, features, and entertainment.

DineSite

http://www.dinesite.com/

This dining directory links menus on a nationwide level. Give and read reviews. Rate experiences. Guide includes celebrity- and cool-theme restaurants.

Did You Know?

...that 68 percent of on-line buyers are over the age of forty?

Directory of Restaurants

http://www.go.com/

Miami

http://miami.diningguide.net/dt2nwc.htm

California & Colorado

http://www.restauranteur.com/

New Jersey & New York

http://www.powerpg.com/

Florida

http://gulfcoastflorida.com/wcfrest.html

Maryland

http://www.marylandrestaurants.org/

United States Dining Guide

http://www.dining-us.com/oindex.cfm

Here you can search the thousands of restaurants in the United States by restaurant name, county, town, cuisine, or price to find the restaurant of your choice. You can also browse the featured restaurants as well as consumer reviews.

Menus On-Line

http://www.onlinemenus.com/

An interactive restaurant information service providing actual menus and other restaurant information. You can even search for a particular food item and find the restaurants that serve it.

MenuHunter.com

http://www.menuhunter.com/

This site features restaurant listings and menus, nutritrional info, recipes, reviews, cookbooks, and more.

World Wide Sushi Restaurant Reference

http://www.cis.unisa.edu.au/~jm/Sushi/

Check out the list of sushi restaurant references, comment on your sushi experience, or learn more about this delicacy.

Diner City

http://www.dinercity.com/

A guide to America's classic diners and roadside architecture. Listings by state include photos, street maps, and menus.

Food.com

http://www.food.com/

The Internet's take-out and delivery service. Quick and efficient, this site is personalized to show you restaurants that will service your address. Food.com allows customers to browse menus on-line, find restaurants in their neighborhoods, see daily specials, and even order their meals hours, days, or weeks in advance.

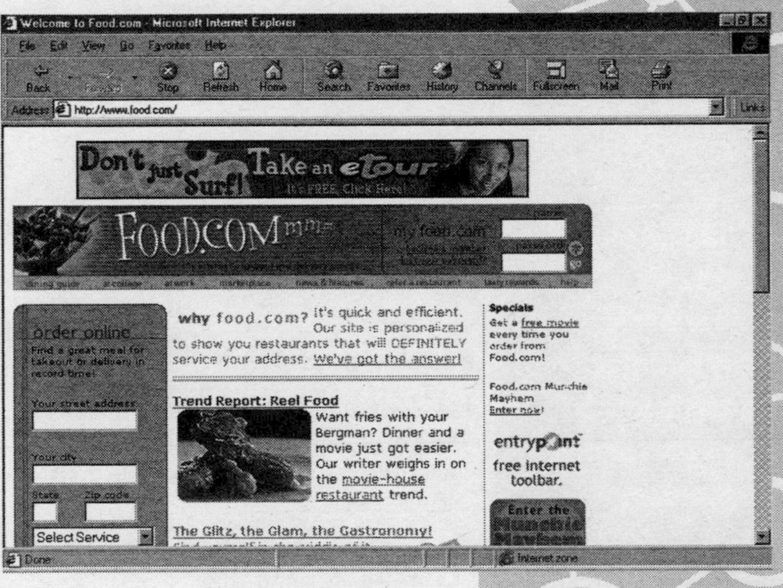

Did You Know?

...that Douglas Engelbart developed the first working hypertext system in 1968? He also invented the graphical user interface and the computer mouse.

REUNIONS

These services on the web can help you

- plan a high school or college reunion,
- track down birth parents,
- find children once adopted,
- reunite with old military buddies,
- and keep in touch with special friends throughout the years.

Connect here in your efforts to stay connected.

Reunions R Us

http://www.gemneye.com/reunions/reunions.html

List your reunion information for free.

ReunionNet

http://www.reunited.com/

A global reunion resource. List your reunion, find reunion products and services, check out reunion-related links, and locate lost friends.

Reunion Research

http://www.reuniontips.com/

This site provides general tips for planning large group reunions. Includes recommended places and other resources.

ClassReunionSearch

http://www.classreunionsearch.com/

This site helps to bring high school classes back together at, and between, reunion time by providing on-line storage of E-mail, phone, and address information.

High School Class Reunions On-Line

http://www.reunionsworld.com/

Their services include reunion web sites and announcements, class directory listings, personal pages, and lost friends and missing persons registries. School reunion database included.

Reunion Network

http://www.reunionfriendly.com/default.html
This site provides a wide variety of resources to help military, voluntary, and family reunion planners throughout the United States.

Reunion Registry: The Difference

http://www.geocities.com/thedifference/
Find free resources for those wishing to reunite—registry, search tools, current news, and more.

Find Me

http://www.findme-registry.com/
A reunion and search registry for adoptees, siblings, birth mothers, and all birth-family members. A private post office enables everyone to participate while protecting the identity of its registrants.

BigHugs: The Magazine

http://www.bighugs.com/mag/
A collection of reunion stories, search services, and advice on reunions, finding missing family and friends, including adoption-related news and topics.

Reunions Magazine

http://www.reunionsmag.com/
Reunions magazine is dedicated to the joy of family, class, and military reunions and everyone who is searching for a reunion—adoption, genealogy, and lost loves. Content focuses on reunion organizing and searching, and helping organizers be well-educated and wise reunion consumers.

Other Links

http://invites.yahoo.com/

http://www.reunionco.com/

http://www.reunionsunlimited.net/

http://www.reunionpro.com/

http://www.greatreunions.com/

http://www.signaturereunions.com/

http://www.reunionswithclassinc.com/

http://www.reunionsmag.com/

http://www.cyndislist.com/reunions.htm

http://www.reunionsunlimited.net/

http://www.reunions.com/

Seeker: Reuniting America

http://www.the-seeker.com/

A magazine helping to reunite America with family, friends, military, and beneficiaries.

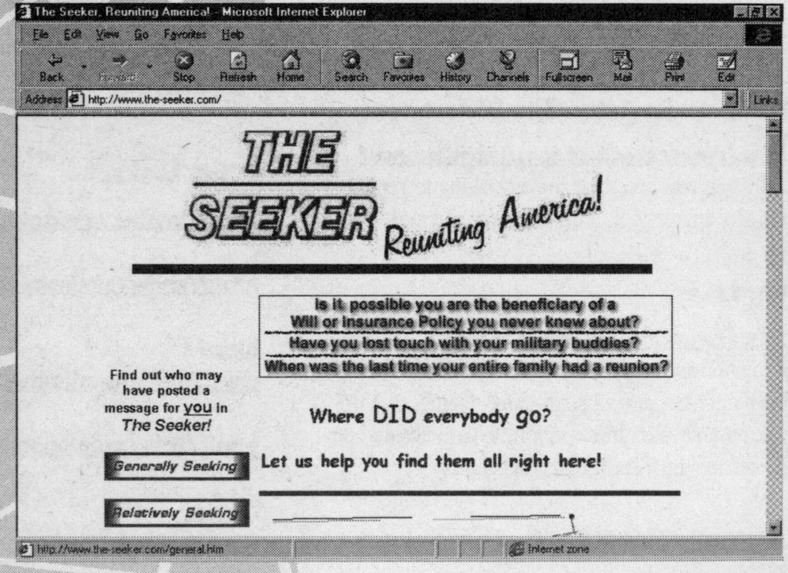

Did You Know?

...that new Internet video conferencing technology can eliminate on-line anonymity, possibly ushering in an era in which coworkers, friends and total strangers can enter each others' worlds with the click of a mouse?

SCIENCE

Christian Students in Science

http://www.csis.org.uk/

Christian Students in Science is a U.K.-based organization set up to promote discussion in the student community on issues relating to science and faith. This site has on-line papers and discussions about faith and science, books to read on-line, and places to ask science-related questions.

Christian Organization

http://asa.calvin.edu/ASA/

The American Scientific Affiliation (ASA) is a fellowship of men and women of science and disciplines that relate to science who share a common fidelity to the Word of God and a commitment to integrity in the practice of science.

Reasons to Believe

http://www.reasons.org/

Reasons To Believe was founded in 1986 to:

- Remove the doubts of skeptics
- Strengthen the faith of believers
- Demonstrate that science and the Bible complement one another

The mission of Reasons To Believe is to show that science and faith are, and always will be,

A topic like science is a biggie. There are specific topics for every specific branch of science. In trying to narrow your search, the best way to start is at a search engine like http://www.yahoo.com/. Search for science and then choose one of the many subcategories it offers.

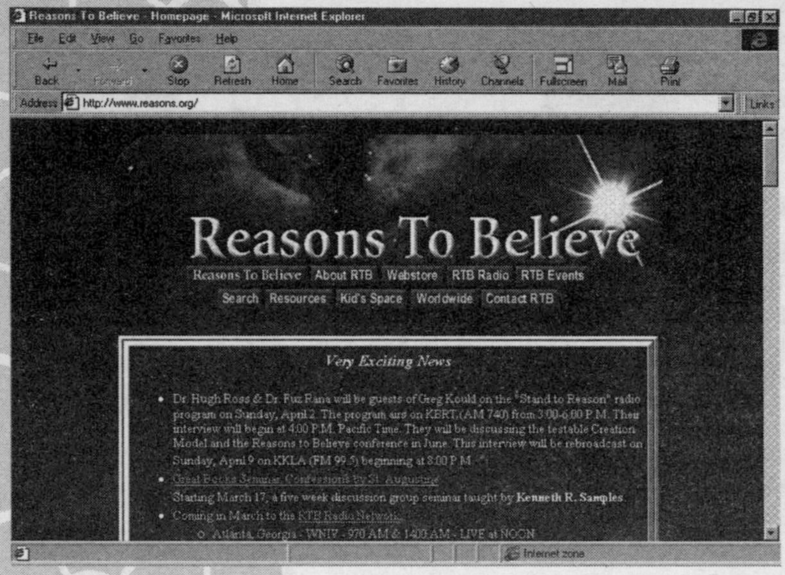

allies, not enemies. This site's mission is to bring that life-changing truth to as many people as possible, both believers and unbelievers.

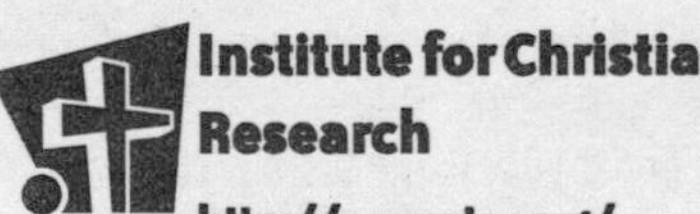

Institute for Christian Research

http://www.icr.org/

The Institute for Christian Research, which has a very vocal position on creation, is devoted to research, publication, and teaching in those fields of science particularly relevant to the study of origins.

Did You Know?

...that the ENIAC, the first electronic computer, appeared fifty years ago, was about 80 feet long, weighed 30 tons, and had 17,000 tubes? By comparison, a desktop computer today can store a million times more information than an ENIAC and is 50,000 times faster.

For Kids

Science Learning Network

http://www.sln.com/

The Science Learning Network helps make

science fun for kids. This site links you to many other sites and helps kids appreciate the world they live in. principle objectives are to involve children in the creative process of science and to help children see how science relates to their lives.

Kids Zone

http://www.pfizerfunzone.com/

This fun site, created by the Pfizer drug company, is for children ages eight to thirteen. It's a place to learn about the science of medicine, play games, and do experiments at home.

Other Links

http://outcast.gene.com/ae/AE/AEC/AEF/

http://outcast.gene.com/ae/AE/ATG/text_files.html

http://biotech.chem.indiana.edu/

http://www.cellsalive.com/

http://www.uq.oz.au/nanoworld/images_1.html

http://www.who.ch/outbreak/outbreak_home.html

http://gto.ncsa.uiuc.edu/pingleto/lobby.html

http://sln2.fi.edu/biosci/heart.html

http://www.vis.colostate.edu/library/gva/gva.html

SEARCH ENGINES

Search engines help you locate a specific site or a many sites on a specific topic. Since each engine searches the web in its own unique way, you'll find that each engine provides slightly different results. Most people find that they have continued success using one particular engine. Try them all to find which one you prefer.

Christian Worldwide Directory

http://www.cwd.com

The CWD is a global Christian marketplace showcasing the most up-to-date products, services, and resources for the Christian community. Whether you are a pastor, church leader, or parent, you can locate companies that will meet your present and future needs to enhance the growth of your "family." Categories include church music, church, homeschool, education, and family resources.

Christian Shopping Mall

http://www.christianet.com/

The Christian Businesses Mall is designed to assist Christians in locating products and services. You will find over 500 Christian business storefronts in over 100 categories.

Christian Links

http://www.christianlinks.com/

Christian Links will help you locate other Christian web sites on the Internet. Christian Links was designed to provide access to thousands of Christian businesses dealing with commerce, computers, devotionals, education, general interest, literature and art, magazines, ministries, missionaries, music and radio, sports and fitness, TV, and youth.

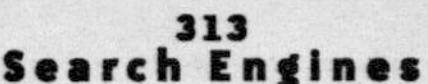

Christian Only

http://www.his-net.com/

His-Net is your source to helpful and edifying Christian web sites that glorify Jesus Christ. Find sites dedicated to Bible study, minsitries, and pastors' helps.

Christian Portal

http://www.711.net/

This site focuses on being a reliable, dependable, and efficient "point of entry" as you search the vast resources of churches, ministries, denominations, organizations, associations, home schools, educational institutions, and the incredible number of products and services by businesses supporting and benefiting the Christian community.

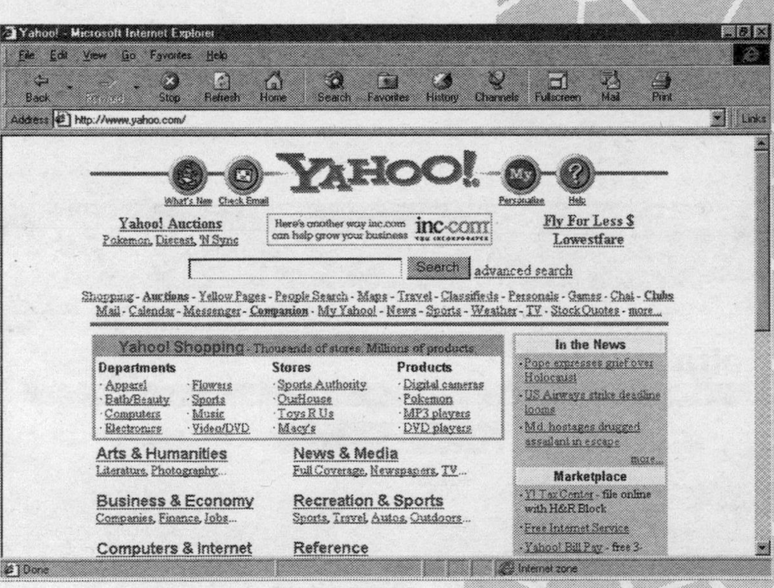

Metasearches

Six Searches in One

http://www.infind.com/

InferenceFind is a metasearch engine. Its search results are generated from calls to other search engines on the web. It's a search tool that calls out in parallel all the best search engines on the Internet, merges the results, removes redundancies, and clusters the results into neat understandable groupings. Finds queries on six search engines on the web, but can be configured to call any search engine. Currently finding results from WebCrawler, Yahoo, Lycos, AltaVista, InfoSeek, and Excite.

Metacrawler

http://www.metacrawler.com/i

This site uses nine search engines to comb the web, auctions, and newsgroups.

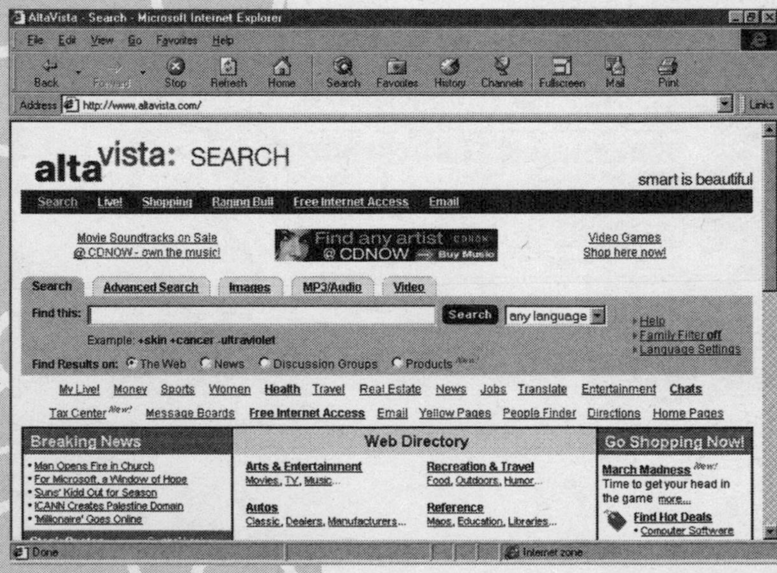

Twenty Searches, One Key Stroke

http://www.savvysearch.com/

A site owned by CNET, this metasearch service allows you to search twenty search engines at the same time.

TOP SITE Classic Search Engines

http://www.yahoo.com
http://www.deja.com
http://www.altavista.com
http://www.hotbot.com
http://www.directhit.com
http://www.excite.com

Many people learn to prefer one search engine over another. Try them all and find the one that best finds the results you're looking for.

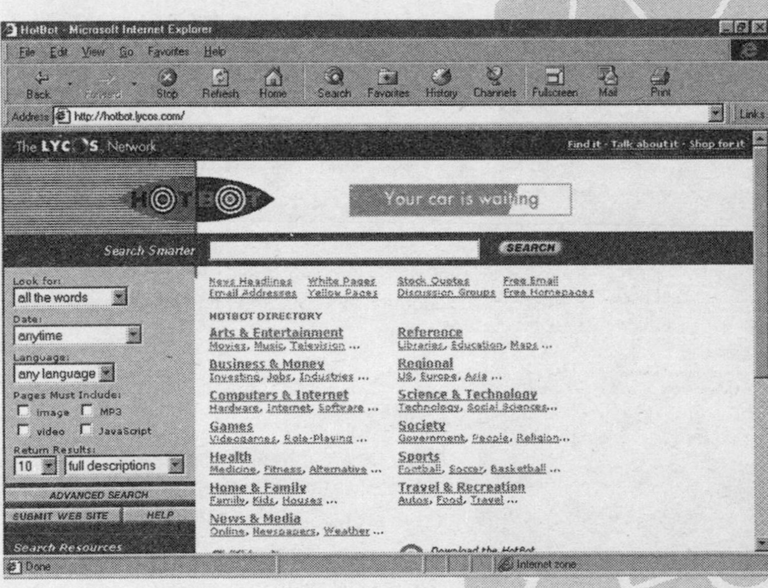

SENIOR'S GUIDE

Seniors are some of the fastest-growing users of the Internet. In addition to other sites listed in this book, these sites are designed to help meet the specific social, living, and health needs of seniors.

AARP

http://www.aarp.org/

AARP is the nation's leading organization for people ages fifty and older. It serves their needs and interests through information and education, advocacy, and community services which are provided by a network of local chapters and experienced volunteers throughout the country. The organization also offers members a wide range of special benefits and services, including *Modern Maturity* magazine and the monthly *Bulletin*.

Government Recommendations

http://www.aoa.dhhs.gov/

Here's the U.S. government's Administration on Aging. Here's the place to find the government's current pending legislation and health recommendations for seniors.

Links Galore

http://www.ageofreason.com/

This site has over 5,000 links to web sites of interest to people ages fifty and over. Sites are organized under category such as travel, government, politics, and sports.

Age Venture News Service

http://www.demko.com/

A news and information source reporting on

lifestyles of boomers and retirees. Services include mature market headlines, syndicated feature columns, personal profiles, and links to Internet resources.

Providing Care

http://www.elderweb.com/
This award-winning site is the oldest and largest eldercare sourcebook on the web. It is a research site for professionals and family members, with a collection of over 5,000 on-site and off-site articles about eldercare and long term care, including legal, financial, medical, and housing issues, as well as policy, research, and statistics.

Focus on the Family

http://www.fotf.org/
This well-known Christian organization includes a ministry to boomers and seniors.

Canada's Seniors

http://www.fifty-plus.net/
Four hundred thousand members have joined this organization—Canada's Association for Retired Persons. Like the AARP, this organization is open to people fifty and older.

News for Seniors

http://www.senior-center.com/
Late-breaking news especially for senior citizens. Featured areas on this site can help you improve your health, wealth, home, cooking, gardening, and more.

Senior Search Engine

http://www.seniorssearch.com/
Here's a search engine that limits its search to those sites of interest to those who are fifty and older.

Other Links

http://www.imall.com/stores/haciendahealthcare/haciendahealthcare6.html

http://www.bancroft.igs.net/Senior_Centre/senior_centre/

Senior Law

http://www.nsclc.org/

National Council

http://www.ncscinc.org/

Hud's Site

http://www.hud.gov/senior.html

Senior Lifestyle

http://www.ezrail.com/

FAVORITE LINKS

Senior Radio

http://www.wiredseniors.com/christianradio/home.htm

This site links you to over fifty Christian radio stations of special interest to seniors. On this site you will also find links to favorite old-time radio shows, history radio, and audio books.

SHOPPING

You can buy *almost* anything on-line. Why fight crowds if you can have each item shipped to you at a discount? For starters, you can quickly buy groceries, furniture, clothing, jewelry, toys, CDs, software, and computers. If you can buy it, you can probably buy it on-line.

BuyCentral

http://www.buycentral.com/
Utilize this shopping guide featuring a store locator and price/product comparison engine.

eSmarts

http://www.esmarts.com/
Find tips for on-line shopping, message boards, coupons, and links to select merchants.

Connect On-Line Shopping

http://www.top20shopping.com/
A directory of shopping web sites for apparel, accessories, food, flowers, home/garden, and more.

800America.com

http://www.800america.com/
Find links to on-line shopping organized into more than twenty categories.

ShopServe.com

http://www.shopserve.com/users/searchmain.asp
A merchant directory with buyer-based rankings. Check out buyers' gripes and get Internet shopping advice.

Safe Shopper

http://www.safershopper.com/

This site has tips for shopping safely on-line, a monthly newsletter, and a directory of safe shopping sites.

StoreSearch

http://www.storesearch.com/

You can locate stores by selecting multiple search criteria to target products, locations, brands, and stores.

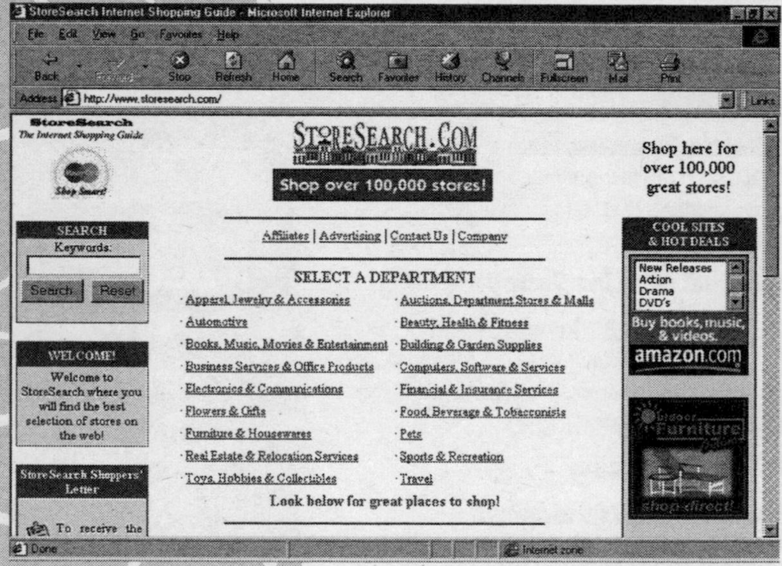

Public Eye

http://www.thepubliceye.com/

Public Eye tests, certifies, and monitors Internet businesses for reliability. Offers a directory of certified safe-shopping web sites.

Better Business Bureau

http://www.bbbonline.org/consumers/safesurfing.html
This site offers shopping tips, consumer information, and assistance. It also has sections on spam and scams.

SafeShopping.org

http://www.safeshopping.org/
This site was created by the American Bar Association to help protect and educate consumers about the legal and practical issues involved in on-line shopping.

E-Commerce and the Internet

http://www.ftc.gov/bcp/menu-internet.htm
Get sound advice from the Federal Trade Commission on how to keep your Internet transactions safe, secure, and private.

Time to Shop!

TOP SITE

Yahoo!Shopping

http://shopping.yahoo.com/
Find thousands of stores and millions and products—and you can shop them all at this one site. Features stores like Eddie Bauer, Sports Authority, Toys R Us, and Macys. Search for products by word with the search engine feature, or use the topical directory to look for everything from apparel to travel.

Mall.com

http://www.mall.com/
Laid out visually like an actual mall, Mall.com is a premier on-line shopping mall facilitating E-commerce by bringing consumers and

Accessories

http://www.ashford.com/

http://www.firstjewelry.com/

http://www.ties.com/

http://www.luggageonline.com/

http://www.sunglasses.com/

Catalog Shopping

http://www.jcrew.com/

http://www.llbean.com/

http://www.eddiebauer.com/

http://www.landsend.com/

merchants together in an interactive and entertaining community. You can find most of your favorite stores here in this one spot.

Shop4.com

http://www.shop4.com/

Shop4.com can get you almost anything you want at up to 60% off Manufacturer's Suggested List Price. Over 500,000 of the best products available. Everything from household appliances, electronics, furniture, tools, jewelry, sporting goods, and much more.

iQVC

http://www.iqvc.com/index.html

QVC has always stood for Quality, Value, and Convenience to its customers nationwide. Now check out their QVC on-line interactive shopping division. Find collectibles, toys, fashion, jewelry, home furnishings—all that and more.

Buy.com

http://www.buy.com/

Buy.com offers the latest computer hardware and software, the newest releases of videos and DVDs, the hottest console and PC games, chart-topping music CD's and the top selling books all at guaranteed everyday low prices. With BuyClearance.com you can save even more on closeout items. Their new design features a state-of-the-art search engine, and gives you the control to track your shipments 24 hours a day.

SKI REPORTS

Ski resorts have quickly networked to use the power of the web. Check these sites to read of snow conditions, see up-to-the-minute pictures of the slopes, or purchase the equipment you need.

TOP SITE

Ski Maps

http://www.skimaps.com/

Complete ski information with trail maps, the ski resort locator, snow reports lodging, shopping for ski gear, ski videos, and ski travel. Also find skiing vacation packages as well as snowfall and weather reports.

Search Engine for Skiers

http://www.ski-search.com

Comprehensive, detailed guide to ski and snowboarding resorts in Spain, Italy, USA, Canada, Andorra, Austria, Bulgaria, Canada, France, Norway, Scotland, and South America.

Ski Resorts

http://skiresorts.com/snowreports/

A worldwide directory of ski resorts featuring travel information and on-line booking services. This particular page gives detailed snow reports so you can compare different slopes in the same area.

Ski Europe

http://www.ski-europe.com/s-report.html

This site focuses on skiing and its conditions in Europe. Here's where you can learn more about different areas, find travel packages, and ask questions about Europe's best slopes.

Snow Reports

http://www.onthesnow.com/

Hourly updated snow news about local, national, and international ski areas including snow conditions, five-day weather forecast, news, free prizes, equipment reviews, free classified ads, and discounts. Web cams allow you to actually see live pictures of the slopes.

Christian Travel Agent

http://www.oakhall.clara.net/

Christian travel company dedicated to providing summer expeditions and winter ski holidays around the world.

DID YOU KNOW?

...that the "save" icon on Microsoft Word shows a floppy disk with the shutters on backwards?

Ski Equipment

Family Owned

http://www.csskiequipment.com

A family-owned and run sports equipment store

designed so that you don't need to pay specialty-store prices for simple accessories.

Snowshack

http://www.snowshack.com/

Your on-line shopping source for ski and other snow sports accessories direct from the manufacturers. Kids' equipment is available, too, as well as a toll-free number for questions.

Bargain Hunting

http://www.bargainsports.net/

Not in the market for brand-new? Try quality used equipment from Play It Again Sports. This is a web page from the chain store.

Did You Know?

...that in 1993 the large network service providers America Online and Delphi started to connect their proprietary E-mail systems to the Internet, beginning the large-scale adoption of Internet E-mail as the global standard?

SMALL BUSINESS

There's lots of help for you if you already run a small business. The challenges you face seem unique, but there is good support. Try these sites to find the tax forms, ideas, resources you need, or help moving your business from red to black.

Yahoo Message Boards

http://messages.yahoo.com/yahoo/Business_and_Finance/Small_Business/

Yahoo hosts message boards on many topics interesting to small business owners. Browse through this site to find the topics that most interest you.

Need a Checklist?

http://www.toolkit.cch.com/

Great, well-organized information covering everything from how to start a small business to advice. Download checklists, model business plans, forms, and other documents you need every day.

Bloomberg

http://www.bloomberg.com/business/

Business tips of the week, articles from Fast Company. Bloomberg's site has teamed up with Let's Talk Business. Their goal is to provide an entrepreneurial support community and to increase the success rate of small business owners around the world.

Motivation

http://edge.lowe.org/

Help with financial questions, human resources leadership, management, legal issues, marketing, sales, and technology. This site is designed o be a peer-learning community for growing your small ɔusiness.

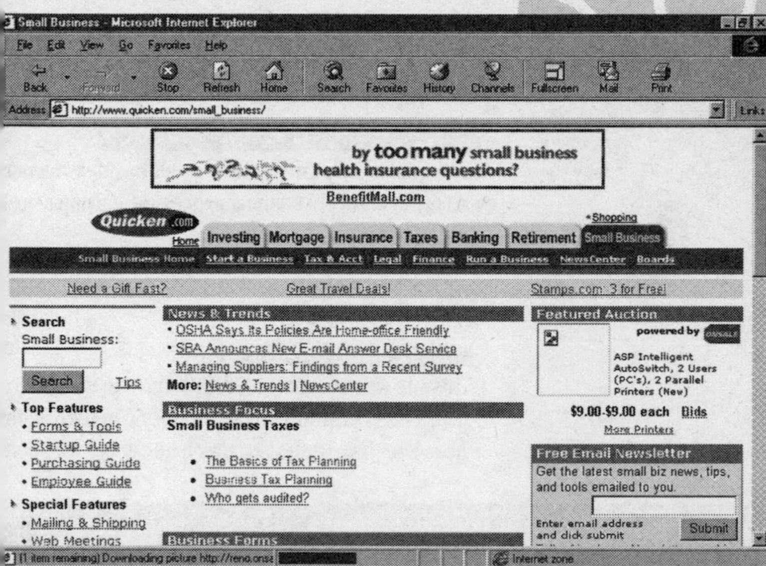

Quicken

http://www.quicken.com/small_business/

When it comes to money, think *Quicken*. This is one of the top money sites, period. Following the web address above will help ou with the money questions about your small usiness.

Expert Advice

http://www.allbusiness.com/

Covering business, financing, law, technology, nd other issues for entrepreneurs and growng businesses. Features expert advice, on-line ools, downloadable forms, and other esources.

Submit a Site
hudson@techie.com

The Home Business

http://www.homebusinessresearch.com/

The site has tutorials, research, resources, software, an newsgroups—all dedicated to people running small businesses out of their homes.

Starting a Businesss

http://www.inreach.com/sbdc/book/

Developed to help prospective small business owner with the often-overwhelming process of starting a business.

Idea Exchange

http://www.ideacafe.com/

This site was created with the premise that entrepreneurs need critical info fast, so they can take actio now. They hate textbooks; they hate people who don

know what it's like trying to tell them what to do. If that describes you, log on to Idea Café to find a fun approach to serious business.

http://www.sbaonline.sba.gov/nonprofit/

http://www.onlinewbc.org

http://www.sba.gov/

http://www.geocities.com/WallStreet/2172

Did You Know?

...that in February 1975 Bill Gates and Paul Allen licensed their newly written BASIC to MITS, their first customer? This was the first computer language program written for a personal computer.

SOCIAL RESEARCH

Many people have occupations that require them to keep track of public interest, opinions, and trends. People in ministry, marketing, sales, teaching, or training will find these sites helpful in staying ahead of the trends in society.

Population

http://www.census.gov/

The census studies conducted by the U.S. government as the information becomes available.

TOP SITE

Social Trends

http://www.gallup.com/

The world leader in the measurement and analysis of people's attitudes, opinions, and behavior.

Christian Research

http://www.barna.org/

Barna Research Group, Ltd. is a full-service marketing research company providing information and analysis regarding cultural trends and the Christian church since 1984. Many archives and studies are available for review on-line.

How Happy Are We?

http://www.eur.nl/fsw/research/happiness/

Here's an ongoing register of research on subjective appreciation of life. Includes a bibliography, statistics of happiness by country, and abstracts of correlational research findings.

Sociology

FAVORITE LINKS

Sociology and Anthropology Sites

http://www.socioweb.com/~markbl/socioweb/

The SocioWeb is an independent guide to the sociological resources available on the Internet.

Yale Library

http://www.library.yale.edu/Internet/sociology.html

Links to on-line discussion lists for sociology. Also included are a list of Yale on-line databases relevant to sociology, an alphabetical listing of sociology associations, organizations, and societies, links to sociology departments worldwide, and Yale Social Science Statistical Laboratory.

Socialogical Tour Through the Web

http://www.trinity.edu/~mkearl/

Here's a site loaded with information in its own right, with links to other sites throughout the net. Also a member of the Sociological Webring, a ring dedicated to sociological professionals and research. Start here, then go through the ring.

Sociology Links

http://www.abacon.com/sociology/soclinks/

This site simply links you to other, more specific sites. Start here if you have a specific topic in mind. You're likely to find the links you need.

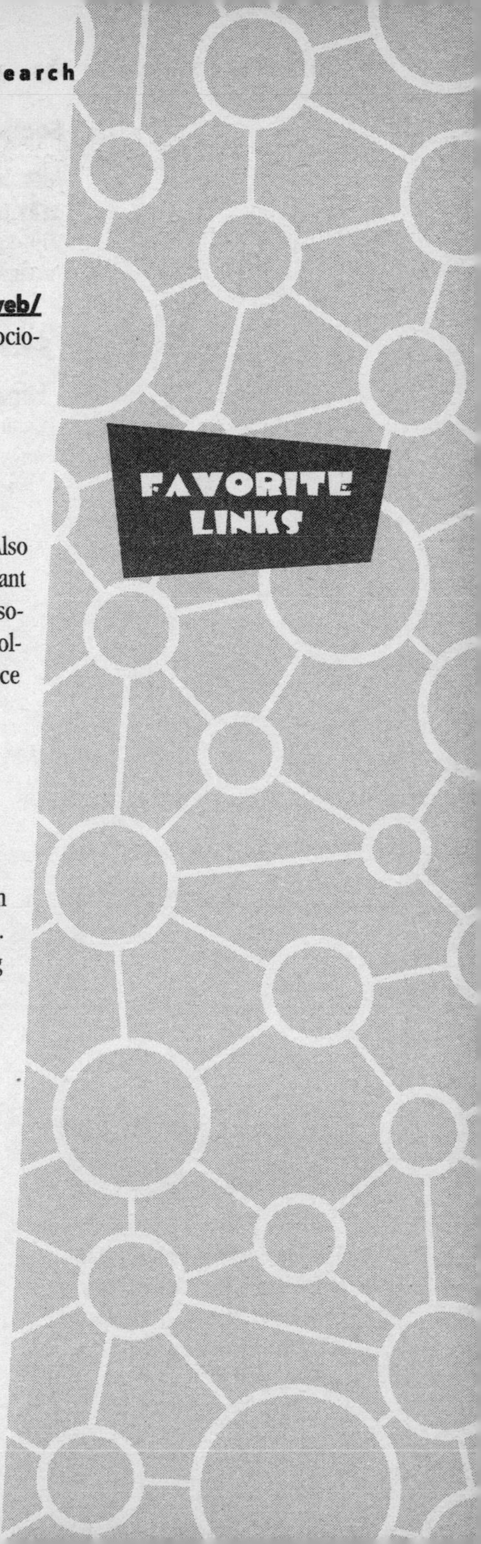

Sociological Library

http://www.mcmaster.ca/socscidocs/w3virtsoclib/index.htm

Surfing this site is like browsing a local library that has an extensive reference section on sociology.

Sociological Dictionary

http://www.iversonsoftware.com/sociology/

Getting lost in sociological terminology? This site defines common terms and concepts.

Did You Know?

...that the first program that Bill Gates wrote was too big to fit in the computer's memory at the time? The PC had 16KB of RAM and his program required 34KB.

SPACE & ASTRONOMY

God told Abraham that his descendants would be as numerous as the stars in the sky. While we still can't count them, we know more than ever before about the those celestial bodies. These sites will help you learn your constellations and cruise God's gallery in the sky.

Explore Space

http://www.finderscope.com/

Information on where and how to observe some of the most interesting objects in the sky, using a variety of techniques. Learn more about all the things you can see in the sky, from stars, constellations, and galaxies to the sun and moon. Find listing of local clubs and organizations.

Frequently Asked Questions About Space

http://www.ksc.nasa.gov/facts/facts.html

Links pointing you to answers.

Space & Flight Launch Pad

http://www.spaceandflight.com/

This site is designed to give you the latest news and informational sites related to the topics of space exploration, astronomy, and aviation. Go for a fascinating journey through the solar system as well as take to the skies for a friendly flight. Send electronic greetings or go to the Space & Flight Message Board Area to talk with others having your interests. Also has special links for kids and teens.

TOP SITE

NASA Human Space Flight

http://spaceflight.nasa.gov/index-m.html

This is an access point to the vast amount of information about NASA's human exploration and development of space. Features include space news and history, real-time data, ask an expert, and a gallery of images, videos, and audio clips.

Links for Kids

http://astroplace.com/

With links for kids, amateurs, and pros, this site has something special for everyone. You can also find information on women in astronomy. Do you have questions? You can ask an astronomer here.

Did You Know?

...that from the smallest microprocessor to the biggest mainframe, the average American depends on over 264 computers per day?

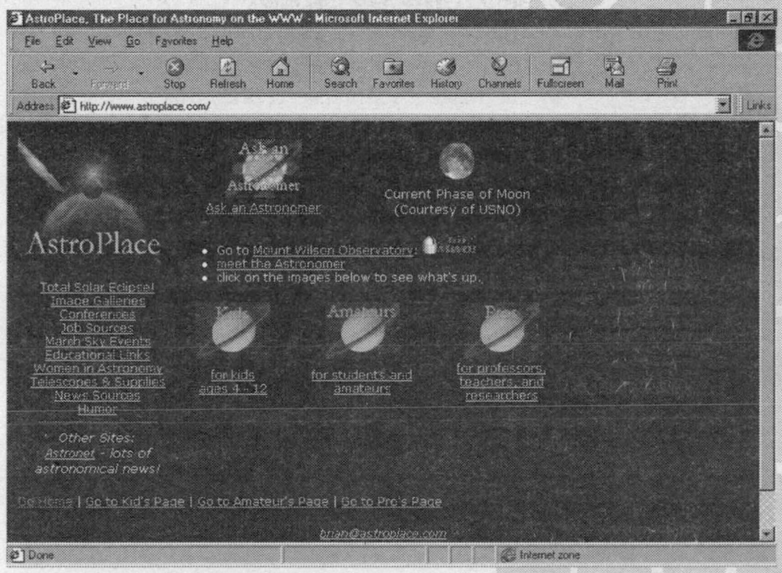

Views of the Solar System

http://www.solarviews.com/

A solar system learning guide for people of all ages, this site presents a vivid multimedia adventure unfolding the splendor of the sun, planets, moons, comets, asteroids, and more. Discover the latest scientific information or study the history of space exploration, rocketry, early astronauts, space missions, and spacecraft through a vast archive of photographs, scientific facts, text, graphics, and videos. Views of the solar system offer enhanced exploration and educational enjoyment of the solar system and beyond.

More Solar System Links

http://astronomy-mall.com/hotlinks/solar.htm

Looking for information on the solar system? You'll find lots of links here to check out.

FAVORITE LINKS

Extraterrestrial Intelligence?

http://www.seti-inst.edu/

The SETI Institute serves as an institutional home for scientific and educational projects relevant to the nature, distribution, and prevalence of life in the universe. Everything you ever wanted to know about the search for life on other planets can be found here.

SPECIAL EDUCATION

Learning doesn't come naturally to all kids. If you're the parent or teacher of someone who needs a little extra help, you can begin to find the support and ideas you may be looking for at these sites.

Special Education Resources on the Internet

http://www.hood.edu/seri/serihome.htm

This is a collection of Internet-accessible resources for those involved in special education. This collection exists in order to make on-line special education resources more easily and readily available in one location; it is continually modified and updated to add additional links.

Federal Resource Center for Special Education

http://www.dssc.org/frc/

This organization helps regional resource centers improve programs, policies, and practices. At this site you can find providers of special education technical assistance and an organized, abstracted list of education-related hyperlinks—plus much more.

Special Needs Opportunity Windows

http://snow.utoronto.ca/

SNOW is a project aimed at supporting educators of students with special needs and at developing innovative ways for learners with special needs to electronically access curriculum materials. This web site serves as a clearinghouse of practical resources and curriculum materials, as a place for educators to meet and share ideas, and as a place for educators to develop their professional skills. Also, links to SNOW Kids, a sister site with activities for young people with special needs.

http://www.iser.com/

http://www.familyvillage.wisc.edu/index.htmlx

http://www.spedex.com

http://www.awesomelibrary.org

http://www.nichcy.org

TOP SITE

Learning Disabilities On-Line

http://www.ldonline.org/

An interactive guide to learning disabilites for parents, teachers, and children. Includes an Ask-the-Expert feature.

Schwab Foundation for Learning

http://www.schwablearning.org/

This web site provides information and resources for all parents, educators, and other professionals who are making a difference in the lives of kids who struggle with learning.

Instant Access Treasure Chest

http://www.fln.vcu.edu/ld/ld.html

A treasure trove of links to web sites and articles on a variety of topics related to learning disabilities.

SPORTS

Total Sports

TOP SITE

http://Sports.yahoo.com/

You want it; they've got it. Up-to-the minute scores. Live audio coverage daily. Video highlights and photo gallery. Expert columns from Sporting News, CNNSports Illustrated. Message boards, clubs, and sports chat. Daily trivia quiz and quote. Shopping and auctions for gear and collectibles. Links to other sports sites. For each sport you'll find information like standings, stats, calendar, and player info—as well as information and links to pages for professional teams. Also features coverage of sporting events from around the world, and sports fantasy games.

Fox Sports

http://www.foxsports.com/

Scoreboards. High school and world sports. Video highlights. Player information. Transactions. Message boards. A marketplace where you can buy team gear and more. Check out regional coverage. Play sports fantasy games. What more could you want? How about the FOXsports.com's GameTracker? With GameTracker, you can get up-to-the-pitch information without having to huddle next to the transistor radio hidden under your desk. Want to know when Mark McGwire goes deep? GameTracker tells you. It lets you view what's going on in the stadium and gives you information on the players and plays as they happen.

Combine the "age of information" with sports and you end up with a sports fanatic's dream. If you have Internet access, you're always just one click away from finding the latest scores, trades, or news. Some of these sites even let you listen to the game live, while Foxsports.com lets you watch a simulation of the game as you're listening. If you're a sports lover, settle in for a long evening.

ESPN.com

http://espn.go.com/

The place to go for sports information. For the latest info, you can read the headline news, top stories, featured columns, or scores. Check out the live ESPN radio, listen to the audio highlights, or view the video highlights. Participate in the contests, polls, message boards, or chat. Go to the Sports Century section for a countdown to the millennium and salute to the greatest North American athletes of the 20th century. Looking for more sports fun? Play the arcade games or purchase tickets to a real game.

Crosswalk Sports

http://sports.crosswalk.com/

This Christian site is loaded with information and features. You can click on the sport/organization (such as golf, tennis, or the NHL, NBA, MLB, etc.) of your choice for news, articles, and info. Or check out the scoreboards (including a live scores sports ticker), team pages, stats, transactions, and more. Find daily quotes, verses, and devotionals. Check out testimonies of well-known athletes, listen to the audio, or view the video clips. Learn more about sports ministries or participate in the chat or forums. You can even send a sports postcard to a fellow sports-fanatic.

Sports Spectrum Online!

http://sports.crosswalk.com/spectrum/

The Web version of *Sports Spectrum* magazine provides in-depth features on major professional Christian athletes and coaches. This site features daily devotional, athlete verse, and athlete quote. Listen to Sports Spectrum radio and the athlete audio quote. Participate in chat or the forums/message board.

Extreme Sports
http://www.extremesports.cjb.net/

Climbing Gear
http://www.sickleclimbing.com

Extreme Scene
http://www.xtremescene.com/

Sports3
http://www.sports3.com/

Christian Skydivers Association
http://members.aol.com/christskyd/

Streetplay.com
http://www.streetplay.com/

Florida Scuba Diving
http://www.terryhudson.com

Christian Sports Flash

http://www.gospelcom.net/gci/sf/

Check out news, including exclusive interviews, sports trivia contests, and more on leading Christian athletes.

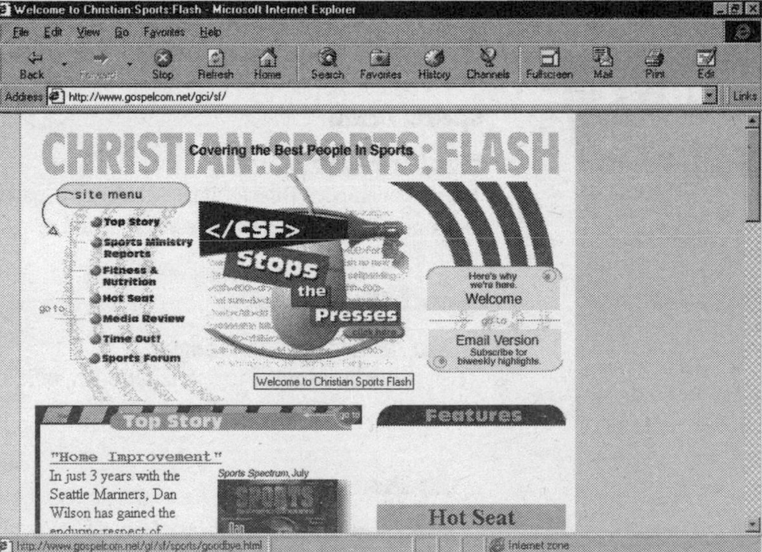

Coach's Edge

http://www.coachsedge.com/

This site is the home of a sports media company dedicated to the entertainment and education of fans, athletes, and coaches. Get the latest happenings in the world of professional sports and find out about contests you can enter. Check out the interactive animations or listen to the audio updates.

Submit a Site

hudson@techie.com

SearchSport

http://www.oldsport.com/search/main.htm

If it's sports, find it here. The award-winning guide to the best sports sites on the web. One of the oldest sports directories, (since 1996), they're striving to put together links to the best resources for you. Also find SearchSport Forum—where you can go to discuss the latest scores, or buy used equipment, or whatever you want that has to do with sports.

Sports7.com

http://www.sports7.com/

International Sports Directory that includes chat, polls, personal sportspages, news, latest results, and more.

SportsPlaces.com

http://www.sportsplaces.com/

Features a directory of top sites, including official team sites, sports news, and sports for kids.

Off the Field

http://www.offthefield.com/

Come get to know your favorite sports celebrities off the field. Check out articles on sports figures from baseball, hockey, basketball, football, golf, and more.

Athlete Direct

http://www.athletedirect.com/AthleteDirect/ad/home.jsp

A place where athletes and fans interact. Find out about chat opportunities, listen to audio clips, view video clips, learn about auctions, and more.

First Base Sports

http://www.firstbasesports.com/fbshome.htm

Learn How To Watch and Understand the Game with their Instructional 'Spectator Guide' Sports Books. On-line you can utilize the sports glossary of terms and phrases with definitions or the guide to officials' hand signals with diagrams and descriptions.

Active USA

http://www.active.com/index.cfm?

A nationwide source for thousands of participatory sports events including registration. Find information on running, cycling, swimming, walking, water sports, and more. Also includes health and training information and weekly on-line radio shows.

Infohub Recreation Page

http://www.infohub.com/TRAVEL/ADVENTURE/recreation.html

Links to recreational adventures from biking and boating to tennis and windsurfing—with lots in between.

Coaching sites

Coaching Staff

http://www.coachingstaff.com/

This is a resource center featuring coaching news, articles, tips, a message board, and a directory of coaching sites.

Sports Coach

http://www.brianmac.demon.co.uk/

This site provides information on a number of coaching and training topics that will help athletes and their coaches achieve their athletic goals.

Did You Know?

...that Andrew Grove, *Time* magazine's Man of the Year 1997, is the pioneer of the modern-day microprocessor chip which is now called the "brain" of all personal computers, cell phones, laptops, and more?

Sports Collectibles

FAVORITE LINKS

SportsNet

http://ini-sportsnet.com/

SportsNet was founded in 1985 as the first computer driven Dealer to Dealer Trading Network. Now SportsNet technology is on the Web to benefit the serious sports memorabilia collector. Check out the marketplace for those rare items you've been looking for, read news and interviews with professionals in the world of sports memorabilia, or learn about upcoming shows and events in your area.

Beckett On-Line

http://www.beckett.com/

This is a one-stop source for sports cards and authentic memorabilia. Browse their selection of more than 75,000 items from the country's top memorabilia dealers. Check out price guides, auction services, and more.

TAXES

Internal Revenue Service (IRS)

http://www.irs.ustreas.gov/

The official site of the IRS. Loaded with services and information including tax stats, electronic services, forms, and a section called Tax Information for You, where you can learn about exemptions, estimating tax liability, and more.

Yahoo! Tax Center

http://taxes.yahoo.com/

Get tax tips, file tax forms on-line, or file for an extension. Calculate your expected tax refund or go over the tax preparation checklist. Loaded with these tax tools and more.

Yahoo! Small Business: Taxes

http://smallbusiness.yahoo.com/smallbusiness/taxes/

Find tips, news, forms, and more for the small businessperson.

Essential Links to Taxes

http://www.el.com/elinks/taxes/

A comprehensive list of tax links. Find on-line resources to taxpayer tips and information on income tax preparation assistance, rules, tax codes, financial planners and tax preparers, forms (from W-2 to Form 1040), publications, instructions, deductions, and filing.

Two things are certain in life today: 1) Taxes and 2) Your ability to freely find the tax help you need on the web.

Take advantage of these sites during the year to estimate what your tax liability might be. Download the forms you'll need to file at tax time or file electronically from one of these sites. Small business owners can also use these sites to find help understanding the tax code.

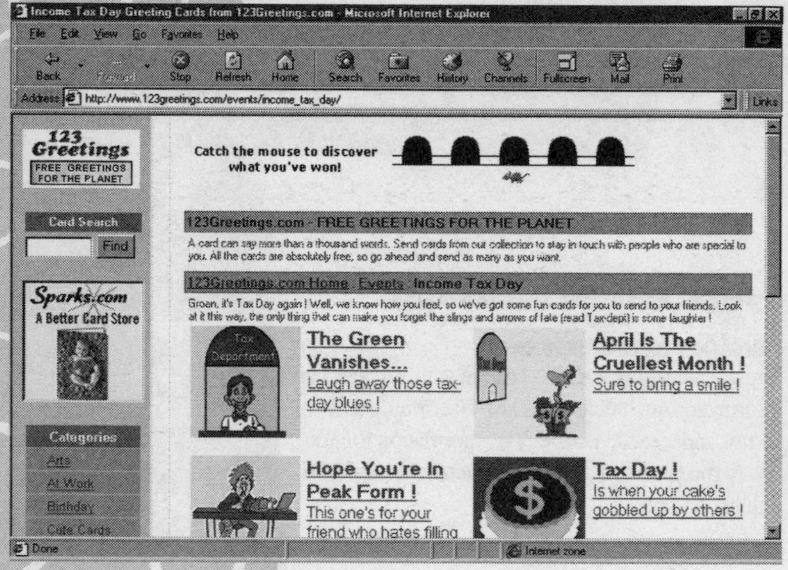

Tax Day E-Greetings

http://www.123greetings.com/events/itreturnsdue/

Take some of the stress out of a taxing situation by sending a humorous virtual card from this site.

Tax Resources

http://www.taxresources.com/

This site provides annotated links to federal and state sites, news articles, and more.

1040.com

http://www.1040.com/

You can find late-breaking tax news to forms to general tax information here. This site also has IRS publications and electronic tax filing information, as well as links to related sites.

Did You Know?

...that logizomechanophobia is the "fear of computers"?

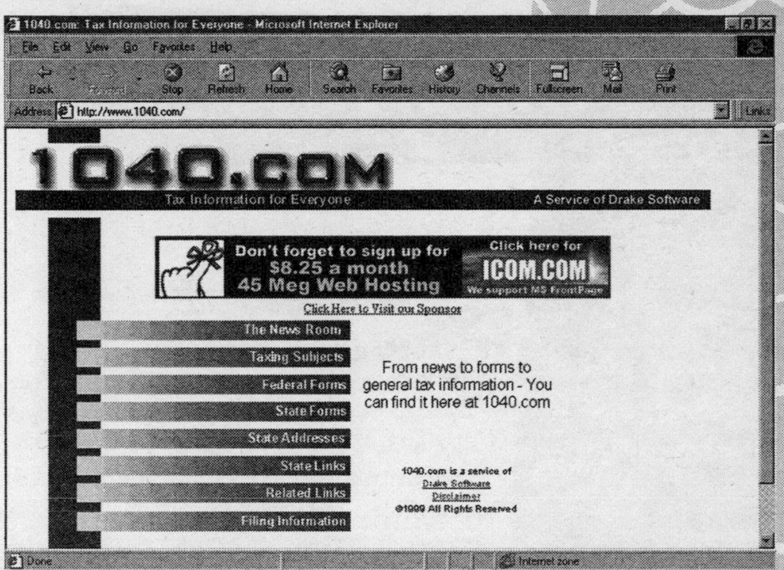

Did You Know?

...that in 1989 MCI Mail and Compuserve provided the first commercial electronic mail connection to the Internet through the Corporation for the National Research Initiative (CNRI) and Ohio State University?

TEACHING

There are many places you might find yourself in the role of teacher:

- classroom
- home
- church
- club
- work

No matter your forum, or the age of your students, these sites can help you chat with other teachers, glean ideas, and brush up on your skills.

TOP SITE

Be Your Best

http://www.adprima.com/

Designed for new teachers and education students—but useful for parents and students as well, this site is a source of serious, quality education information. You can find lots of practical information on curriculum, instruction, learning, thinking skills, lesson plans, teaching, homeschooling, colleges, writing assistance, classroom management, education reform, and a whole lot more. Links to many sites with useful education information, as well as original work and information. Also hosts a discussion forum.

Global Schoolhouse

http://www.gsh.org/

Internet resources and classroom projects for the education community.

Teacher's Edition On-Line

http://www.teachnet.com/

Targeting elementary education, this site features teaching ideas, hints, tips, lesson plans, room ideas, and even an advice column.

Virtual Teachers' Center

http://www.timeplan.com/vtc/index.htm

A great resource for both teachers and students. A wide variety of curriculum and teaching-related topics are contained in a set of menus with a short description for each link.

Teachers First

http://www.teachersfirst.com/

TeachersFirst is a web resource for K–12 classroom teachers who want useful resources and lesson plans to use with their students. Includes lesson plans, interdisciplinary activities, library resources, free downloads, and tutorials on using the Internet.

Awesome Library

http://www.awesomelibrary.org/

This site organizes carefully reviewed education resources for teachers, students, parents, and librarians. It contains a directory, an index, and a search engine.

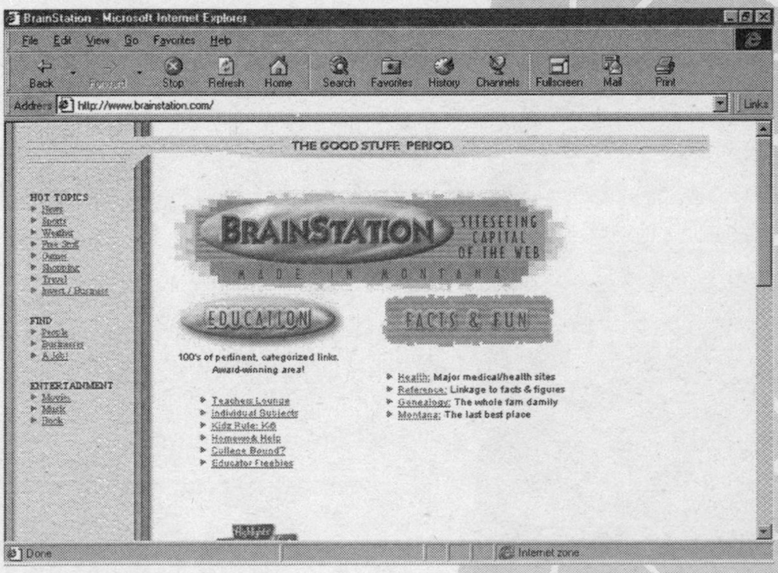

FAVORITE LINKS

BrainStation

http://www.brainstation.com/

Calling itself the siteseeing capital of the web, this site has hundreds of pertinent, categorized links in the area of education (and lots of others, too!). Features an extensive listing of individual subjects, resources for teachers and parents, fun sites for kids, on-line museums, and help for the college-bound student.

TELECOMMUNICATIONS

Telecoms Virtual Library

http://www.analysys.com/vlib/

An annotated directory of all things relating to telecommunications.

TOP SITE

AT&T Lab's Brain Spin

http://www.att.com/technology/forstudents/brainspin/

Enjoy interactive modules that will teach you about phone numbers, the Internet, fiber optics, call routing, and more.

Telecommunications Information

http://telecom.tbi.net/

This is an indispensable reference for the telecommunications professional and a great educational tool for those wishing to learn more about telecommunications. Includes the history of telecommunications and advanced technology overviews.

Telecom Update

http://www.angustel.ca/update/up.html

A weekly summary of telecommunications news.

Telecommunications is a key part of our lives: phone, pagers, voice mail, even E-mail and the web is based on it.

As telecommunications change, your web experience will change. Keep up with the changes and the new technology through these sites.

http://www.its.bldrdoc.gov/ITS

http://www.americancomm.org/

http://www.thephoneguy.com/FCC/index.shtml

http://www.mwtdd.comTELEPHONE DIRECTORY/

http://www.collegegrad.com/book/6-2.shtml

http://www.lifeintheusa.com/services1/phoneetiquette.htm

http://www.lifeintheusa.com/services1/payperminute.htm

http://www.biztalk.com/articles/phone.shtml

Telecommuting Knowledge

http://www.telecommuting.org/

This is a comprehensive on-line sourcebook and information center for telecommuting technologies. It provides access to an extensive resource of telecommuting literature, vendors, consultants, products, services, and events. All of these items have been categorized to make it easy to research specific telecommuting topics.

Telecom Policy and Regulation

http://china.si.umich.edu/telecom/policy.html

A web directory of telecommunciation information resources on the Internet.

TELEPHONE DIRECTORY

TOP SITE

Reverse Phone Directory

http://www.reversephonedirectory.com/

Do you have a phone number but don't remember who it's for? Or maybe you have caller ID and want to know who is calling. This site will identify a name and address from a telephone number.

International Directories

http://www.infobel.be/inter/world.asp

Find anyone anywhere in the world. All the white and yellow pages telephone directories available on the web.

Yellow Pages Resources

http://www.ypr.com/

The home of the telephone directory marketing specialists. Their on-line offerings include *free* tips on how to develop a yellow pages program, opportunities to win prizes, a chance to test your yellow pages knowledge, and more.

Home Numbers

http://superpages.com/
http://www.bigbook.com/

The home of GTE's SuperPages Interactive Services, this is a whole new kind of yellow pages

Track down an old classmate or find a particular kind of business in any part of the country.

The reverse phone directory is especially interesting—just type in a phone number and find the name and address of its owner.

that combines a complete list of businesses with street-level maps, customer voting, reviews, and personal address books.

International White and Yellow Pages

http://www.walens.no/
International inquiry of names, addresses, telephones, and faxes.

BigYellow

http://www.bigyellow.com/
This national on-line shopping directory has over 17 million business listings, thousands of advertisers, 277 million residential listings, 10 million E-mail addresses, and links to directories in seventy foreign countries.

AnyWho Directory Services

http://www.anywho.com/
AnyWho features residential, business, and government white and yellow pages listings. This site

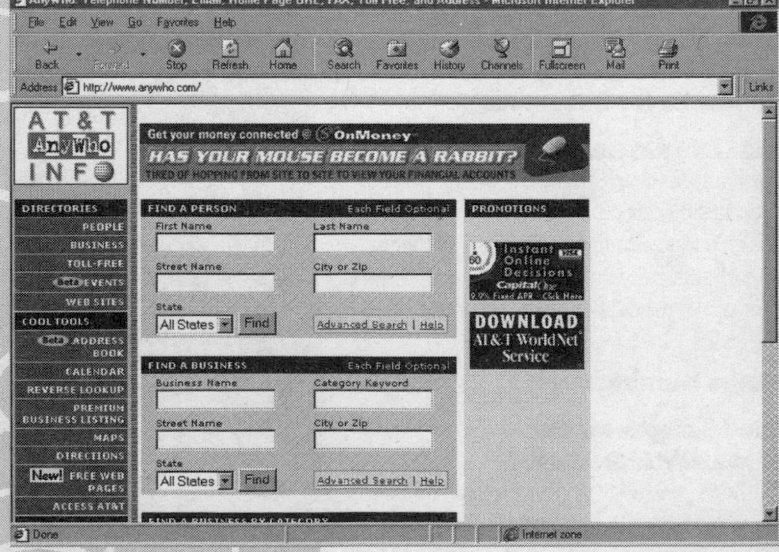

demonstrates some of the fastest search response times on the web and features web pages designed to provide consumers with quick, easy-to-use access to business information over dial-up Internet connections. Consumers can search by a variety of criteria including business category, name, city, and state.

Ameritech Internet Yellow Pages

http://yp.ameritech.com/

This is an on-line yellow pages directory and shopping resource that gives consumers the opportunity to find businesses, shop on-line, research products before buying, bid through on-line auctions, or list items for sale with Ameritech's classifieds. They offer coverage of over 10 million U.S. businesses. For advertisers, Ameritech yellowpages.net provides a variety of effective advertising solutions.

TODAY'S NEWS

Access the world or local news that interest you most. Many sites allow you to customize your browsing experience to display only the stories that interest you. Some allow you to have custom headlines E-mailed to you throughout the day.

Kidon Media-Link

http://www.kidon.com/media-link/index.shtml

This site tries to give a complete directory of newspapers and other news sources on the Internet. According to Altavista, over 1,700 Internet sites link to the Kidon Media-Link.

My Virtual Newspaper

http://www.refdesk.com/paper.html

A great reference with well-organized links to U.S. and worldwide news sources.

News365

http://www.news365.com/

News and information at your fingertips—over 10,000 news media sites and 300 topics. Search by topic or region.

All Newspapers.com, Inc.

http://www.allnewspapers.com/

Find today's headline news, business reports, sports events, and more; news stories are updated as soon as they are available. Also links to local, national, and international newspapers, magazines, radio and TV stations, and other news sources. Read the news from where it is happening and in the language of your choice.

NewsFrontier

http://www.newsfrontier.com/

Provides a guide to major news stories from top news sources, including national, international, business, sports, and entertainment news with links to a variety of columnists.

Interlope News

http://www.interlope.com/

This site provides continuously updated news headlines.

Newshub

http://www.newshub.com/

This site integrates and reports headlines from the world's premiere news sources every fifteen minutes. It is the way to stay informed about important topics because news stories are current and reported by the most respected sources in the world.

NewsMaps

http://www.newsmaps.com/

Here news stories, newsgroups, and discussion forums are mapped by topic onto a visual landscape. The underlying technology actually reads the articles and discussion forums before you do, and then organizes them onto a NewsMap based on the information they contain. It acts as a visual table of contents that shows you what information is available, but links you directly to the originating site to read the article or posting.

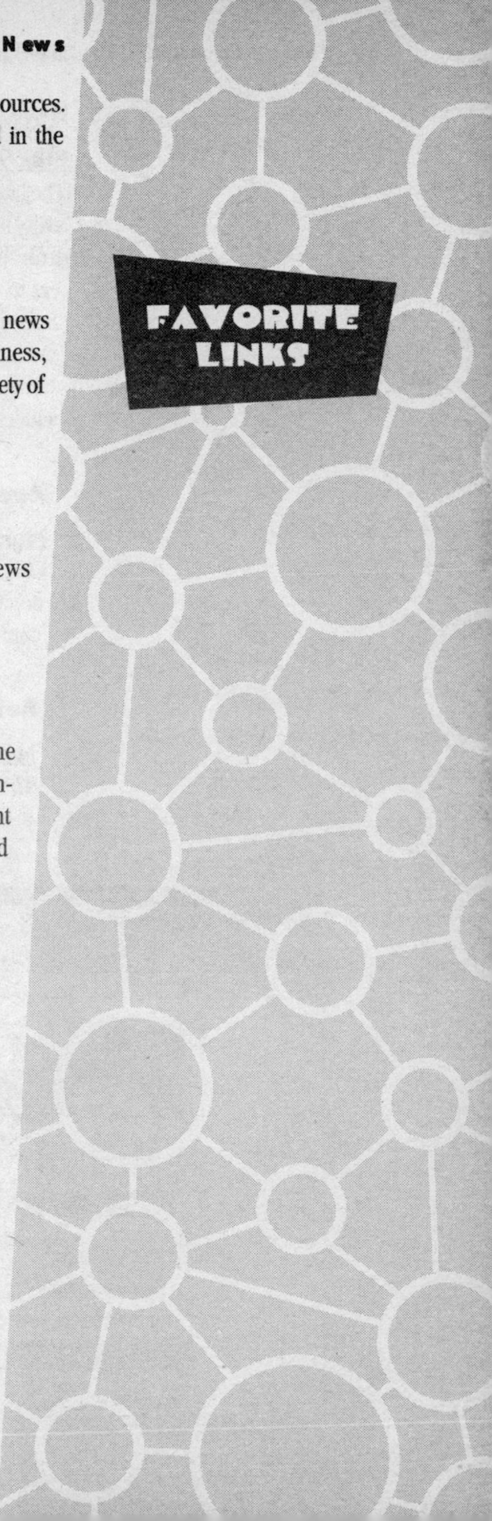

NewsNow

http://www.newsnow.co.uk/

The latest headlines from leading news sources, updated every five minutes. This site works like a TV remote control, allowing professionals, journalists, and casual surfers to click easily and quickly between latest headlines from more than 1,000 leading news sources without visiting each site separately, and then to read their choice of stories in full on the publishers' web sites. Also includes an extensive archive.

NewsMax

http://www.newsmax.com/

Check out breaking stories on politics and other national issues. Also find E-mail news alerts, cartoons, columnists, classifieds, and more.

Religious News Service

http://www.religionnews.com/

This news service specializes in religious news. While it covers all religions, you can always find updated Christian news.

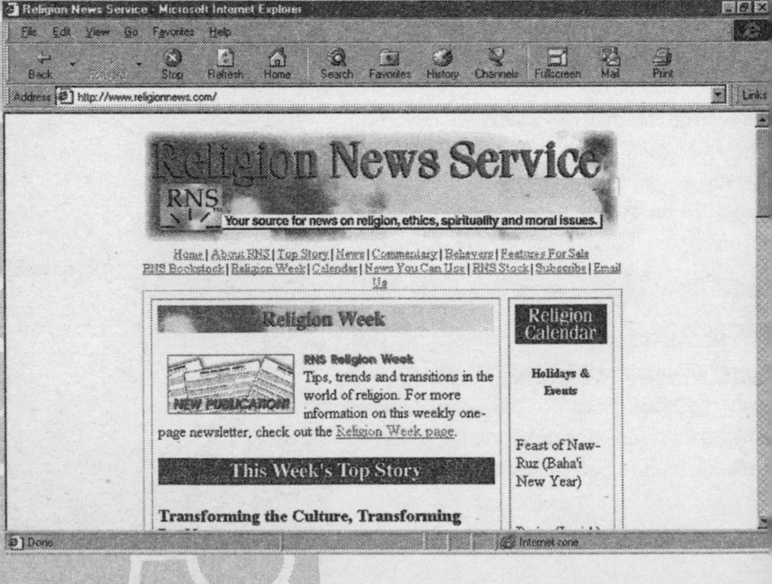

TRAFFIC & ROAD CONDITIONS

If you're someone who listens for (and actually understands) traffic reports on the radio, this section is for you.

Check out road conditions before you get into the car. If you don't understand radio traffic reports, but still need the same information delivered in plain English, these sites can help.

AccuTraffic

http://www.accutraffic.com/www/accutraffic/traffic.html

Get real-time conditions, construction notices, road closures, and more.

Weather & Traffic Reports

http://www.2it.com/

Access real-time traffic reports, as well as other information like current weather, latest news, and live web casts.

TOP SITE

Regional Reports

http://www.4traffic.com/

Avoid gridlock at 4traffic.com. Find regional traffic reports, maps, photos, traffic services, and alternative transportation resources. The site's researchers have found the sites to help you avoid rush hour. Information from AAA Road Report, SmarTraveler, MapQuest, Amtrak, Travel Wise, and more.

Road Conditions and Traveler Information

http://www.carsafety.com/road_cnd.html

Provides USA road conditions and traveler information by giving a list of links by state.

Other Links

http://www.smartraveler.com/

http://www.aaa.com/road/hotspots/hotspots.htm

Traffic Cams

Phoenix

http://www.azfms.com/Travel/Map/camera.html

Toronto

http://www.mto.gov.on.ca/english/traveller/compass/camera/cammain2.htm

Honolulu

http://www.eng.hawaii.edu/Trafficam/index.html

Denver

http://www.9news.com/eoc/alleoc.htm

Truckers.com

http://www.truckers.com/road.htm

What's the weather like for your drive? Click on the ma for the forecast of the cities along your route. Also chec out links for road conditions and traffic reports from a over the U.S.

Road Condition Reports

http://www.beaverbear.com/hwycond.html

Get the latest weather and construction information fro state departments of transportation. Select from a ma of the United States or Canada.

Yahoo! Traffic

http://traffic.yahoo.com/

Check out traffic reports, maps, and advisories.

TRAVEL

Planning a trip has never been easier. Find out more information about a destination no matter where it is. Get the best airline prices even if your travel agent is closed. These sites put you in charge of your travel and ensure that you get the best possible deals.

True Trip

http://www.truetrip.com/

A directory of travelogues, travel tips and classifieds, and destination information. Use their Travel Guide to find hundreds of links to airlines, hotels, cruise lines, maps, weather, world destinations, and more. You can also send a Travel Postcard to a friend or colleague.

Budget Travel

http://www.budgettravel.com/

Budget Travel's web site provides thorough information on domestic and worldwide travel destinations. Developed for those who don't want to pay five-star prices, this is the place to go to make traveling on a budget easier and more fun.

Eurotrip.com

http://www.eurotrip.com/

A great guide to budget travel in Europe. Offers information on travel basics, hostel reviews, destination information, packing and travel advice, accomodations, live travelogues, and cheap flights. Also offers a free E-mail newsletter and live travel chat.

About.com Travel

http://home.about.com/travel/index.htm

This is part of the About.com network of sites

which features highly targeted, topic-specific sites with Internet link directories, original content and perspective, community features, and E-shopping opportunities; each is overseen by a company-certified subject specialist to make sure you get what you want quickly and easily. Find links to destinations, lodging and transportation, vacation travel, cultures, languages, travel chat, "expert insight," and loads more. Also sign up for their newsletter and receive "the latest in travel news."

TOP SITE

Cheap Tickets

http://www.cheaptickets.com/

This site specializes in low-fare and discount airline tickets for regularly scheduled flights out of all major airports in the U.S., Europe, Asia, and South America, and on all major airlines. They have recently added discount cruises and hotels as well. You can also book car rentals at this site.

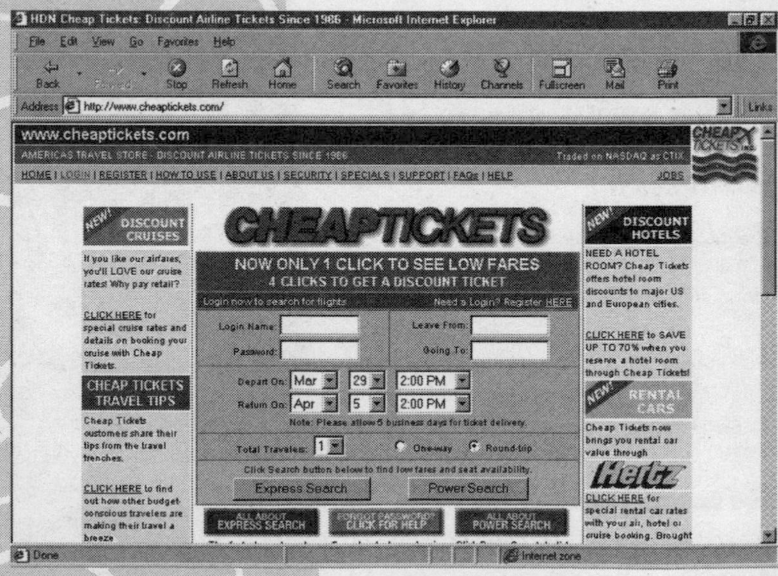

Priceline.com

http://www.priceline.com/

Priceline.com is a revolutionary new buying service where you can save money by naming your own price for the things you need. You tell Priceline how much you want to spend for an airline ticket or a hotel room, and they see if they can find someone willing to provide that for you at that price; this often works because many planes fly with empty seats, and hotels are left with empty rooms each night, and those companies are willing to consider what you're offering. Rental cars are also available here. In addition, you can even name your own price for home mortgages, home equity loans, mortgage refinancing, new cars and trucks, and groceries (currently only available in a few states). Soon to come . . .name your own long-distance phone rates.

Family Travel Files

http://www.thefamilytravelfiles.com/

This site offers a directory of family-friendly vacation spots, advice, and an e-zine with personal travel articles on topics ranging from road trips, campgrounds, and hostels to historic hotels, spas, and cruise ships. A great resource for parents and grandparents who want to enjoy traveling with children.

Adventuremom.com

http://www.adventuremom.com/

An on-line forum for moms who travel and want up- to-date information about traveling with children. Includes reviews, travel journals, and destination information.

Travel Agent Locator

http://www.locateatravelagency.com/

Need a travel agency to help you plan your vacation, business trip, or weekend getaway? This site will tell you why it is beneficial to use a

Airlines

http://www.americanair.com/

http://www.nwa.com/

http://www.ual.com/

http://www.twa.com/

http://www.alaska-air.com/

http://www.hawaiianair.com/

http://www.americawest.com/

http://www.flyvanguard.com/

http://www.flyfrontier.com/

http://www.midwayair.com/

http://www.delta-air.com/

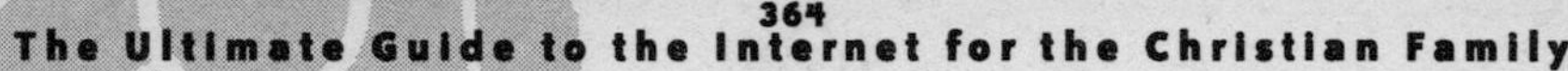

travel agency and help you find one anywhere in the USA.

Travel Hub

http://www.travelhub.com/

A doorway to specialized travel agencies, this site offers a newsletter, tour packages for destinations worldwide, airfares, and more. See the latest specials from over 500 certified travel agencies.

Information USA

http://www.information-usa.com/

A searchable guide to tourism organizations, lodging, and vacation information. With useful links to all fifty states, Information USA is your one stop for travel and vacation information when planning your USA vacation.

Web Travel Secrets

http://www.web-travel-secrets.com/

Web Travel Secrets is for the savvy on-line traveler looking for relevant and helpful travel information to plan their next trip or vacation. Reference how to find airlines, hotels, and cruises; find the best fares and deals; purchase tickets and make reservations; even when and how to best utilize your local travel agent. Provides an organized current list of links to the the most popular travel sites on the Internet.

Tourism Library

http://www.travel-library.com/

A comprehensive collection of travel and tourism information.

Fodor's

http://www.fodors.com/

Your guide to destinations around the world with a trip-planning center, forums, on-line reservations, hotel and restaurant index, bed-

and-breakfast guide, North American parks feature, adventure trips information, and more.You can create and customize a concise guide to any of 110 destinations worldwide and even learn up to 500 essential phrases in the foreign language of your choice.

Lonely Planet

http://www.lonelyplanet.com/

This site features down-to-earth travel information designed to kick-start your travels and help you on your way. Find destination information with links to relevant sites, weekly travel news, important health information, and a travel bulletin board where others can share their "know-how and no-ways." This is also the home of eKno—a budget phone system, a global answering machine, and a free E-mail service rolled into one—to help you stay in touch while you're on the road.

Submit a Site
hudson@techie.com

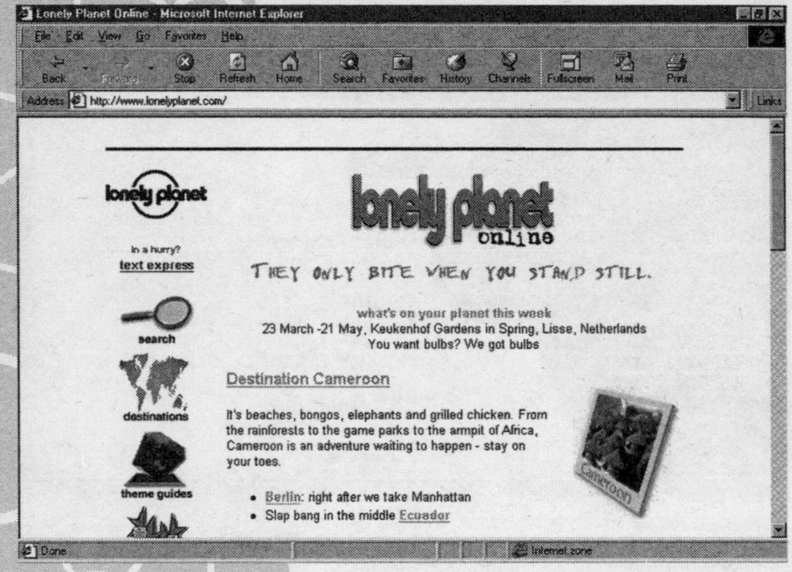

TheTrip.com

http://www.thetrip.com/

This site features resources for business travelers. From the small-business owner or remote office to the schedule-weary "road warrior" who travels all too often, Trip.com seeks to meet and redefine the needs of this influential audience. On-line flight availability and reservations, real-time flight tracking, airport guides, ground transportation schedules, and more.

CyberTrip

http://www.cybertrip.com/

Whether you travel by cruise ship, bus, train, or rental car, CyberTrip can help you with your international or domestic vacations. From airlines to weather and exchange rates to time change, this

Did You Know?

...that about 19 percent of Australians used the Internet in 1998?

site can help. Make air, hotel, and car reservations online and link to other helpful sites for everything else you need.

Events Worldwide

http://www.eventsworldwide.com/

To find details of locations, dates, and how to get tickets for leading, unusual, and exotic arts, sports, entertainment, and special events around the world, search this database and discover the best ways to have fun. Select from five languages. Also find fun stuff like trivia, contests, and hot news.

The Ultimate Directory of Travel Sites

http://www.tudots.com/

This is a directory of major travel resources on the web. Links to major web sites are provided along with a description, a review, and a rating. Find

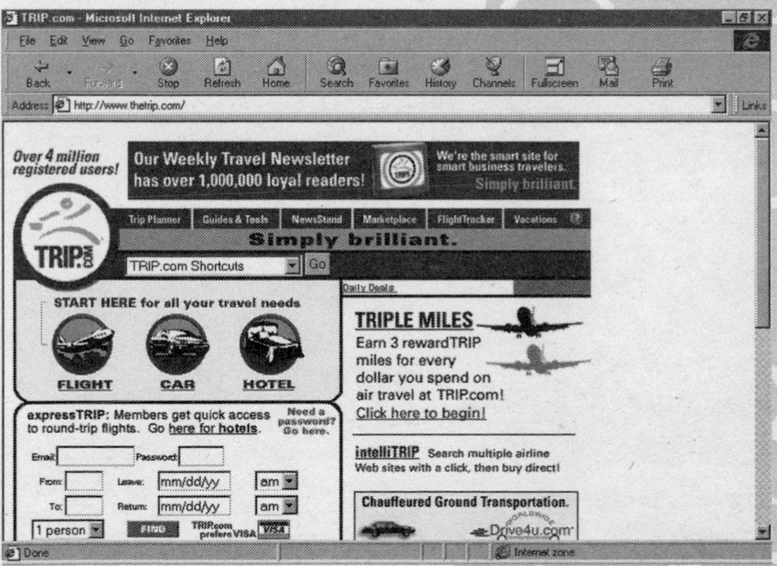

travel sites, airlines, accomodations, ground transportation, tours, events, hot deals, travel agents, and specialty travel (like eco-travel, adventure, romantic getaways, spas. . .). A complete, hands-on guide to travel.

FAVORITE LINKS

TRIVIA

What's the name of the actor who played Greg on the *Brady Bunch*? What was the name of President Reagan's would-be assassin? If you are a trivia nut, all you'll need is some spare time to join in the fun at some of these sites.

Some sites exist just for fun. Others let you win prizes as a reward for knowing the strangest details.

Trivia Contest Locator

http://www.beststock.com/trivia.html

The best of trivia on the Internet—located for you. No long lists, dead links, or two-year-old contest answers. Just a few links. . .the best that each category offers.

Thinks.com

http://thinks.com/webguide/trivia/index.htm

Your guide to the best web sites for trivia on a variety of subjects. You can also download free games, send E-postcards, win prizes, and sign up for their weekly *Brain Games* newsletter.

Riffnet Trivia

http://www.riffnet.com/trivia/

At this site, there are currently four categories in which you can play; three general games that are updated each week with new questions, and one themed after events happening in each month. Score well, and you can be entered in the weekly cash giveaway, just for playing a fun game. To play, you'll need to use a Java-enabled browser.

Planet Trivia

http://www.planet-trivia.com/

A large collection of interactive, real-time trivia challenges on the Internet. Have fun and win prizes!

MindFun.com

http://www.mindfun.com/

Trivia questions, trivia games, word puzzles, trivia chat room, interactive trivia games, Java games and puzzles . . . it's all here. Created by Jeopardy champion Mike Dupee, you'll find links to all of the best the net has to offer, including Acrophobia, You Don't Know Jack, Uproar games, card games, plus the fifteen original MindFun.com games, including the Cerebral Vortex trivia chat room, and the Knowledge Chamber Trivia Game. Find live trivia contests and register for weekly prize drawings and contests.

Trivia Web

http://www.trivia.net/

Trivia game with thousands of TV, music, kid, sports, and history questions. TriviaWeb is a free interactive trivia game which will allow you to test your knowledge in several topic categories. Your scores will be calculated and saved and compared against other participants' scores.

Find By Subject

http://onnow.com/excite/listing/GamesTrivia5.htmpl

A guide to live trivia events on-line.

Music Trivia

http://www.triviamusica.com

Trivia Musica is a music trivia site *for* the fans and *by* the fans, where you can share cool trivia about your favorite band, or ask questions you want to know the answer to, or even submit answers to other fans' questions.

Trivia Wars

http://www.triviawars.com/

Challenging trivia questions to

test your knowledge and awareness of the world around you. Features at this site include advanced scoring, personal history page, top-scorers honor roll, achievement levels, top-level performers, question submission tracking, and the chance to win cash prizes. Over 200 fun categories such as kid-friendly topics, art and literature, science and technology, "for women," eat and drink, wheels, and business—as well as the usual sports, entertainment, and general topics.

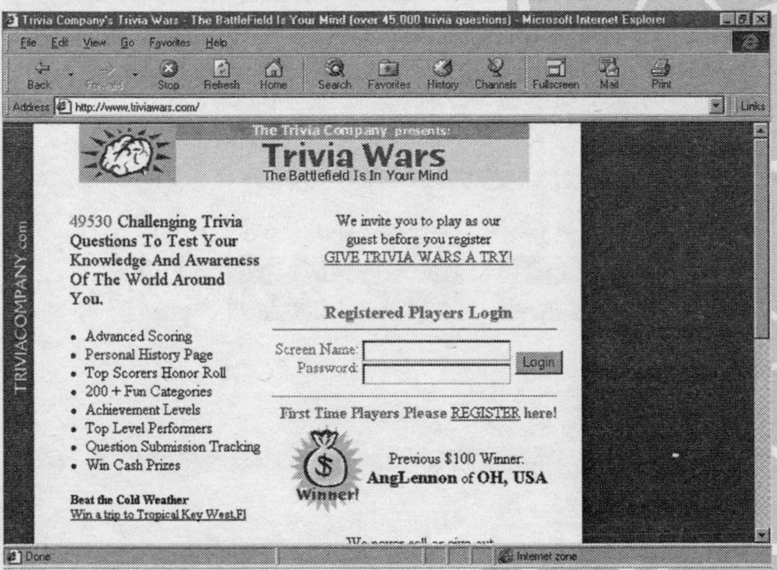

Trivia Links

http://members.home.net/destro/trivia/

Here you will find hundreds of links to trivia sites across the net. The links have been separated by category—music, movies, television, sports, and geography, with a miscellaneous category that contains links to sites that don't fit into the other categories and sites that fit into more than one of the other categories.

Amazing Facts

http://amazing-facts.org

Some of the most amazing facts found in the Bible. Many come from stories you've heard over and over. Family fun Bible trivia designed to surprise and amaze.

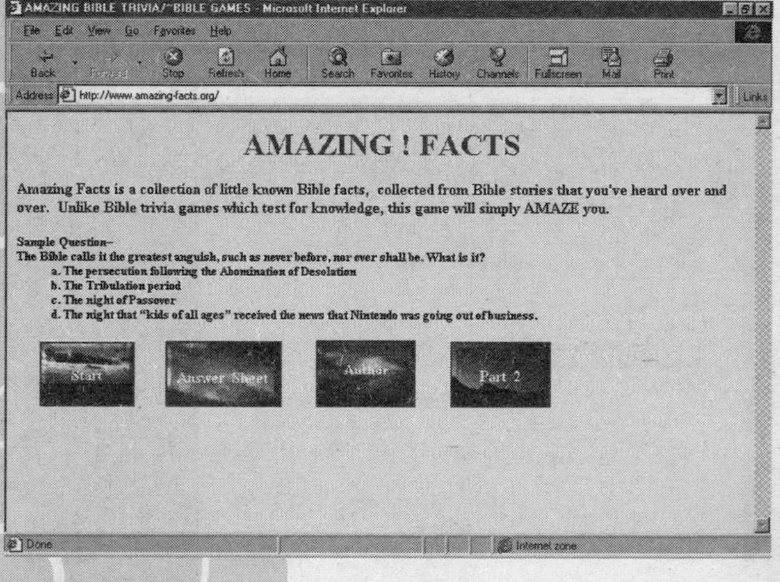

Wilesworld

http://www.angelfire.com/oh/wilesworld/trivia.html

Four trivia games: sports, entertainment, general, and a category that changes each month. Play each of these trivia games daily to win prizes; score enough points, fill out a form, and you are entered into a drawing. Good clean fun!

hudson@techie.com

For Christians

http://www.techline.com/~forchristians/bible_trivia.htm

Bible trivia from a site dedicated to Christian living according to God's Word.

Amen Ministries

http://www.jcxpress.com/bibletrivia/

An interactive Bible trivia game developed by *Amen Ministries* webzine where players can play against Bible triva and win prizes.

Did You Know?

...that in 1964 John Kemeny and Thomas Kurtz developed the BASIC programming language at Dartmouth College? (BASIC is an acronym for Beginners All-purpose Symbolic Instruction Code.)

TV

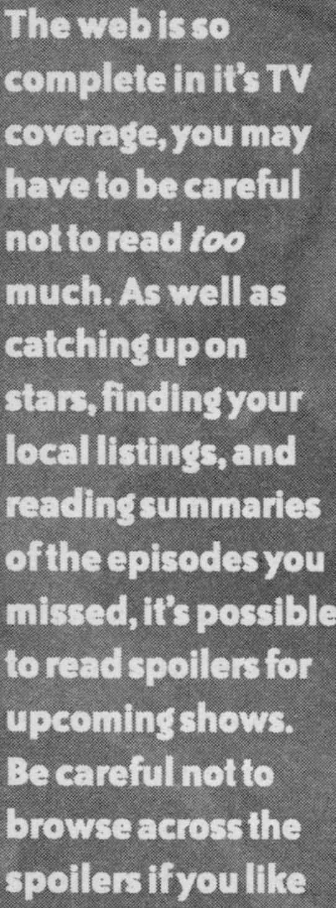

The web is so complete in it's TV coverage, you may have to be careful not to read *too* much. As well as catching up on stars, finding your local listings, and reading summaries of the episodes you missed, it's possible to read spoilers for upcoming shows. Be careful not to browse across the spoilers if you like to surprised.

Yahoo! TV

http://tv.yahoo.com/

Enter your zip code and get the TV listings in your area. You can also search for a specific show.

Entertainment Network News Television

http://www.slip.net/~scmetro/tv.htm

Check out links to all networks, favorite current and past TV programs, '60s-70's sitcoms, TV industry news, listings, and latest TV entertainment news.

Special TV Resources

http://www.specialweb.com/tv/

A constantly updated and extensive list of TV-related links to sites in a variety of categories including TV headline news, networks, shows, actors/actresses, TV-related reading, and TV newsgroups.

Xplore Television

http://www.xplore.com/xplore500/medium/television.html

Xplore Television has a carefully chosen list of good TV sites, from A&E to the *X-Files,* to help you view selectively and intelligently.

Classic TV Page

http://www.classic-tv.com/

Search an extensive database for information on classic shows. Check out the top 100 shows of all time, download theme songs, purchase classic TV collectibles, and find out where the stars of your favorite shows are now.

Episode Guides

http://epguides.com/

This site contains episode lists for over 1,475 TV shows. Each list contains titles and airdates. For over 310 shows there is a more detailed episode guide containing guest stars and plot summaries.

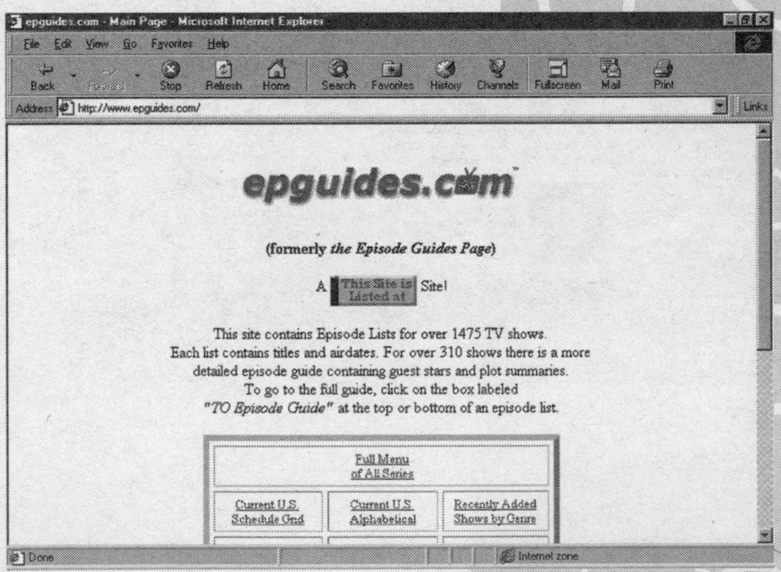

epguides.com - Main Page - Microsoft Internet Explorer
File Edit View Go Favorites Help
Back Forward Stop Refresh Home Search Favorites History Channels Fullscreen Mail Print
Address http://www.epguides.com/
Links
epguides.com
(formerly the Episode Guides Page)
A This Site is Listed at Site!
This site contains Episode Lists for over 1475 TV shows.
Each list contains titles and airdates. For over 310 shows there is a more detailed episode guide containing guest stars and plot summaries.
To go to the full guide, click on the box labeled
"TO Episode Guide" at the top or bottom of an episode list.
Full Menu of All Series
Current U.S. Schedule Grid
Current U.S. Alphabetical
Recently Added Shows by Genre
Done
Internet zone

TOP SITE TV news; cover story; what's on tonight; TV listings; and comprehensive information on shows, stars, networks and stations—local and national. See TV listings and watch actual clips from upcoming shows.

Ultimate TV Guide

http://www.tvgen.com

Find preview information for your local television shows.

Did You Know?

. . .that 40 percent of on-line users watch their TV and PC screens simultaneously?

USENET

These are the newsgroups of the Internet. These bulletin boards are places you can follow discussions and news about topics that interest you.

Remember: These are public forums and the views and opinions expressed aren't always professional (and are sometimes fueled by rumors). A word of caution: *Anyone* can access these sites. Even a seemingly innocent newsgroup may receive posts from obscene parties.

List of Newsgroups

http://www.liszt.com/news/

This is not a Christian site, but catalogues 30,000 newsgroups (both Christian and nonChristian alike). You can visit these, subscribe, and keep up on your hobbies or professional interests.

TOP SITE Christian Sites at Deja.com

If any of these sites interest you, type in their address into the Quick Search at http://www.deja.com. The search results should reveal the latest posts on each message board. The advantage to discussions through deja.com is that you don't need any special downloads to view postings.

Moderated

alt.current-events.cc-news

Conservative Christian news items.

alt.education.home-school.christian

Christian homeschoolers.

bit.listserv.christia

Practical Christian life.

christnet.christianlife

Applied Christianity.

christnet.christnews
Your news on the Christian scene.

christnet.ethics
Christian Scripture and ethics.

christnet.ladies
Discussion group for Christian women.

christnet.philosophy
Philosophy in Christianity.

christnet.poetry
Christian poetry.

christnet.theology
Christian theology.

christnet.writers
Discussion group for Christian writers.

Other Groups (some unmoderated)

soc.religion.christian
christianity and related topics.

soc.religion.christian.bible-study
Examining the Holy Bible.

soc.religion.christian.promisekeepers
The Christian group Promise Keepers.

soc.religion.christian.youth-work
Christians working with young people.

alt.christnet
Gathering place for Christian ministers and users.

Did You Know?

...that newsgroups are the town square of the Internet; a place where literally millions of people gather to debate, preach, get information or just leave a group message for anyone who cares about the same subject?

alt.christnet.christianlife
How to live what Christians believe.

alt.christnet.philosophy
Philosophical implications of Christianity.

alt.christnet.prayer
Prayer in the lives of Christians.

alt.christnet.racism
Christian talk about racism.

alt.christnet.songwriters
For composers of Christian music.

alt.christnet.theology
The distinctives of God of Christian theology.

alt.recovery.fundamentalism
People who left fundamentalist Christianity.

alt.religion.christian
Unmoderated forum for discussing Christianity.

alt.religion.christian-teen
Discussion area for Christian teens.

alt.religion.christian.20-something
Discussion for the twentysomething.

alt.religion.christian.baptist
Baptist churches.

alt.religion.christian.east-orthodox
Eastern Orthodox churches.

alt.religion.christian.episcopal
Episcopal churches.

alt.religion.christian.last-days
In anticipation of Christ's second coming.

Other unmoderated boards

alt.religion.christian.intervarsity

alt.religion.christian.ywam

soc.religion.christian

soc.religion.christian.bible-study

soc.religion.christian.youth-work

tamu.religion.christian

alt.music.christian.rock

alt.religion.christian.biblestudy

alt.religion.christian.calvary-chapel

alt.religion.christian.campus-crusade

alt.religion.christian.lutheran
Lutheran churches.

alt.religion.christian.methodist
Methodist churches.

alt.religion.christian.pentecostal
Pentecostal churches.

alt.religion.christian.plymouth.brethren
Forum for discussion among Plymouth Brethren.

alt.religion.christian.presbyterian
Presbyterian church.

utexas.religion.christian
Christianity at University of Texas.

alt.religion.christian.roman-catholic
Roman Catholic Church.

alt.religion.christian.youth-ministry
Discussion of youth ministry.

bit.listserv.christia
Another Christian discussion (not a typo).

aus.religion.christian
Christianity and issues relevant to Christianity.

git.club.ccf gt
Christian campus fellowship.

han.soc.religion.christianity.catholic
Discussions on Catholicism.

han.soc.religion.christianity.protestant
Discussions on Protestantism.

hk.soc.religion.christianity
Discussion about Christianity in Hong Kong.

DID YOU KNOW?

...that there are 186,000 miles of undersea telephone cables?

misc.education.home-school.christian
Christian homeschooling.

pdaxs.religion.christian
Christian religion and activities.

rec.music.christian
Christian music, both contemporary and traditional.

WEATHER

Plan your outdoor events with confidence. These sites link you to live radar data, seven-day forecasts, and even some specialized services—ski reports, travel forecasts, aviation and boating forecastsand even golf reports. Look at these sites when gearing up for a business trip or just a vacation to get national or international forecasts.

AccuWeather — The World's Weather Authority

http://www.accuweather.com/

A great site for weather information. Check out your five-day forecast, current conditions, ten-day forecast, moon phases, sunrise and sunset information. View short- and long-range weather maps, such as temperature, precipitation, and weather systems. Want to know where the precipitation is now? Check the radar section. Look at satellite imagery showing cloud cover, water vapor, etc. Get information on winter storms, hurricanes, severe weather, and lightning. There's even a place for those people who want more weather detail, and those affectionately known as "weather weenies" can link to the meteorologist section. Get weather information as it relates to topics like skiing, gardening, golfing, aviation, travel, and agriculture. Filled with news and interesting facts about weather, this site just about has it all.

TOP SITE

The Weather Channel

http://www.weather.com/

This is the home page for the Weather Channel, and it offers forecasts for over 1,600 cities worldwide, as well as numerous radar and satellite maps. Go to the news center for the latest stories, find out how the weather relates to topics like golf or gardening or driving, or check out the lesson plans and other teaching resources for those

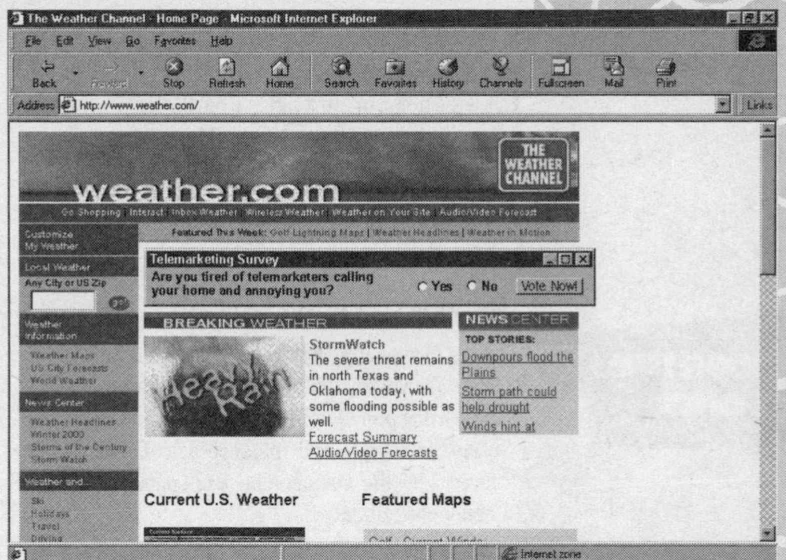

involved in education. Or join in some chat about the weather and check out the photo gallery.

Intellicast.com

http://www.intellicast.com/

Intellicast.com provides extensive specialized weather information to help plan all outdoor and weather-sensitive activities—whether golfing, sailing, hiking, skiing, or relaxing at the beach. Drawing on the meteorological knowledge of its staff, Intellicast.com now provides over 250,000 pages of detailed weather information.

WeatherLabs

http://www.weatherlabs.com/

WeatherLabs offers current conditions and 24-hour forecasting for all major Unites States and international cities. Features high-tech Doppler radar and satellite imagery maps.

DID YOU KNOW?

...that 50 percent of computer users do not like using a mouse?

Weather.gov

http://weather.gov/

This is the home of live weather from the National Weather Service, the entry point for the Emergency Manager's Weather Information Network (EMWIN), and the National Weather Service's home pages. Over 10,000 web sites link directly into this system.

National Weather Service

http://www.nws.noaa.gov/

This is the government Internet service home page. It's the starting point for official government weather forecasts, warnings, and meteorological products for forecasting the weather. Check out national and international weather.

The Weather Page

http://www.esdim.noaa.gov/weather_page.html

From the U.S. Department of Commerce National Oceanic and Atmospheric Administration, the NOAA weather page provides links to sources of weather information on the web.

Yahoo! Weather

http://weather.yahoo.com/

Yahoo's weather forecast. Search by zip code or city, or browse to locate a city.

University of Michigan Weather

http://cirrus.sprl.umich.edu/wxnet/

This site provides access to thousands of forecasts, images, and a large collection of weather links. Get your local forecast, check out ski weather, learn the latest on tropical storm conditions, and access the weather software archive.

Weather & Climate Images

http://grads.iges.org/pix/head.html

Features a navy tropical storms page, intellicast tropical storms page, hurricane potential maps, current conditions and forecast, climate outlooks, and other interesting links.

Unisys Weather

http://weather.unisys.com/

The intent of this weather site is to provide a complete source of graphical weather information. It is designed to satisfy the needs of the weather professional but can be a tool for the casual user as well. The graphics and data are displayed as a meteorologist would expect to see. For the novice user, there are detailed explanation pages to guide them through the various plots, charts, and images.

Dan's Wild Wild Weather Page

http://www.whnt19.com/kidwx/

This is an interactive weather page for kids—geared

especially towards those ages six to sixteen.

Weather Dude

http://www.wxdude.com/
This site helps kids learn about weather and meteorology.

Submit a Site
hudson@techie.com

WOMEN'S HEALTH

The Obstetrics & Gynecology Network

http://www.obgyn.net/

A physician-reviewed service offering doctors, nurses, practitioners, students, researchers, and women a home for publishing and accessing information. Site includes a Reuters Woman's Health daily update.

National Women's Health Information Center

http://www.4woman.gov/

The National Women's Health Information Center is a free, one-stop gateway for women seeking health information. NWHIC is a free information and resource service on women's health issues designed just for you, whether you're a professional or layperson.

Midwifery, Gynecology, & Prenatal Care

http://www.acnm.org/

Information on nurse-midwifery care, women's health, prenatal care, childbirth, finding nurse-midwives, education, certification, and questions to ask your health care provider.

Women's Health Center

http://www.betterhealth.com/womens/

Information on many women's health issues such as eating disorders, fertility, menopause, and other emotional and physical ailments.

There is no shortage of women's health sites available. These sites are designed to provide general medical information and assist women to take the best care of themselves. Here's a good place to begin researching answers to the questions you have—but might be embarrassed to ask your doctor about. The favorite is http://www.amereicasdoctor.com, which allows you to chat one-on-one with a real doctor.

FAVORITE LINKS

Women's Health News

http://cnn.com/HEALTH/women/

Imagine CNN's trademark coverage on a topic like women's health. Go to the page above and imagine no further. News articles about women's health issues, plus information on a variety of conditions and illnesses—all with CNN timeliness and quality.

FDA Information for Women

http://vm.cfsan.fda.gov/~dms/wh-toc.html

Here's the place to keep up with what the FDA has to say on women's health, nutrition, and pregnancy. Specifically, they target cardiovascular disease, cancer screening, and treatment for sexually transmitted diseases, pregnancy and childbirth, hormone replacement therapy for menopause, osteoporosis, and other diseases affecting older women, as well as autoimmune diseases.

Health Answers

http://www.healthanswers.com/Centers/topic/topic.asp?id=women's+health

Over twenty-five specific women's health subtopics, important relevant links, and up-to-the-minute women's health news, as well as over 1,000 articles, news releases, and videos all relating to women's health issues.

HealthGate.com's Healthy Woman

http://bewell.com/healthy/woman/index.asp

Information on a variety of women's health issues. This site includes health calculators as well as overviews on different medical tests.

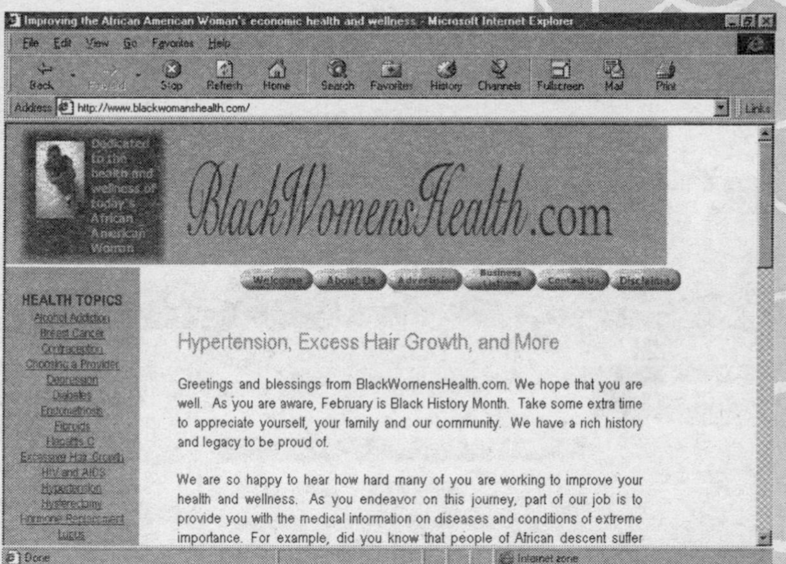

African-American Women

http://www.blackwomenshealth.com/

Dedicated to the health and wellness of today's African-American woman. Topics include preventative health, mental health, and nutrition.

HeartStrong Woman

http://www.heartstrongwoman.com/

HeartStrong Woman is a public awareness site developed by the American College of Obstetricians and Gynecologists and Bayer Corporation to provide women with information about how to protect their cardiovascular health.

HeliosHealth

http://www.helioshealth.com/

Women's health issues from pregnancy to menopause in a well-arranged, informative site. This site, useful for both professional medical workers and laypeople, is distinct from others in its

Did You Know?

. . .that in 1952, CBS made computer history by being the first to use a computer, the UNIVAC I, to forecast the U.S. presidential election?

extensive discussion forums, hundreds of animations and videos, and a HealthAlert E-mail newsletter.

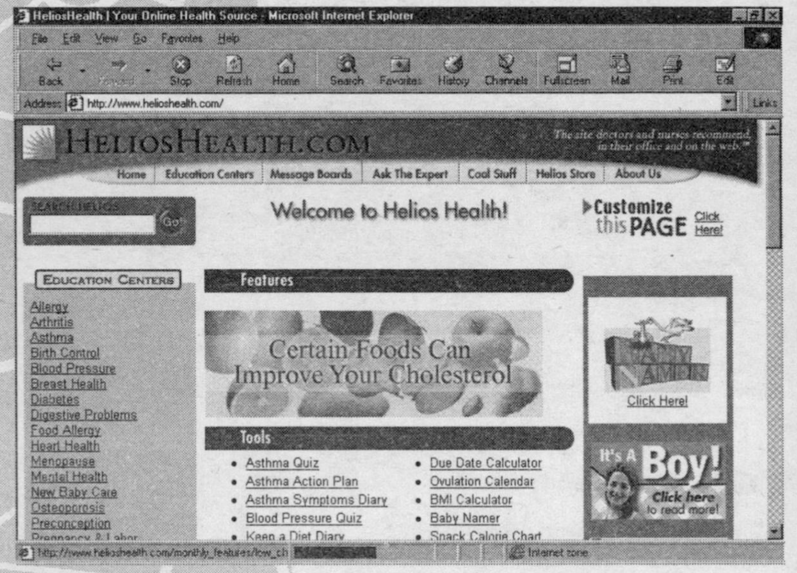

Her Health

http://www.thriveonline.com/health/herhealth/

A comprehensive women's health site covering medical topics, healthy lifestyle issues, inspirational stories, and controversies. It's a place to get advice and ask health-related questions.

Just for Women

http://www.j-f-w.com/

This site is filled with facts you need to make informed health care decisions. It offers useful links to valuable resources as well as helpful advice on talking to your health care provider.

Did You Know?

...that there has been a live Internet chat with Koko the gorilla?

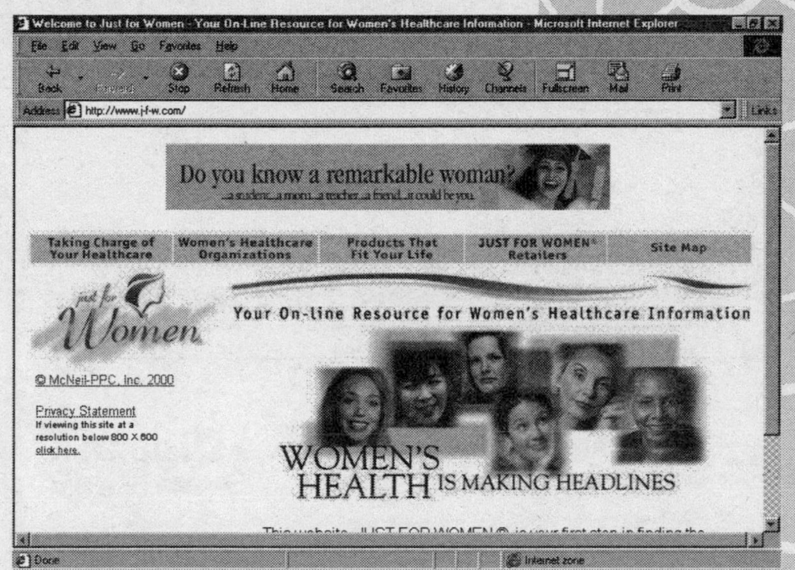

Mediconsult.com: Women's Health Educational Material

http://www.mediconsult.com/mc/mcsite.nsf/conditionnav/women~educationalmaterial

Fact sheets, charts, and articles on topics including medications, breast cancer, osteoporosis, depression, nutrition, headaches, taking control of your health care, and more.

Motherstuff

http://www.motherstuff.com/

Information and links for mothers, parents, and pregnant women. This site is owned by an individual, rather than a large company, which gives it a friendly feel.

Did You Know?

...that the top purchasing categories overall are Books, CDs/videos, computers, clothing, and software?

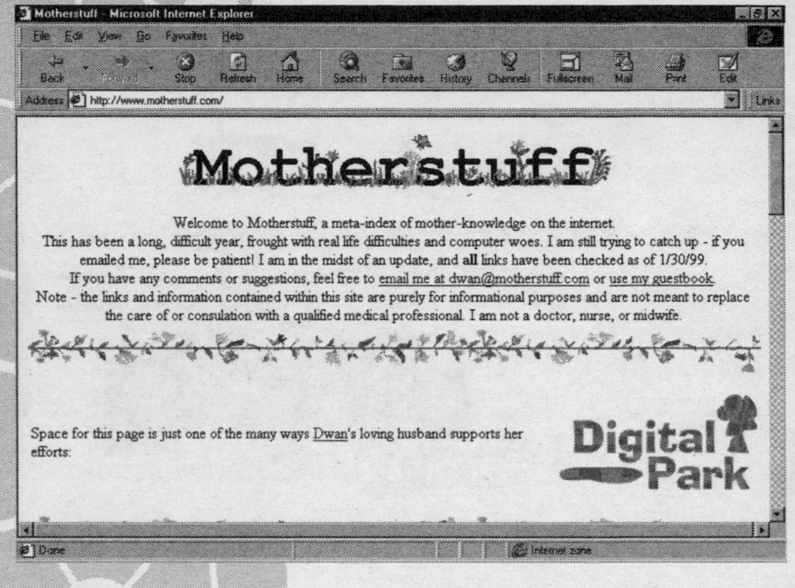

The Women's Wellness Network

http://www.wwn.on.ca/

Here's a health site that goes beyond physical health. This site also includes emotional, social, and financial well-being.

Woman's Diagnostic Cyber

http://www.wdxcyber.com/

While no web site can replace a trip to the doctor's office, this site might help answer questions and aid diagnosis of a problem before the office visit. As well as descriptions and charts, a physician-maintained message board exists here to ask personal questions.

Did You Know?

...that the major on-line computer services provided access to the web in 1995, quickly making it a household word, and spreading its use to millions of new users?

Women's Health

http://womenshealth.about.com/

Frequently updated comprehensive resource provides articles, thousands of annotated net links,

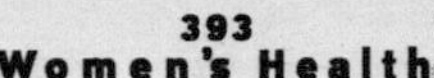

an active bulletin board and chats, and a biweekly newsletter.

AmericasDoctor.com

http://www.americasdoctor.com/communities/community.cfm?community=21

Information from doctors about women's health. Feature articles, message boards, chat, drug encyclopedia and overviews of clinical trials. This site offers free, one-on-one chats with real physicians who are available 24/7.

Forty and Older

http://www.thirdage.com/health/women/

The physical and emotional roller coaster ride of your life could start in your forties—and last another ten years. But take heart, ThirdAge provides you with the best ways to stay energized and empowered.

Women's Health Interactive

http://www.womens-health.com/

This site encourages you to learn as much as you can and tries to motivate you to take care of yourself.

FAVORITE LINKS

WOMEN'S ISSUES

Most of these sites are not Christian-based and many might be antagonistic to Christianity. They are, however, sites with lots of information on the study of women in the United States. Use your discernment as you surf.

Christian Communities

http://www.christianity.net/community/women/

Here's a Christian refuge for women—many of whom are in the same situations as you. Chat with other women and post or respond to messages left by others.

Women on Crosswalk

http://women.crosswalk.com/

This Christian community includes women in the news and women's history, as well as support for what you're facing today. Daily devotionals written for women and inspiring stories of women who made a difference.

Christian Support

http://www.christianworkingwoman.org/

Christian Working Woman is a ministry and a radio program that is centered on bringing a fresh, Christian perspective to workplace situations. With daily and weekly radio programs, bimonthly newsletters, speaking engagements, and resource materials, TCWW gives Christian women in the working world a place to turn for hope and encouragement.

Mothers with Children

http://www.gospelcom.net/mops/

MOPS is dedicated to the message that "mothering matters" and that moms of young children need encouragement during these critical and formative years.

Concerned Women for America

http://www.cwfa.org/

This site and organization is dedicated to allowing Christian women to come together and restore the family to its traditional purpose and thereby allow each member of the family to realize their God-given potential and be more responsible citizens.

Hearts at Home

http://www.hearts-at-home.org/

Hearts at Home is a nondenominational, Christ-centered, professional organization for mothers at home or those who want to be.

Women in the Arts

http://www.nmwa.org/

Women have made a tremendous impact in the the arts. This site exhibits, preserves, acquires, and researches art by women in order to educate others on their accomplishments.

National Women's History

http://www.nwhp.org/

This nonprofit organization educates by promoting gender equity through education. This site features the accomplishments of women and highlights their diversity.

Other Links

http://www.TheCyberMom.com/

http://www.women.ca/violence/candle.html

http://www.cc.rochester.edu:80/SBA/95-75/wave.html

http://whoa.femail.com/

http://www.women.ca/

http://www.islandnet.com/~vwsac

http://www.wwwomen.com/

A Celebration of Women Writers

http://www.cs.cmu.edu/People/mmbt/women/writers.html

Celebration of Women Writers recognizes the contributions of women writers throughout history. The goal of this site is to promote awareness of the breadth and variety of women's writing.

Women in Science

http://www.astr.ua.edu/4000WS/4000WS.html

Women are, and always have been, scientists. This site lists over 125 names from our scientific and technical past. Lists includes inventors, scholars, and writers. This interesting site include biographies and photographs.

Women in the Workplace

http://www.womenconnect.com/

This site is dedicated to women in business with features in business, career, politics, family, health, and finance. You'll find articles, links, and message forums on many topics of interest to you.

Advancing Women

http://www.advancingwomen.com/

This site is dedicated to offering women the information they need to level the playing field in the workplace. A great source for networking with women across the country and around the world.

Women@Work

http://www.nafe.com/

The mission statement for this organization says it is the "largest women's professional association and the largest women business owners' organization in the country, providing resources and services—through education, networking, and public advocacy—to empower its members to achieve career success and financial security."

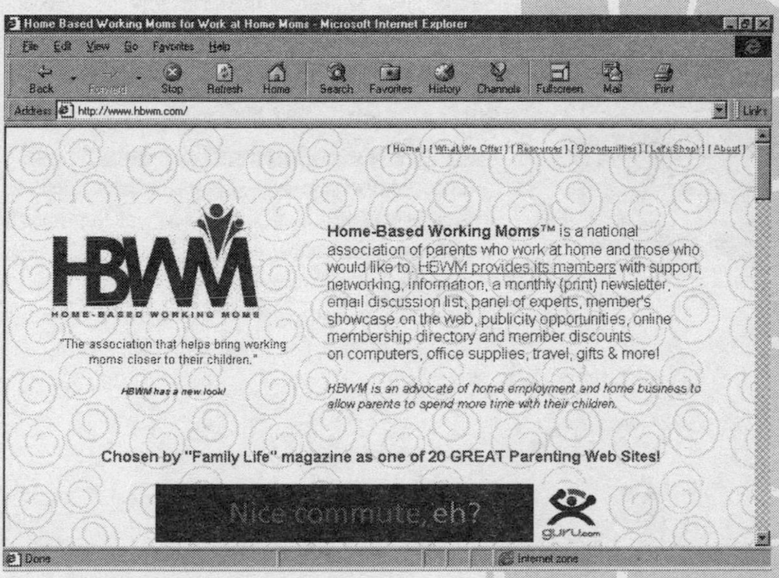

Home-Based Working Moms

http://www.hbwm.com/

Work at home and feel out of touch? Or would you like to work at home? This organization provides its members with support, networking, a monthly newsletter, membership directory, and discounts on various products and services.

Women in Society

http://www.rci.rutgers.edu/~cawp/

The Center for American Women and Politics (CAWP) is a Rutgers University-based research, education, and public service center. This organization promotes greater understanding and knowledge about women's participation in

FAVORITE LINKS

politics and government.

Women and Research

http://www.umich.edu/~irwg/

This site contains the social of history in the United States, research about women in the workplace, as well as access to the site's regular newsletter.

Women's Studies Programs

http://www.users.interport.net/~kater/

Want to contact a college that has a department or degree in women's studies? Here's a guide to women's studies programs in the country.

YELLOW PAGES

TOP SITE

WorldPages.com

http://www.worldpages.com/

WorldPages.com features 117 million U.S. and Canadian white and yellow pages listings, 30 million URLs, 125,000 web sites hosted for local businesses, and government listings. Also find driving directions or search for companies within a certain distance of a chosen zip code.

Yahoo! Yellow Pages

http://yp.yahoo.com/

Here's Yahoo's powerful search engine at work as a yellow pages. Enter the name of business or the category of business you're searching for. Yahoo will ask you what part of the country you'd like to see results and get you what you need. Try http://dir.yahoo.com/Regional/U_S__States if you want to start your search regionally.

Big Book

http://www.ndiyp.com/

While some Macintosh users will have trouble if they use Netscape, everyone else can access 2 million entries and a set of classifieds, too.

Yellow Pages

http://www.yellow-pg.com/

While this database is much smaller than some,

Not all yellow pages are created equal—and no yellow pages have *everything* you might be looking for. When trying to track down a business you may have to consult many different yellow pages.

If you're looking to buy or send a gift from a store in a certain part of the country, these sites can often help you search for stores in a zip code or county.

search results include an E-mail, phone number, fax, and name of a contact.

Yellow Pages

http://yp.ameritech.net/
http://www.yp.bellsouth.com/
http://yp7.superpages.com/sform.phtml
Fill in the form to find information on local or distant businesses or click on another tab to shop on-line or find driving directions to the store you choose.

Yellow Pages Superhighway

http://www.bestyellow.com/
This site has a database that equals 300 printed yellow pages books for both national and international business. So complete, this site calls itself the "Yellow Pages Superhighway."

Down-Under Yellow Pages

http://www.yellowpages.com.au/
Search Australia's yellow pages to do business with companies "down under." Here you'll find 1.6 million business listings.

Music Yellow Pages On-line

http://www.musicyellowpages.com/
A terrific resource for the music and entertainment professionals and consumers, with phone, fax Internet links, toll-free numbers, and trade shows. The site's goal is to list every company that manufactures, distributes, or sells music and entertainment equipment.

Off-Road.com Searchable Off-Road Yellow Pages

http://www.off-road.com/yp
Own an ATV, motorcycle, snowmobile, or truck?

DID YOU KNOW?

...that some of today's leading Internet minds are already seeing the day when the Net is so ubiquitous it's virtually unnoticed? It will eventually be in the streets, the air, even part of the clothing people wear.

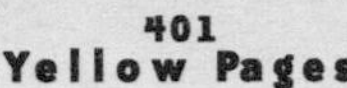

Want one? This site is a yellow pages dedicated to supporting people with an interest in this area.

20 Million Listings On-Line

http://asp.sbn.com/

These yellow pages by Superior Business Network (SBN.com) provide you with more than 50 million businesses. You can browse these by category or by area of the country. Do you have a cousin living somewhere out East? Click on the map where they live and find the businesses near them.

One Stop

http://www.teldir.com/eng/

This site is jammed with 350 links to yellow pages, white pages, business directories, E-mail addresses, and fax listings from over 150 countries all around the world. If you're not able to find it through this site, the information may not be available.

Super Pages

http://www.bigbook.com/

Here you can find yellow pages phone listings, directions, on-line shopping sites, maps, and addresses for U.S. business. This site is unique in that it adds consumer guides for many items you might be searching for.

A Yellow Page Portal

http://www.zip2.com/

If you need the yellow pages a lot, this one might be a good start-up page for you. This page tries to be your portal—offering headline news and many links in addition to business access.

Submit a Site
hudson@techie.com

GLOSSARY

Acrobat Reader

A program created by Adobe (http://www.adobe.com/) that allows you to view a PDF (Portable Document Format) file. Acrobat is quickly becoming a web standard and a necessity for viewing documents on-line. Acrobat Reader is free and can be downloaded from Adobe.

Access provider

See Internet Service Provider.

ActiveX

Many browsers support ActiveX technology (developed by Microsoft). This technology allows exciting sound and graphics to be added to many web pages.

ADSL—Asymmetrical Digital Subscriber Line

This is a high speed Internet connection made available by telephone companies. This connection is constant and uses a dedicated phone line. Much faster than a regular modem, this Internet access is growing in popularity.

Anonymous FTP

See FTP. Anonymous FTP differs from regular FTP in that it allows anyone to use the site. No user ID or password is required.

Applet

This is a small Java program that may exist on a web page. The applet downloads to your computer while you view the page. Not all browsers support Java.

AVI—Audio Video Interleave

This video file format was created by Microsoft and can be recognized in file names that end with ".avi." This file can be viewed by Media Player.

Bandwidth

This is the data transmission capacity of your Internet connection. You'll notice that your Internet connection seems to slow down when you use more bandwidth. You use more bandwidth by opening more than one web page at a time, downloading a program, listening to streaming audio, or watching streaming video.

Banner

These are the billboards of the web. When you arrive at the page you may find long, skinny advertisements at the top or bottom of the page. They usually allow you to click on them to learn more about the advertiser.

Baud

Your modem has a baud rate. The faster, the better. Baud rates are measured in "bits per second" and they tell you how fast data is transmitted through them. Modems using standard phone lines can go as fast as 56,000 kbs.

Beta

Beta programs are versions of software applications that are released for consumer testing. They are generally buggy and can be unreliable, but they also allow you to "test drive" a new program and it's new features. Once a company collects feedback from beta users, subtle changes are made to the program and it is released for general distribution.

B-ISDN—Broadband Integrated Services Digital Network

This kind of Internet connection allows a transmission speed of one and a half million bits per second and is the fiber optic connection standard.

Bit

You often hear about bits when talking about how many bits per second are transmitted by your modem. Bits are the smallest components of computerized data that make up E-mail, programs, and web pages.

Bookmark

All popular browsers let you save the address of your favorite web pages. This feature allows you to easily return to the web page at a later date.

Browser—Web Browser

Programs such as Internet Explorer and Netscape Navigator allow you to surf the web. Browsers are usually free. Service providers that require you to use proprietary software (like AOL) have their own browser that comes in the software. Proprietary browsers usually aren't as powerful as Internet Explorer and Netscape Navigator.

Cable Modem

An alternative to tying up your phone line, this modem allows you to connect to the Internet through the same lines that bring you cable TV service. These connections are usually faster than a regular phone line connection.

Cache

When you return to a web page, you may notice that it loads quicker than it did the first time you visited that page. That's because some of the page has been stored in your computer's cache. The cache keeps track of the sites you view so that they load faster when you return to them.

Chat

Chat allows you to type messages to other people in real time. Your typed messages take the place of speaking them. This activity usually happens in a chat room. If you're chatting, you might need this decoder to common acronyms:

AFAIK	As Far As I Know
AIUI	As I Understand It
BTDT	Been There. Done That
BTW	By The Way
FWIW	For What It's Worth
HAND	Have A Nice Day
HTH	Hope This Helps/Happy To Help
IIRC	If I Recall Correctly
IMHO	In My Humble/Honest Opinion
IMO	In My Opinion
IOW	In Other Words
ISTR	I Seem To Recall
ITYM	I Think You Mean
LOL	Laughing Out Loud
OTOH	On The Other Hand
ROTFL	Rolling On The Floor, Laughing.
TIA	Thanks In Advance
TTBOMK	To The Best Of My Knowledge
TTFN	Ta Ta for Now
WADR	With All Due Respect

Cookie

Some web sites place a cookie on your hard drive. This small file serves many different functions: 1) it lets web sites know when surfers come back to a site 2) it stores your login information if a site requires it 3) It tells a site what version of a page to load if you have customized it (i.e., requested local weather).

Cyberspace

This term was invented by William Gibson in *Neruomancer*. Today, cyberspace is a synonym for the Word Wide Web.

Daemon

A daemon is a system, not a person. It awaits to perform tasks, such as returning an E-mail when it has been improperly addressed.

Data encryption key

If you upload or download a file to a secure site, it may require you to enter a key. This key is a series of characters that is used to encode the file or message—allowing it to be viewed or used only by people who also have they key.

Dedicated line

A direct phone line that is connected twenty-four hours a day between your computer and your Internet Service Provider.

Dial-up Connection

This connection to the Internet is gained by calling and connecting to your Internet service provider. This is what most home users have, unless they have ADSL or a cable modem.

Domain name

Every Internet site has a unique name and address that identifies it. By entering your domain into the web browser, you are directed to the correct site. You can find who owns a domain, see if it's available, or purchase one through http://www.register.com/.

Download

You download whenever your computer receives data from another computer. You download programs, files, and emails.

E-mail—Electronic Mail

E-mails are like letters, notes, or memos sent from one person to another through their computer. E-mail addresses are usually in the form of yourname@provider.com.

Emoticon

Those sideways faces help you combine what your feeling (your emotions) with a clever icon. These symbols are commonly used in chat rooms and in E-mail. Here's a list of popular ones: *(List adapted from http://members.aol.com/bearpage/smileys.htm)*

:-) Your basic smiley
;-) Winky smiley
:-(Frowning smiley
:-I Indifferent smiley
8-) User is wearing sunglasses
::-) User wears normal glasses
:'-(User is crying
:-& User is tongue tied
O :-) User is an angel (at heart, at least)
:-D User is laughing (at you!)
:-o Uh oh!
:-9 User is licking his/her lips
:-0 Yelling!
:) Midget smiley
=) Variation on a theme...
:) Happy
:D Laughter
:(Sad
:[Real Downer

FAQ—Frequently Asked Questions

Many websites have a FAQ section, which answers the most Frequently Asked Questions at a particular site.

Frame

Netscape Navigator invented frames, but now they are available through all popular browsers. This feature allows web sites to divide your browser window into smaller windows. Each smaller window can open a different page. This feature is popularly used two ways: 1) to allow advertisements to stay on your screen even after you've clicked somewhere else 2) to launch another web page but leave you with the navigational commands of the page you were just at.

FTP—File Transfer Protocol

This is the system for exchanging files from one computer to another via the Internet. With FTP you can upload files to a remote computer or download them. You may need an FTP browser, which you can find for free. One free option is available at http://www.tripod.com/.

GIF—Graphics Interchange Format

This is one of the web's most common graphics file formats. This format is popular for showing small art or short animations.

Hacker

Someone who breaks into computers or user accounts without authorization.

Home Page

The page your browser opens to each time you log on to the net. A home page is also the phrase used to describe the main page of a web site.

HTML—Hypertext Mark-up Language

Many web pages are created with HTML. A simple set of codes, this language tells your browser basic information, such as how big a font should be, what color should be used, and where it can find the graphics needed for viewing.

Hyperlink

A word or graphic that allows you to be redirected by clicking on it.

Information superhighway

A synonym for the Internet.

Internet

The system of computers throughout the world that are connected and sharing information.

Internet Explorer

Microsoft's web browser can be downloaded from http://www.microsoft.com/.

IRC—Internet Relay Chat

See Chat.

ISDN—Integrated Services Digital Network

This digital phone line provides high-speed data exchange. While popular a few years ago, it is falling in popularity to cable modems and ADSL.

ISP—Internet Service Provider

Your ISP is the company that provides your access to the Internet. See the front of this book for free and fee-based options.

Java

A programming language for the web that allows web pages to have animations and other special effects.

JavaScript

Created by Netscape, JavaScripts are inserted into HTML documents to add bells and whistles to web pages that HTML coding can't deliver.

JPEG—Joint Photographic Experts Group

This is the web standard for viewing full color photographs. They compress in size very well, becoming very small, yet maintain much of their color.

Login

Many web pages require you to login. This provides you a customized viewing experience. It also lets you perform secure actions (like banking on-line).

Lurk

To lurk is to watch a chat room without entering the conversation or to read a message board without posting.

Mailing list

These are often discussion groups or forums in which all posts are sent directly to you.

MIME—Multipurpose Internet Mail Extensions

This is file compression used to attach non-text files or multiple files to your E-mail. Some E-mail programs (like AOL) require you to uncompress these yourself. You can do so with a program like Winzip (http://www.winzip.com/). The Macintosh equivalent is called StuffIt and can be downloaded from http://www.aladdinsys.com/.

Mirror

An FTP site that has a duplicate copy of a web site or files that may be downloaded. They are often created when traffic to a web site becomes overwhelming to it.

Modem

A modem is the hardware you need that allows your computer to exchange information with other computers via telephone lines.

Moderated

Some newsgroups (see Usenet chapter) are moderated. Moderators review posts before they are submitted to ensure they are appropriate, relevant, and interesting.

MP3 or MPEG 3

This standard file format allows music to be compressed and transmitted over the Internet.

MPEG—Moving Pictures Expert Group

This standard video format allows videos to be compressed and transmitted over the Internet. It is often viewed with a program like Real Player.

Net

Short for Internet.

Netizen

Someone who surfs responsibly.

Netscape Navigator

The web browser created by Netscape. It can be downloaded from http://www.netscape.com/.

Newbie

A newcomer to the Internet.

Newsgroup

See Usenet.

Newsreader

A program that allows you to read postings to newsgroups. Some web browsers include this feature. Some sites, like http://www.deja.com/, allow you to read newsgroups without special software.

On-line

Your status when you connected to the Internet. (When you're not connected, you're off-line.)

PDF—Portable Document Format

This file format was invented by Adobe. See Acrobat.

Portal

A web site that is a point of entry to your surfing experience. These sites usually update their information and news on a daily basis and allow you to search the Internet for what you're looking for. The most popular Christian portal is http://www.crosswalk.com/. Other popular portals include http://www.yahoo.com/ and http://www.msn.com/.

Posting

An article or message placed on a message board or forum.

Search engine

A site that allows you to search for topics or key words found on other sites. These sites are often the best tools for finding the information you need on the web.

SMTP—Simple Mail Transfer Protocol

This is the main system set up for sending and receiving E-mail on the Internet.

Streaming audio/video

Files that allow you to listen or watch while they are still downloading.

StuffIt

See MIME.

Surfing

The action of traveling from site to site.

Sysop

An abbreviation for the System operator.

T-1 and T-3

A high speed Internet connection that uses a dedicated line. T-3 is substantially faster than T-1. Home users do not generally have this kind of connection.

Thread

A collection of replies to a single post on a message board.

Upload

Transferring your files or mail from your machine to another machine via the Internet.

URL—Uniform Resource Locator

The address of any page on the web.

Usenet

Is a term that covers many discussions and newsgroups on the net. People can post their message in a public forum that may be read by thousands of users.

Virus

Programming codes or commands that come embedded in a file. Many virus writers are malicious and cause their scripts to do damage to programs on your machine or to your computer itself. Virus can be avoided by running anti-virus software and only downloading files from reputable sources.

Webmaster

The person who has created, designed, or maintains a particular web site.

World Wide Web

A system for connecting computers and exchanging information based on HTML programming language. Created in 1991.

Zip file

See MIME.

INDEX